Senex

The British Empire

Senex
The British Empire
ISBN/EAN: 9783337168537
Printed in Europe, USA, Canada, Australia, Japan
Cover: Foto ©ninafisch / pixelio.de

More available books at **www.hansebooks.com**

THE BRITISH EMPIRE:

CAN IT BE LONG MAINTAINED

IN ALL ITS INTEGRITY,

UNDER THE UNRESTRICTED AND UNRECIPROCATED

FREE-TRADE (RATHER, FREE IMPORTS)

POLICY?

BY

SENEX.

A TRUE CONSERVATIVE.

"In reckoning up the *significance* of this grand aggregate of machinery, it is impossible not to feel *that an important change* is approaching. A century ago no conditions existed which could have enabled *Adam Smith to anticipate* a time when the *producing*" (it would be more correct to say *transforming*) "power of Automatic Machinery would exceed the requirements of the *human race.* That state of things is rapidly approaching, and it is for the Philosopher and Political Economist to *consider carefully beforehand the impending revolution*, so that it may all work for good to the family of mankind."—*Conclusion of the last communication from Philadelphia respecting the late International Exhibition, by the* "*Times*'" *Special Correspondent* "*Mechanician.*"—*Times,* 18*th November,* 1876, *see* p. 77.

Salus populi suprema lex.

LONDON:
WILLIAM RIDGWAY, 169, PICCADILLY.

1878.

"A State is equally desperate when there are *no* remedies to be found that are equal to the distempers of it, and when there *are such to be found*, but neither hands to administer them, nor, perhaps, *strength of Constitution sufficient* to bear them."—*Bolingbroke.*

" Good Government is a machine for *developing the resources of a country* in such a manner as shall *advance* the best interests *of the people.*"—*Burke.*

"Nations are not made by alliances, nor will anything except *actual and intrinsic strength be recognized as constituting a first-rate power.*"—*The Leader in the "Times,"* 24th August, 1864.

" The false man sees false shows, plausibilities, *expediences ;* the *true* man is needed to discern even *practical truth.*"—*Carlyle's Lectures on Heroes.*

" In the youth of a State, arms do flourish ; in the middle age of a State, learning ; and then both of them together for a time ; in the declining age of a State, mechanical arts and merchandize."—*Bacon's Essays, " Of Vicissitude of Things."*

NOTICE.

Many will no doubt remember that a few years after "the great experiment" of the late Sir Robert Peel—the Free Imports' Policy of 1846—had been in operation, *national* prosperity was trumpeted forth as the result of that measure; whereas Sir Robert himself had said that, for any beneficial results, *he* relied upon Foreign nations soon following the example he had set. In fact, upon Free TRADE becoming then soon established. In this, however, he was mistaken, and no doubt greatly disappointed.

Hence it was that the author of the present volume, perceiving many painful signs in the country—amongst them the rapid increase of Strikes, and the still more rapid increase of *insanity* amongst the labouring classes—soon became convinced that the prosperity resulting from the Free Imports measure was not at all general, but confined to a few of the largest capitalists and manufacturers, and could not rightly be termed *National* Prosperity; and not being promotive of sober steady native industry, but founded and relying on the quicksand, excess, instead of on the rock, moderation, it seemed to the writer of this volume ("Senex") that such prosperity must inevitably be short-lived.

In the course of 1854-5, he, therefore, sent a few letters to that constitutional journal, *John Bull*, under the heading: " Is Free Trade " (rather the Free Imports) " Prosperity a NATIONAL Blessing ?" and though a perfect stranger to the editor, both then and up to the present time, he most willingly and courteously afforded them space in his Journal.

These letters, with a few of later date, were to have been included in the present volume, but the Publisher thinking, and no doubt rightly, that such an addition would make it rather too thick, the letters with some Miscellanies calculated to interest all anxious to promote the Commonweal, will form a supplemental volume, to be published as quickly as possible.

PREFACE.

ROBERT SOUTH, the eminent Divine, who was born in 1633, and died in 1716, is said to have been a great wit, and his sermons possess the merit of great earnestness and originality. In one of them, on the text, St. Luke xi. 34, 35, " The light of the body is the eye; therefore, when thine eye is *single*, thy whole body also is full of light; but when thine eye is evil, thy body also is full of darkness.

" Take heed, therefore, that the light which is in thee be not darkness." He says,

" The three grand disturbers of the '*singleness*' of the eye are *covetousness, sensuality,* and *ambition*. These are the three passions which most perniciously *darken the conscience and judgment*." And a later Divine, Charles Webb Le Bas, A.M., who was Professor in the East India College, Herts, and Rector of St. Paul's, Shadwell, and died so lately as 1861 (in a Sermon preached in the Chapel of the East India College in 1825, on

St. Matt. vi. 22, 23,* says, "Time would fail, if we were to trace out all the fatal influences of ill-governed emotion upon the *mental discernment*, and to describe all the halting and *obliquity of movement* which follow from such a distemper of the faculties. There are, however, three grand disturbers of 'the singleness of the eye' (or conscience), which seem to demand a more attentive notice, viz., *pride, sensuality*, and *avarice:* of which *in their excess* it is scarcely too much to affirm, that they *envelope* the whole man in *the shadows of night;* that they crowd his path with *phantoms which lure him to perdition* ; that they blot out, as it were, the very sun from heaven, and wrap the firmament in one deadly mist."

In the short Dedication of the first volume of his Sermons to the Honourable Court of Directors of the East India Company, Mr. Le Bas says, "The Discourses, with few exceptions, have been selected from a number delivered within the last eight years (his dedication is dated 1st of March, 1822) *in the Chapel of the East India College.* They were addressed *to young men destined by you for a service, the importance of which none but a thoroughly well-informed judgment can duly estimate.* It is true they were not written originally

---

* "The light of the body is the eye; if therefore thine eye be single, thy whole body shall be full of light. But if thine eye be evil, thy whole body shall be full of darkness. If therefore the light that is in thee be darkness, *how great* is *that darkness.*"

with a view to publication. They were, however, composed under a deep and *constant sense of the solemn responsibility* attached to this office of training men to fulfil *a momentous destination in this life*, and to stand *before the presence of their God in that which is to come.*"

One of the old Lecturers on Theology "to the King's Scholars of St. Peter's College, Westminster," in his *first* Lecture delivered in Westminster Abbey, on "Justice, or Righteousness," says,—

"I *add Righteousness*, because in the originals, as well Hebrew as Greek, there is but *one word for both*, and therefore we should have one and the same notion of both. It is peculiar to our English translators of the Bible, that they render the single term by two words, sometimes Righteousness, sometimes Justice; both which were, I suppose, *quite synonymous* (as we may collect from that part of the Litany, where we deprecate those evils which we *most righteously* have deserved)."

"*Justice* is the compendious name *for all duty*, because to give to each thing its due, and treat it according to its desert, which is the office of *justice, comprehends the whole of religion and morality.* Righteousness does indeed imply the same notion; but I shall always keep to the word *justice* in my interpretation, because the terms which relate to it, viz., the *Just, to Justify*, and *Justification*, being of the same derivation, the sense of the many passages wherein they occur will be more obvious. And besides, *to some ears* at least, cant and fanaticism have tarnished and debased the words *righteous* and *righteousness;* whereas as long as *any spark of conscience remains, Justice* will be a venerable, an *awful name.* The obligations of Justice are the most sensible and pressing to the human mind."*

Imbued no doubt with the spirit of *patriotism and justice*, the late Sir Edward Bulwer Lytton (afterwards created Lord Lytton), father of the present Governor-General of India, in his unanswered and unanswerable " Letters to John Bull, Esquire, on Affairs connected with his *Landed Property*, and the *Persons who live thereon*,"† says,—

"Our foreign trade, the exports of our cotton

---

* The following appeared in the *Times* of the 28th August:—" Midhat Pasha. (By Telegraph.) (From our own Correspondent.) Paris, August 27, 1877. A deputation of the Society of Positivists waited yesterday on Midhat Pasha, to express to him their sympathy with the cause of Turkey and with his own efforts. Midhat Pasha, in his reply, complained of the prejudice in Europe against the spirit of the Mussulman religion, which he assured them was, at least, as much adapted as Christianity to the spirit of civilization and modern institutions. . . . . He complained especially of those European statesmen whose religious sentiments had overbalanced their reason, and who, despite all that Russia had been doing for two years, heaped only on Turkey their indignant rebukes: 'What,' he asked, 'was the use of religion, if it did not make people just?'" The writer of these pages, however, wishes not to be understood, in giving this note, to offer any opinion, direct or indirect, relative to the merits or demerits of either Russia or Turkey, in relation to the miserable war still going on.

† Tenth edition. Chapman and Hall, Piccadilly, 1851.

manufacture, are worthy objects of attention; but they are *not the sole ones*. The *wealth of the State itself cannot so absorb* the attention of a *thoughtful legislator*, but what he will also regard *the moral and social circumstances by which alone that wealth can be permanently secured.** Let me care ever so much for money, it is not only to *make* money that *I must care;* I must also look to the *safeguards* that are to prevent me from *losing it.*"

"Defence," says Adam Smith, "is of much more importance than opulence."

"Our debt—the fundholder—the *safety* of the *Empire* in its actual and necessary defences—all these I must look to *as a Citizen*, as well as the quantity of cotton I can sell to the foreigner." (See Letter iii., p. 98, 10th ed.)

In his first Letter, p. 28, he had said—

"Whether or not Political Economy be a science based upon induction, rather than logic, is it a study affording *the most valuable suggestions.* . . *But* I must be permitted to observe, that it is a common mistake with the ordinary run of students

* The late Prince Metternich, who for more than a quarter of a century conducted the affairs of the Austrian Empire, once said to Count Z——y:—"My dear Count, you wish to do good to your country, but you go the *wrong way* about it. The *material advantages* you procure it turn to its *moral d*isadvantage, and when the *moral* evil shall be accomplished IT will *remain*, but the *material* good will *disappear* in the terrible convulsions of civil war. The credit you obtain by *flattering* the passions you will lose when you endeavour to *restrain* them."

at *least, cant and fanaticism* have tarnished and debased the words *righteous* and *righteousness;* whereas as long as *any spark of conscience remains,* *Justice* will be a venerable, an *awful name.* The obligations of Justice are the most sensible and pressing to the human mind."*

Imbued no doubt with the spirit of *patriotism and justice,* the late Sir Edward Bulwer Lytton (afterwards created Lord Lytton), father of the present Governor-General of India, in his unanswered and unanswerable " Letters to John Bull, Esquire, on Affairs connected with his *Landed Property,* and the *Persons who live thereon,*"† says,—

" Our foreign trade, the exports of our cotton

---

* The following appeared in the *Times* of the 28th August: —" Midhat Pasha. (By Telegraph.) (From our own Correspondent.) Paris, August 27, 1877. A deputation of the Society of Positivists waited yesterday on Midhat Pasha, to express to him their sympathy with the cause of Turkey and with his own efforts. Midhat Pasha, in his reply, complained of the prejudice in Europe against the spirit of the Mussulman religion, which he assured them was, at least, as much adapted as Christianity to the spirit of civilization and modern institutions. . . . . He complained especially of those European statesmen whose religious sentiments had overbalanced their reason, and who, despite all that Russia had been doing for two years, heaped only on Turkey their indignant rebukes : ' What,' he asked, ' was the use of religion, if it did not make people just ?' " The writer of these pages, however, wishes not to be understood, in giving this note, to offer any opinion, direct or indirect, relative to the merits or demerits of either Russia or Turkey, in relation to the miserable war still going on.

† Tenth edition. Chapman and Hall, Piccadilly, 1851.

manufacture, are worthy objects of attention ; but they are *not the sole ones.* The *wealth of the State itself cannot so absorb* the attention of a *thoughtful legislator*, but what he will also regard *the moral and social circumstances by which alone that wealth can be permanently secured.** Let me care ever so much for money, it is not only to *make* money that *I must care;* I must also look to the *safeguards* that are to prevent me from *losing it.*"

" Defence," says Adam Smith, "is of much more importance than opulence."

" Our debt—the fundholder—the *safety* of the *Empire* in its actual and necessary defences—all these I must look to *as a Citizen*, as well as the quantity of cotton I can sell to the foreigner." (See Letter iii., p. 98, 10th ed.)

In his first Letter, p. 28, he had said—

" Whether or not Political Economy be a science based upon induction, rather than logic, is it a study affording *the most valuable suggestions.* . . *But* I must be permitted to observe, that it is a common mistake with the ordinary run of students

* The late Prince Metternich, who for more than a quarter of a century conducted the affairs of the Austrian Empire, once said to Count Z———y :—" My dear Count, you wish to do good to your country, but you go the *wrong way* about it. The *material advantages* you procure it turn to its *moral dis*advantage, and when the *moral* evil shall be accomplished IT will *remain*, but the *material* good will *disappear* in the terrible convulsions of civil war. The credit you obtain by *flattering* the passions you will lose when you endeavour to *restrain* them."

in Political Economy, *to mistake altogether the nature of that science, and the reservation imposed upon the practical adoption of its principles.* Political Economy *deals with but one element* in a State, viz., its *wealth;* and the *soundest political* economists will be found *cautiously stopping short* of what would seem *the goal of* an argument, with some such expression as 'But *this belongs to National Policy.*' Political Economy goes *strictly and sternly,* as it were, towards the *investigation of the rigid principle it is pursuing;* it has only incidentally to do with the modifications which it would be *wise to adopt* when you *apply* the principle to *living men.* Of *living men,* their *passions,* and *habits,* and *prejudices,* it often thinks no more than Euclid does when he is demonstrating the properties of a triangle. All this is *out* of the province of the Political Economist, and *within* that of *the Statesman.*"

And a writer of more recent date—the author of " *Physical Science compared with the Second Beast or False Prophet of the Revelation,*" (Rivingtons, Waterloo Place, 1865), says—

" It may be quite true that acting upon the principles of Political Economy may bring *wealth* to a man or to a nation ; but whether it be *right* to act on them for this purpose is the *really important question.*

" I think I am justified in saying that Political Economy has too much of *temptation* mixed up with it, for it *to be right; since not even its greatest admirer will, I believe, declare that it would be right to follow it to its last consequences.* Now, a system which will produce certain *apparently* desirable results if *followed out, but which cannot be fully followed out, unless a man were to get rid of his feelings and his conscience,* seems to me to be a system of *temptation,* and, therefore, *anti-Christian.*

"For Political Economy teaches a man, that by working in obedience to certain general laws, and *for his own interest solely,* he will really in the end be doing more good to the *whole community,* than he would be doing if he allowed *present, and perhaps local, distress to turn him from following those principles, and to lead him to sacrifice himself for others.* And that, therefore, true wisdom and true charity are to be found in obeying those *natural* laws, by *which we shall be led in the end to the greatest material prosperity.*

"*If this* theory *can* be reconciled with the doctrine of the *Bible* about wealth and men's duty, *then* Political Economy is *not* that mark which the Beast causeth all, both small and great, rich and poor, free and bond, to receive.

"But, contrast with this 'true wisdom,' as it is often called, which springs from the *brain of man,*[*] and is not revealed from Heaven, the words

---

[*] A note, by the Author of *Physical Science,* &c., says: "Dr. Adam Smith, the father of the Modern Science of

of Him who is the wisdom and the power of God."

The author then gives several verses from St. Matt. vi. 28-34; Luke xii. 33, 34; and amongst them, " Ye cannot *serve God and Mammon,*" "For where your treasure is, there will your heart be also," and thus concludes the Chapter (X.)

" This is true wisdom, for it is God's, and it seems to me contrary to that human wisdom called ' Political Economy,' for I cannot understand how that desire for wealth, which has worked out a science of getting it, can be reconciled with such a sacrifice of the world as that described in what I have quoted.

"I think then that ' Political Economy ' may be ' the buying and selling mark.' Now it is said, that the Beast ' causeth all, both *small* and great, rich and poor, free and bond,' to receive the mark. The ' small ' may be those of small account, yet there is another way in which (in this case at least) the ' small ' may be understood. In England, Political Economy is taught in Schools."* I mention this because, though *all know how it is forced* upon ' rich and poor, free and bond,' all may not know how some of the ' small ' have it *stamped upon their helpless little foreheads.*"†

Political Economy, was an *avowed infidel.* Whose is this image and superscription ?"

* See Appendix, No. 1.

† POLITICAL ECONOMISTS.—Of seven prizes given this year by the Cobden Club to the most successful students in Politi-

In Mr. J. A. Froude's still more recent volume of *Short Studies on Great Subjects* as reviewed in the *Times* of the 15th August, 1877, it is said:—

" The State has lost its legitimate influence, the nation is a mere *sum of atoms*, without *coherence or real dependence;* authority is a *vain shadow*, and *wholesome order* has ceased to exist; and the great body of the people is a brainless multitude, weltering loosely about in wild confusion, fierce with *angry jealousies, and filled with discontent and destructive longings.* We have broken down the bonds that upheld the *Commonwealth;* we have sawed through the bulk-head that kept the ship together; and society with us *is an aggregate of dust,* or a *universal scramble of selfishness,* nursed in '*political economy,*' the most *barefaced attempt that has yet been openly made on this earth to regulate human society without God or recognition of the moral law.*"

In order to enlighten any whose politics are influenced by the impression that the " Unrestricted Competition Policy" of 1846 was instigated

cal Economy in connection with the Cambridge University Extension Syndicate for conducting Local Lectures, five have been awarded to female competitors. The winners are Gertrude Gregson, of Highbury-Bowdon; Sarah Smithson, York; Hannah Cheetham, Southport; Annie Hankinson, Altrincham; Elizabeth H. Sturge, Cheltenham; H. R. Krüger, Hull; and Alfred W. Tarbotton, Hull.—*Times,* 11th Dec., 1877.

and carried by the aid of the *labouring classes,* it is well that such persons should be undeceived and learn the truth from the Right Hon. Robert Lowe.

In addressing the constituency of Kidderminster in 1858 when he was standing for re-election, in the *Times* of the 10th December, 1858, Mr. Lowe is reported to have said, " I have told you very plainly that I think the Reform Bill (1832) has fully and satisfactorily answered the purpose of those who framed it, and I have told you that in my opinion the present state of the question of Reform does not arise from any feeling on the part of the people that the Reform Bill has not worked well for them (*some disapprobation from a part of the audience*) : *of this I am certain* that if the *working-classes* had had their destinies in *their own hands* some years ago, they would not have been in as good a position as now they are. (Oh! Oh!) *Look at the abolition of the tax upon corn,* which was perhaps the greatest blessing that any government could offer to a people, but *that* was accomplished *for* the people and *not by them.**
In fact so far as their organization *enabled them* to do so, *they* offered *the greatest opposition to that measure* (Cheers). Now what are the *people of America*—where *every one has a vote*—about to do ?

---

* The right hon. gentleman said what was no doubt true, for in America and other countries, where the voice of the people prevails, there is no *reciprocity* with England in her Free Imports System.

To restore and to strengthen the system of Protection," &c.

This was in 1858, and the Americans have continued and will continue to do so, and whoever has read the great work of their countryman " Carey," — the eminent statistician, — entitled, " *The Harmony of Interests*—agricultural, manufacturing, and commercial," wherein he has so clearly shown the danger of the Free Imports policy, will know how small a chance there is of their ever adopting it. The work was published in 1851, at Philadelphia (J. S. Skinner, 79, Walnut Street). For the aid of those who are seeking for *truth*, extracts from the two first pages are given,* and all who wish to investigate the causes of the progress and decline of industrial communities will do well to procure, if possible, a copy of this work, and ponder over it.

The President of America in 1869 (General Grant, the writer believes, who has lately visited this country and been deservedly honoured) in his Address to Congress, in a spirit of true patriotism, said in relation to Canada.

"The reciprocal trade with Canada has not been favourably considered by the Administration as the *advantages of* such *Treaty* would be *wholly* in favour of *Canada*. Except *possibly a few engaged in trade between* the two countries, no citizen in the *United States* would be *benefited* by

* See Appendix, No. 2.

reciprocity, as our *inland taxes* would give the *British producer* a protection almost equal to the *protection* given to *domestic manufactures* by *Tariff*. .... American manufactures are now *increasing with great rapidity* under the *encouragement they receive*, and this will probably cause *imports* to fall off in a *few years. Manufactures* are becoming *diffused over all sections of the country*. The extension of railways in Europe, and in *the East* is bringing *into competition* with *our agricultural* products, *like products of other countries;* and therefore *self-preservation* dictates *caution* and the necessity for other markets for the sale of our supplies."* The Message concluded by an expression of belief that " the patriotism and statesmanship of Congress will suggest topics for legislation *most conducive to the interests of the whole people.*"

May similar patriotism and statesmanship be found to suggest topics for legislation conducive to the same end in England!

Happily the path of *duty* is ever the *safest* course to enter on, and if, as Adam Smith said— " Defence is of much more importance than opulence "—

We must *above all things strive* to improve and preserve the health and vigour of the labouring population of the kingdom.

The writer of the following pages has imposed

* See Appendix, No. 3.

on himself a by-no-means pleasing task. He has felt himself bound to point out unpleasant truths, for the smoothness of flattery will not avail us.

Conscience, as well as judgment, teaches him that however duty and interest may at any time seem to clash, yet, that, whether in public or private, or national concerns, integrity, and *a love of justice* is the true and only path to safety, honour, and success. *A true Conservative* knows his duty as a subject and performs it cheerfully. He regards the poor and helpless, not as burdens upon his land, who have scarcely a right to live, except as they minister to the pride and convenience of the rich, but as a sacred charge to be especially protected and cherished.*

He has no idea of politics apart from morals: of morals not founded on religion; of religion not derived from Revelation. He holds conservative principles as comprehending our duty to our neighbour, our country, and our Queen, *all* with reference to God as our supreme ruler and judge.

During each session of Parliament, may all sincerely pray that God "will be pleased to direct and prosper all their consultations to the advancement of His glory, the good of His Church, the safety, honour and welfare of our sovereign and her dominions." Let all remember what is recorded of a nation of old and was "written for our learning." In addressing the Israelites God

* See Appendix, No. 4.

said—"*Hear*, O my people, and I will assure thee, O Israel, if thou *wilt* hearken unto me. There shall no *strange* god be in thee; neither shalt thou worship any other God. *I* am the Lord thy God, who brought thee out of the land of Egypt; open thy mouth wide, and I will fill it. But my people would not hear *my* voice, and Israel would not obey me. So I gave them up unto their own hearts' lusts; and let them follow their own imaginations."* (Ps. lxxxi.)

In order that any reader of the first part of this volume may be able to judge how far the anticipations of the writer as to the ultimate effect of the Free Imports policy of 1846 (without *reciprocity* by other nations) have been realized, a few letters which appeared in 1854-5, in a weekly journal of sound constitutional principles, and conducted with great ability, are herewith republished.

---

* Bishop Horne, in his well-known and valuable *Commentary on the Book of Psalms*, says:—"When we see men enabled, by wealth and power, to accomplish the inordinate desire of their hearts, and carry their worldly schemes into execution, without meeting any obstructions in their way, we are apt to envy their felicity; whereas such prosperity in wickedness is the surest mark of divine displeasure, the heaviest punishment of disobedience, both in individuals and communities."—"My people would not hearken to *my* voice, and Israel *would none of me:* so I gave them up unto *their own hearts'* lust; and they *walked in their own counsels.*—(Bible Translation)*.

Shakspeare tells us :—

> Sweet are the uses of adversity,
> Which, like the toad, ugly and venomous,
> Wears yet a precious jewel in his head.
>
> *As You Like It*, ii. 1.

It was after experiencing "Adversity,"—*after his Fall*,—that Wolsey gave *that* advice to his Secretary, Thomas Cromwell, by heeding which we should all be, and *do*, the better, perhaps:—

> "Cromwell, I charge thee, fling away ambition;
> By that sin fell the angels; how can man then,
> The image of his Maker, hope to win by 't?
> Love thyself last; cherish those hearts that hate thee;
> Corruption wins not more than honesty.
> Still in thy right hand carry gentle peace,
> To silence envious tongues. BE JUST AND FEAR NOT.
> Let all the ends thou aim'st at be thy country's,
> Thy God's and Truth's; then if thou fall'st, O Cromwell,
> Thou fall'st a blessed martyr."
>
> *Henry VIII.*, Act iii., Scene 2.

GOD SAVE THE QUEEN.

O Thou, by whose almighty nod the *scale*
Of Empire rises, or alternate falls;
Send forth the saving virtues round the land,
In bright patrol; white Peace, and social Love;
The tender-looking Charity, intent
On greater deeds, and shedding tears through smiles.
Undaunted Truth, and *Dignity of Mind:*
Courage compos'd, and keen sound Temperance
Healthful in heart and look; clear Chastity
With blushes reddening as she moves along,
Disordered at the deep regard she draws;
Rough Industry; Activity untired,
With copious life informed, and all awake;
While, in the radiant front, superior shines
That *first paternal virtue—Public Zeal*;
Which throws on all an equal wide survey;
And, *ever-musing on the Common Weal,*
Still labours gloriously with some great design.

THE TENDENCIES OF THE POLICY OF 1846 ARE TO DENATIONALIZE AND DECOLONIZE.

It is not unnatural that it should take a long time to convince a man, born with a good constitution, and who from his youth up to manhood has enjoyed robust health, that he has, with *advancing age*, contracted, and is suffering from, some INTERNAL *disease* inducing weakness. Rather than become *convinced* of this, he will have recourse to a variety of physicians, and change them frequently. Either, however, for lack of true wisdom, or courage, on the part of the patient to make known fairly and fully to his medical advisers *all* his sensations, or candidly to confess some act to which the origin of the derangement of his system, and consequent failing health might be surely traced, or from the medical men thinking that the *only* means that would *eradicate* the disease would operate *too slowly to satisfy the patient*, or to increase, or *even uphold* their own fame and interest, the remedies from time to time administered are found not really to invigorate the patient's health and constitution, though perhaps just as a cosmetic might do, if used, as a cure for jaundice, it may afford occasionally, for a short time, *a fallacious external* appearance, while, *all the time*, the disease is becoming more complicated and general, and undermining more and more the patient's constitutional power. Unfavourable symptoms return, therefore, quicker and quicker, and with increased severity; and if the patient's originally good constitution has become too exhausted (by the delay of the only sure, though, perhaps, SLOW remedy) to bear the process *absolutely necessary* for restoration to a healthy condition, the patient may linger on for a time in a diseased condition, but with very little enjoyment, and he finds himself unable to occupy the position he once did in the world's eye.

Let us then, for our present purpose, assume that, in the case put, the nation is the *patient*. True it is, all empires have been subject to decay; but the domination of the mighty nations of antiquity was prolonged or shortened *as their inherent capacity for maintaining power* was more or less active, or as the races around them were more or less feeble. Therefore, though constrained perhaps to admit the principle that every empire must eventually yield the sceptre to a younger and more impetuous rival, it may be laid down as an axiom that it is in the power of the people of a dominant nation to *lengthen the period of its supremacy to an extent not calculable by them.** The

* See Appendix.

whole end of statesmanship and politics* is in the *prolongation of the national status;* or, it may be, *supremacy;* consequently if we can arrive at the TRUE *causes* of the *symptoms* of decay, we may, by removing them, tend to preserve our progress *in the proper path*, if not by *positively indicating* whither it lies, which *may* be not possible, at any rate indicating what *course it is dangerous to pursue.*

It is now two-and-thirty years since our present Premier (then Mr. Disraeli, now Earl of Beaconsfield) wrote of England:—

"The disease we labour under is *social disorganization.*" The grand and all-important question then is, What has induced this disease? Nothing could be gained by finding fault with any particular Ministry or parties in the State conscientiously labouring to discharge their duties. The difficulties *any* Ministry, in these our days, has to

---

* The sphere of the Civil Government may be briefly defined to be the maintenance of peace and good order, and the careful attention to everything that tends to promote the highest temporal well-being of all. Wise legislation, equal administration of law and justice, security to life, health, and property, DEVELOPMENT OF MATERIAL RESOURCES, promotion of education, are all means towards the great object of securing for all the most favourable opportunity possible in this present world for living that life, and attaining that growth and development in all the elements of our human nature, in body and mind, in heart and soul, and spirit, for which our Creator sent us into the world. St. Paul says in his Epistle to the Romans, ch. xiii., "Let every soul be subject unto the higher powers;" and also, "Render unto all their due."

contend with, are great indeed; and every lover of his country ought to do his best in endeavouring to aid, not embarrass, their endeavours to advance *the* NATIONAL interest."

Whether *this* has been or can be the result of the policy of 1846, it is the object of the writer of these pages to enable readers to form an opinion from the facts disclosed. When commenting on these, he has always been influenced by the maxim, " Nothing extenuate, or set down aught in malice."

The present Dean of Westminster, writing of the late Samuel Taylor Coleridge, says, " His *Table-Talk* marks him, in my judgment, as a very great man indeed, *whose equal* I know not where to find in England." (See Stanley's *Life of Arnold*, vol. ii., p. 432.) It must be admitted then that Coleridge is no mean authority in what he said in relation to Corn Laws and modern Political Economy. In his *Table-Talk* we find that in 1834, not long before his death, he said—

" In the argument of the Corn Laws there is a μετάβασις εἰς ἄλλο γένος. It may be admitted that the great principles of commerce require the interchange of commodities to be free; but commerce, which is *barter, has no proper range beyond luxuries or conveniences ;*—it is *properly* the *complement* to the full existence and development of a State. But *how can it be shown that the principles* applicable to an interchange of *conveniences* or *luxuries* apply also to *an interchange of necessaries?** *No State can be such properly which is not self-subsistent at least;* for no State that *is not so, is essentially independent.* The nation that cannot even EXIST

* Since these pages were sent for publication, the *Times* of the 12th January, 1878, had a leader, of which the following is the commencement. The writer of that leader will perhaps now not feel inclined to differ with the sentiments of Coleridge, expressed in 1834, for mark, reader, in rather (and rightly) a tone of regret, he says, "the case may be stated by saying that our foreign custom has declined," (he might have added, and our Home-trade also), "but that our population nevertheless increasing, we have not been relieved from the necessity of seeking our food from abroad," &c.

We lately had occasion to refer to the alarm which has been produced in certain quarters by the discovery that the imports of this country have for some years past been exceeding the exports to a constantly increasing extent; and we published on Wednesday the official returns, which show the amount of the difference for the year which has just been brought to a conclusion. It appears, from these returns, that the balance of international trade was against us during 1877 to the extent of about 145 millions, and that this amount exceeds by no less than 30 millions the similar difference of the preceding year. When we look into the particulars of the account, and ask what are the articles of foreign production which we have required in such excess of our power to send goods in exchange for them, it appears that the explanation of our transactions lies within a very narrow compass. Our imports of food grains and flour exceeded those of 1876 by about 12 millions, and the increased value of such articles as cheese, coffee, fresh and preserved meats, currants, hops, potatoes and sugar, represent another sum of the same amount. The value of our sugar import exceeds that of 1876 by more than 6 millions, but this represents a larger quantity, as well as a larger value, and partly, at least, depends upon a great increase in the amount of English-made preserves, which have

without the COMMODITY of *another nation,* is in effect the slave of that other nation. In *common times,* indeed, *pecuniary interest will prevail,* and prevent a *ruinous exercise of the power* which the nation supplying the necessary must have over the nation which has *only the convenience or luxury* to return; but such interest, both in *individuals and nations,* will yield to many stronger passions. Is Holland any authority to the contrary? If so, Tyre and Sidon and Carthage were so! Would you put ENGLAND on a footing with a *country* which can be *overrun in a campaign, and starved in a year?"*

And of "the modern Political Economy" he adds—"The entire tendency of the modern or Malthusian political economy is to *denationalize.*

to a considerable extent superseded those imported from foreign countries. However certain details of the account may be explained, it is manifest, upon the whole, that the larger balance against us depends entirely upon the importation of articles of NECESSITY; and hence that the case may be stated by saying that our foreign custom has DECLINED, but that, our population nevertheless increasing, we have not been relieved from the necessity of seeking our food from abroad. Our expenditure, within certain limits, cannot be curtailed in consequence of a decreasing income, and the slackness of our trade has not reached a degree which has compelled us to deny ourselves enjoyments which habit has rendered necessary to our comfort. We have, doubtless, drawn upon our foreign investments to pay for the luxuries to which we have become accustomed, but we have done so in the full expectation that a short period of time would see the commencement of a beneficial change in our affairs. It is of the first importance to consider whether such an expectation is well-founded.

It would dig up the charcoal foundations of the temple of Ephesus to burn as fuel for a steam-engine."*

In 1851, five letters "addressed to the Public on Free Trade, by Agricola," were published (by Seeleys, Fleet Street), and at the present time, when the minds of so many who, when the late Sir Robert Peel introduced his " great experiment" in 1846, thought favourably of it, are, after thirty-two years' experience of its results, beginning to doubt the wisdom of free imports without reciprocity on the part of other nations, and to think that the "great experiment" has been tried as long as it can be with a due regard to *national* interests, the following extracts from " Agricola's" letters

* See pp. 303-4, in *Specimens of the Table Talk of Samuel Taylor Coleridge*, 2nd Ed., London. John Murray, Albemarle Street, 1836.

Of "Machinery" he says, "The wonderful powers of Machinery can, by multiplying production, render the mere *arte facta* of life actually cheaper; thus, money and all other things being supposed the same in value, a silk gown is five times cheaper now than it was in Queen Elizabeth's time; but machinery cannot cheapen, in anything like an equal degree, the immediate growths of nature or the immediate necessaries of man. Now, the *arte facta* are sought by the higher classes of society in a proportion incalculably beyond that in which they are sought by the lower classes; and therefore it is that the vast increase of mechanical powers has not cheapened life and pleasure to the poor as it has done to the rich. In some respects, no doubt, it has done so, as in giving cotton dresses to maid-servants, and penny gin to all. A pretty benefit truly;" Page 224. See Extract from M'Culloch in Letter II., *post*.

will be read with greater interest, and, perhaps, advantage, than when the letters were first published:—

Letter I.
"*The Tendency of Free Trade to impoverish all Classes.*

"Fellow-Countrymen,

"There is one simple view of the question of Free Trade which, it has always appeared to myself, ought to carry with it more than ordinary weight. It is the *tendencies* of a system which stamp its character, and its *ulterior* results which claim attention in *a higher degree* than any *present* indications. The *immediate* results are *temporary;* the *ultimate, permanent.* Now, it must be admitted by every advocate of Free Trade, that one *inevitable* tendency of that system is the following:— to reduce the prices of *all production, the profits of every business, and the wages of every description of labour, to the lowest point.* Mr. Cobden certainly did maintain, if my recollection be correct, that Free Trade would have the effect of raising wages; but such an assertion is not deserving of notice. It is, I think, perfectly evident, and will be admitted upon the slightest reflection by every candid mind, that the effect stated above *is inevitable.*

"Where *unlimited* competition is the accepted principle of traffic, prices *must fall*, and fall to the *lowest extreme; profits must* fall with them, and *wages too.* Custom, it is true, has some share in the regulation of wages; and on *that* account employers may FOR A TIME *continue to maintain* a scale of wages which *is not proportionate to the rate of profit:* but *eventually a low rate of profit* must produce a *corresponding low scale of wages.* But is it desirable that the prices of all production, the profits of every business, and the *wages of every description* of labour, *should be reduced to the lowest point?* Is not this subject deserving of very serious consideration? One which ought not to be lightly dismissed by the politician, or by any private individual personally interested in the matter, as *indeed all* are? Is it not a strange plan for advancing the prosperity of the country, and promoting *the comfort* of its *different classes?* Will any advocate of Free Trade confidently maintain that such means are well adapted *to their end?"*

In his fifth (last) letter, " Agricola" wrote, " Next to the ruin that is gradually overtaking the agricultural population, the principal danger to the country is the loss of its *Colonies* — Colonies, whose interests and welfare are placed upon *a par with those of foreign States,* cannot retain their allegiance to the *Mother-*Country — a Mother-Country, which adopts and carries out in practice *cosmopolitan theories,* cannot recognize the use of Colonies. And, accordingly, the more advanced disciples of Free-trade are prepared at once to cast off the Colonies as useless incumbrances. Government, following at humble distance, are gradually opening their eyes to the same enlightened views. Useless incumbrances the Colonies may be *under the rule of Free-trade:* but when the folly of Free-trade has passed away, more just opinions will prevail upon this subject. To think that there are men, men high in political influence, calling themselves, and reputed to be Statesmen (a name how little deserved!), who, in order to carry out their fantastic schemes, can, knowingly and deliberately, incur the risk of losing the British Colonies, nay, can seriously entertain the question whether Colonial connection shall not be voluntarily abandoned, would be incredible, if it were not fact. Under a *wise system of rule the value* of the Colonies to the *Mother-Country is incalculable;* and so is that of the Mother-Country to them. England, with her circumscribed insular limits, finds in Colonies a substitute for a wider home-domain. In some respects, from their more varied capabilities, she derives from them advantages superior to those of a more compact territory. Surrounded by great and flourishing Colonies, *accessories to her power*, and her magnificence, she sits in queenly dignity, pre-eminent among the nations. Deprived of those colonies, *her sceptre drops from her hands;* her majesty is made to stoop; her power passes away; she ceases *to be the most favoured instrument* in fulfilling the highest purposes of Providence,* and *her very existence* is endangered. Instead of severing the connection between herself and them, let every means be adopted to cement a closer union. *Admit representatives from the Colonies into the British Parliament, thus converting the Colonies from dependencies into equal and integral portions of the Empire—an Empire then of which the world might be proud.* It is generally supposed that, as the Colonies grow into importance, that is to say, as they become an ornament and advantage to the Mother-Country, separation is inevitable. *It might be so upon the present plan;* it would not upon the one named. Let the Colonies go. What then? The *reality* of its situation would burst *upon the country* with the force and the *terror of a thunderclap.* The country would instantly attain sufficient perception of the truth to recognize and deplore its loss. Then behold Britain, no longer *Great*, seated in the midst of the ocean, not now its Queen, but a forlorn and desolate widow. *Foreign competition grows upon her:* in all the *markets of the world she is successfully*

* May 4, 1833.—" Colonization is not only a manifest expedient for, but an imperative duty on, Great Britain. God seems to hold out His finger to us over the sea. But it must be a National colonization, such as was that of the Scotch to America; a colonization of hope, and not such as we have alone encouraged and effected for the last fifty years, a colonization of despair."—*Coleridge's Table Talk*, p. 223, 2nd Ed.

met; *prices come down, profits are reduced, wages are lowered,* wide-spread destitution prevails; and that *destitution,* be it observed, is *permanent.* Foreign countries, by a change of their tariffs—a stroke of the pen—torture her at pleasure. She is bound hand and foot *in the fetters of a grinding commercial slavery.*

Suppose a war breaks out. She has been sacrificing her own maritime resources; she has been fostering those of her opponents; she is beaten at sea. Foreign navies ride triumphant on that ocean, of which she formerly was mistress; her *shores are blockaded:* her *people cry for bread;* and cry in vain; for *America* grows it, *not England.* Her insular position, *once her pride and strength,* is now *weakness and death to her.* The horrors of starvation set in, and she is glad to make an exchange of liberty for life.*

---

* Perhaps some will recollect that a letter, bearing the signature, "John Michel Trutz-Baumwoll" appeared in the *Times* and other journals in 1871, said to be a translation of a German letter, suggesting "Invasion of England by the Germans." This letter was published as a pamphlet by Houlston and Sons, 65, Paternoster Row, 1871.

"Forewarned, Forearmed!"

A copy of the 4th edition is now before the writer, and at p. 9 is the following:—

"Why should England not become a part and a member of the country which rejoices in the possession of such a ruler as the great and humane victor of France?"

Whoever was the author, he was one who knows English habits well, and says, too truly (p. 3), "Nothing remains of the subordination of the different classes which was once so

Or, suppose a commercial crisis arrives, such as is constantly recurring in the course of every few years in this commercial country! but then possibly and probably" (it would be more correct to say, *certainly*) "on a *scale of much greater magnitude*. Formerly, on an occasion of this description, she has fallen back for *support upon her agriculture: that has upheld and carried her safely through the difficulty;* in a little time trade has resumed its accustomed channels, and the stream of prosperity once more flowed in full tide. But *now* the case is altered; her *agriculture is not so productive;* while the *solid rock lay at hand*, she has selected in preference *the foundation of a quicksand:* she has built upon *one huge manufacturing interest*, without a *counterpoise;* there *is no sustaining principle left*, and she sinks, *overwhelmed, into ruin.*

These are no images of *fanciful impossibility*; but descriptions consistent with sober practical truth. But to enumerate all the dangers to the country which this *insane system is gathering round it*, would be an endless task. *At present*, however, all is still. For *some time longer* we may be *amused*

remarkable a feature in English society. There is no longer that mutual confidence and dependence of one class upon another which formerly softened the differences of birth and wealth."

In fact, as Burke said in his *Reflections on the French Revolution*, "the unbought grace of life" no longer exists in England.

by assurances, on the part of *Her Majesty's Ministers, of unbounded prosperity,* coupled with the expression of a hope that, as regards one exception, that of the *agricultural body,* the satisfactory state of trade, *combined with the impetus of the new system,* will soon react upon it with the most beneficial results. Ridiculous hope! The agriculturists are suffering from the *want of remunerative prices,* and Free-Trade *comes* to their assistance *with a further reduction.* At present, all is still, except the slighted murmurs of the agricultural and shipping interests—the first spatterings of the coming storm. Meanwhile the sun is seen shining, red and lurid, in the cloudy horizon, and it is proclaimed by *false prophets* that its appearance *indicates fine weather.* But *come that storm will,* and with a *fury sufficient to rend up by its roots the venerable British Oak. England is playing a desperate game.* She is *gambling with her destiny,* while the *odds are a thousand to one against* her, and, if she escape ruin, it must be by the intervention of a miracle. If she *persist in her present policy a train of causes must come into gradual operation which will exert over her a more and more fatal influence,* and, at length, *seal her destruction.*

Englishmen! awake from your stupor, and shake off these fatal delusions. Abandon your blind attachment to this *misnamed theory,* this struggle of *misery,* this *impoverishing starving competition!* Provide for your comfort, maintain your independence, *secure your safety, retain your Colonies, look to your Home and Colonial trades, and adopt means for their adequate development:* examine also into the state of your *domestic* affairs, and set about the *reduction of your debt,* that heavy mortgage upon your property. Estimate *too* the Foreign trade at its *proper* value: *but do not struggle for it at a cost which may render even its acquisition a curse:* do not sacrifice for it *everything you possess; greatness, comfort, independence, existence.* Thus acting, and relying upon the blessing of *Him, who raises and destroys Empires at pleasure,* you will long retain your place at the head of the nations of the world, present an impregnable front to the assaults of all your foes, enjoy the largest measure of national and individual prosperity, and reach, hereafter, a position to which your present, exalted though it be, is but an infancy preparatory to manhood.

This was addressed to his fellow-countrymen by "Agricola" in 1851, but, alas! his warning remains unheeded to the present time, and "dangers to the country, it is to be feared, have been *gathering* round it by continuing the insane system."

About the same time, or a little earlier than these letters were published, a very clever and amusing work appeared, intitled, *Sam Slick, the Clock-maker,* by the late Colonial Judge, Mr. Halliburton, and, it will doubtless be remembered, created no slight sensation.

And when, some years later, *Nature and Human Nature*, by the same Author, was published (1855), it was found that years had not impaired, but improved and matured his powers of mind. There were in the later volumes the same *keen insight into life*—the same appreciation of men and things, *not according to a conventional and merely nominal price*, but *according to their real and intrinsic value*—the same *practical wisdom, the fruit of much deep and grave meditation*. Both works abound in graphic and racy sketches of *Transatlantic life*, in laughable anecdotes and amusing tales, *but also in instructive discussions on public questions, affecting the social and political condition both of the Mother-Country, and of her still faithful as well as of her emancipated Colonies*. One of the most important of these questions, and one on which Mr. Halliburton is no mean authority, is the question, "*what is the destiny of British North America?*" and the question might well be extended to others, if not to all, of our Colonies. The able Article, " Greater or Lesser Britain " (in the July number of the *Nineteenth Century*), by Sir Julius Vogel, and the object he has in view, gives at this time a peculiar interest to the facetious reply made to the foregoing question.

"Oh," says I, "I could tell you if I was Colonial Minister, because, *I should then have the power to guide that destiny. I know full well what ought to be done*, and the *importance of doing it* soon, but I am not in the position to *give them the right direction:* no *English* statesmen have the information, the time, or the inclination to meddle with the subject. To get rid of the bother of them, they have given up all control and said to them 'there is responsible government for you, now toddle off home, and manage your own affairs.' Yes, yes, so far, so good—they can manage their own *domestic* matters, but who is to manage their *foreign affairs*, as I said *once* to *a Member* of Parliament. They have *outgrown Colonial dependence, their minority is ended;* the clerkship is out; they *are of age* now; they never did well in your house; they were put out to nurse at a *distance;* they had their schooling; they learnt figures easily; they can add and multiply faster than you can to save your soul; and *now they are uneasy.* They have your name, for *they are your children,* but they are *younger sons.* The *estates and all the honours* go to the ELDEST, who *resides at home.* They know but little about THEIR PARENTS, further than their bills have been liberally paid, but they have no PERSONAL *acquaintance with you. You are tired of maintaining them,* and they have too much ENERGY to continue to be a burden to you. They *can and they* WILL *do for themselves.*

"Have you ever thought of setting them up in business on *their own account,* or of *taking them into partnership with yourself?* In the *course of nature they must form some* CONNEXION SOON,

Shall they *seek it* with *you or the States,* or *intermarry among themselves* and *begin the world on their own hook?* These *are important questions* and they must *be answered* soon. Have you acquired their *confidence and affection?* What has been your manner to them? Do you treat *them* like *your other younger children that remain at home?* Them you put with your army and navy, place a sword in their hand and say, *distinguish yourselves* and the highest *rewards are open to you,* or you send them to the *Church or the Bar,* and *say a mitre or a coronet* shall be *the prize to contend* for. If you prefer diplomacy, you shall be *attaché* to your elder brother. I will place the ladder before you; ascend it. If you like politics, I will place you in Parliament, and if you have no talents sufficient for the House of Commons, you shall go out as Governor of one of our colonies. *Those appointments belong of right to them; but they can't help themselves* AT PRESENT (sic). Get one while you can.

"Have you done this, or anything like it for your *children abroad?* If you have, perhaps you will be good enough to furnish me with some names that I may mention them when I hear you accused of *neglect.* You are very hospitable and considerate to *strangers.* The representative of any *little insignificant German state,* of the size of a *Canadian township, has a place* assigned him on *State* occasions. Do you ever show the *same* attention to the *delegate of a colony* of *infinitely more* extent and value than even Ireland? There can't be a *doubt* you *have*, though *I* have never heard of it. Such little trifles are matters of course, but still as *great interests are at stake*, perhaps it would *be as well to notice such things occasionally* in *the Gazette*, for *distant and humble* RELATIONS are always *trusting*.

"Ah, Doctor," says I, "THINGS CAN'T AND WON'T REMAIN LONG AS THEY ARE, (in original *sic*) England has three things among which to choose for her North American Colonies:—First; *incorporation with herself*, and *representation* in *Parliament*.* Secondly: *independence*. Thirdly:

* Since these pages were sent to the publisher, a most interesting letter, full of sound advice, and proving the great advantage to us of the "incorporation of our Colonies with the Mother-Country," appeared in the *Times* of the 10th of January, 1878; and the writer of these pages hopes our statesmen and legislators will ponder over the advice given.

THE CANADIAN MILITIA.
To the Editor of the *Times*.

SIR,—During my service in India I was greatly impressed with the fact that the large force of British troops we maintain there is to a certain extent locked up, the effect of which would eventually show itself in crippling the movements of the English Army, and also in giving weight to the arguments of other Powers who, being aware of the situation, may differ from us on points seriously affecting the interests of England and her Colonial Empire.

That the situation is known may be seen in the friendly criticisms of intelligent foreigners. Herr Wickede wrote freely about our Army some months since to the *Cologne*

annexation with the States. Instead of deliberating and selecting what will be most conducive to the *interest* of *herself and her dependencies* she is *allowing* things to take *their chance.* Now, this is

Gazette, and last month a friendly critic in a leading New York newspaper, pointed out that the days of foreign legions are past. "Austrians and Hessians," he remarks, "do not want to be hired, they have their own fighting to do; and if England has any fear for her Empire, she must do as the Germans and Americans did—fight for it." I am no advocate for fighting; my object in writing is merely to hint that some steps might be considered by which it could be made plain to all interested that the whole of our English Army in India could be set free, not so much for the object of fighting, as for giving reasonable weight to the counsels of England in troublesome times.

Although we can no longer count on foreign legions, I believe the time is approaching when our colonies will be able to afford us unlimited help. I have just returned from a tour in Canada, and through the kindness of Lieutenant-General Sir Selby Smyth, K.C.M.G., commanding Militia, I have his reports of 1875 and 1876 before me. Before reading his reports I was struck with the military spirit of the Canadians and the conflict in consequence with their Government, which has little money to spare for the Militia, from the cost of continually extending its possessions in the magnificent western territory of the Dominion. Sir Selby Smyth says in his report of 1876 :—

"There is a great military spirit among all classes of the population of Canada, which would insure immense efforts and sacrifices in the event of alarm or apprehension of danger. It has been frequently exhibited and it is hardly necessary for me to bring it again to notice so prominently except with the view of adding that, given that valuable element of zealous patriotism, it should be cultivated and encouraged in every possible way to serve the country efficiently, if ever suddenly required to be called into action."

all very well in matters over which we have no control, because Providence directs things better than we can; but if one of these three alternatives is *infinitely better than the other*, and it *is* in

The active Militia of 10 out of 12 districts were called out in 1876 for training. This force consisted of five regiments of Cavalry, 15 field batteries, 40 garrison batteries, and 90 battalions of Infantry. Sir Selby Smyth remarks, " It must be borne in mind that the active Militia is but the advance guard of the army of Canada, in case a general call to arms should occur. The real force of the country should then be represented by the Reserve Militia, amounting to some 600,000 men."

This prodigious force actually exists and is enrolled ! Sir Selby Smyth recommended that a reliable officer in each division should assure himself every year and report that all the men on the rolls were effective. The country, however, is poor, and in consequence of want of funds the active Militia were of necessity much below their strength when called out. The Artillery, however, under the careful inspection of Lieutenant-Colonel T. Bland Strange, R.A., Dominion Inspector of Artillery, is in fine condition, and the field guns are of the latest and most approved pattern. All that is wanted is a little more money expended in arms and in the training of complete regiments to fully develope and satisfy the military spirit of the Canadian officers. I cannot help thinking this is the moment for the English Government to step in and invite, say, 30 battalions to volunteer and place themselves on the list for two years' garrison duty in England. It would be no great tax on the Mother-Country to pay for their yearly training compared with so great a step towards the consolidation of our Empire. During the Crimean War the English Militia volunteered readily for garrison duty in Malta and Gibraltar ; and as I have some knowledge of the Militia service, my father having commanded his county regiment for 50 years, and having myself served as a Captain, I feel that an application to the Militia of Great Britain and

our power to adopt it, *it is the height of folly* not to do so. I know it is said, for I have often heard it myself, WHY WE CAN *but lose the Colonies at last.* Pardon me, you *can do more than that*, for you can lose their *affections* also.* If the partnership is to

Ireland for 30 regiments to place themselves on the list for two years' garrison duty in India for a moderate bounty and a year's pension on return home would be attended with success. The innate love of an outing alone would bring it about, together with the knowledge every Militiaman has that India is popular with the British soldier, and that he volunteers from regiment to regiment to remain there. As the English regiments embarked for India, the Canadian regiments could come to England to take their place. It may be urged that the readiest plan would be to increase our Militia at home, but it is well-known that already their enlisting clashes with that of the Line.

It is to be hoped that it may be long before our Militia have to go to India, but the knowledge throughout the world that they are ready to embark, and that our right arm is no longer tied up in that country, would give greater weight to the advice or remonstrances which our Government may be called on to make in future.

Your obedient servant,
OBSERVER.

* " If there is any lesson which we should draw from the loss of the United States, it is the misfortune of parting from those Colonies in ill-will and irritation. We parted with those great Colonies because we attempted to coerce them; and if we now part with our present Colonies it will be because we expel them from our dominion. The circumstances are different, but the result will be the same, and that result must be the bitter alienation and undying enmity of those great countries. For my own part I see with dismay the course which is now being taken, a part at once cheese-paring in point of economy, and spendthrift in point of national character. I will be no

be dissolved, it had better be done by *mutual consent*, and it would be for the *interest of both that you should part friends*. You *didn't shake hands with*, but *fists* AT us, when *we separated*. We had a stand-up fight and you got licked, and wounds were given, that the best part of a century hasn't healed, and wounds that will leave tender spots *for ever*, so don't talk *nonsense*.

"Now, Doctor, mark my words, I say again, things *won't remain long as they are*."

Connected with this topic Mr. Halliburton has some stringent remarks on the management of colonial affairs in general, and of those in Canada in particular :—

"Well, there is one thing you *can* boast, *Canada is the most valuable and beautiful appendage of the British Crown*.

"*England* may boast of it as such" he said, "but *I* have no right to do so. I prefer being one of the pariahs of the Empire, a *mere colonist*, having NEITHER *grade nor caste, without a country* party to it, and I beg to enter my humble and earnest protest against a course which I conceive to be ruinous to the honour and fatal to the best interests of the Empire."—*Lord Carnarvon in the House of Lords, Feb.* 1870.

When are we likely to have a Ministry more able than the present, and with the Premier and Colonial Secretary possessing such strong feelings as to the importance of the consolidation of our Colonies with the Mother-Country? If the present Ministry could carry out this most desirable policy their names would indeed shine brightly in a future History of England.

of my own, and *without nationality.* I am an humble man, and when I am asked where I come from, readily answer the Chaudiere river. Where is that? Out of the world? *Extra flammantia limina mundi.* What is the name of your *country?* It is not a *country,* it is only a *place.* It is better to have no flag than a borrowed one. If *I had one, I should* have *to defend* it. If it were wrested from me I should be disgraced, while my victorious enemy would be thanked by the *Imperial Legislature,* and rewarded by his sovereign. If I *were triumphant,* the affair *would* be deemed *too small to merit a notice in the Gazette.* He who called out the Militia and quelled amid a shower of *balls,* the late rebellion, was *knighted.* He who assented amid a shower of *eggs* to a Bill to indemnify the rebels, was created an earl. Now, to pelt a Governor-General with eggs, is an overt act of treason, for it is an attempt to throw off the *yoke.* If therefore, he was advanced in the peerage for remunerating traitors for their losses, he ought now to assent to another Act for reimbursing the expenses of the exhausted stores of the poultry yards, and be made a marquess, unless the British see a difference between a rebel mob and an indignant crowd, between those whose life has been spent in hatching mischief, and those who desired to scare the foul birds from their nests.

"If that man had been a colonist, the despatch marked 'private' would have said 'it served you right' whereas it announced to him '*you are one of us*,' and to mark our approbation of your conduct, you may add one of those savoury missiles to your coat of arms, that others may be *egged* on to do their duty. Indeed we *couldn't well have a flag of our own*. The Americans have a very appropriate and elegant one, containing stripes emblematical of their slaves, and stars to represent their free states, while a Connecticut goose typifies the good cheer of thanksgiving day. It *is true* we have the honour of fighting under that of England ;[*] but there is, as we have seen, this *hard condition*

[*] Another letter from "Observer," in the *Times* of the 12th January, 1878 is interesting :—

The Canadian Militia.

To the Editor of the *Times*.

Sir,—During a profound peace with a friendly neighbour, whose standing army is less than 25,000 men, it would be most uncalled for the Canadian Government, even if it had the means, to call out, arm, and equip its reserve Militia of 600,000 men. I repeat, however, that this enormous force is enrolled, and every man must turn out when called on or take the consequences. No such law, I believe, exists in any other part of the empire, and the Canadians deserve credit for it. With regard to the active Militia, it is seven years since the Fenian raid mentioned by your correspondent "Linesman," during which time there has been a great improvement. I saw very fine regiments last September in Canada, and from that time have been impressed with the source of strength stored up in such young and loyal nations as Canada and Australia on the flanks of our empire. Their hearty co-operation, which is to be had for the asking, alone is wanted to enable us to garrison India in case of war, and set our army

annexed to it, we must consent to be taxed, to reimburse the losses of those whom by our gallantry we subdue. If we take Sebastopol, we must pay for the damage we have done. We are not entitled to a separate flag, and I am afraid if we had one we should be subject to ridicule. A pure white ground would prefigure our snow-drifts; a gull with outspread wings, our credulous qualities; and a few discoloured eggs, portray our celebrated missiles. But what sort of a flag would that be? No, sir, *these provinces should be united*, and *they would, from their territorial extent, their commercial enterprise, their mineral wealth, their wonderful agricultural productions, and above all, their intelligent, industrious, and still loyal population, in time form a nation second to none on earth;* until *then* I prefer to be a citizen of the world.

"I once asked an Indian *where he* lived; I meant of course where his camp was, but the question was too broad and puzzled him. Stretching out his arm and describing a circle with his heel, he said, 'I live in all these woods!' Like him, I live in *all this world*. Those who, like the English and Americans, *have appropriated so large a portion of it to themselves*, may severally boast if they think proper of their respective governments there free to support the interests of England where it may be most required.

Your obedient servant,
Observer.

and territories. My boast sir, is a peculiar one, that I *have nothing to boast of.*

"If such are your views," I said, "I must say I do not understand that absurd act of firing from Parliament House. It is, I assure you, reprobated everywhere. Our folks say your party commenced as old *hunkers* and ended as *barn-burners.*

"That remark threw him off his guard; he rose up greatly agitated; his eyes flashed fire, and he extended out his arm as if he intended by gesticulation to give full force to what he was about to say. He stood in this attitude for a moment without uttering a word, when, by a sudden effort, he mastered himself, and took up his hat to walk on the terrace and recover his composure.

"As he reached the door he turned, and said; 'The assenting to that *infamous Indemnity Act,* Mr. Slick, and the still more disreputable manner in which it received the *gubernatorial function,* has produced an impression in Canada *that no loyal man'*——but he again checked himself and left the sentence unfinished.

"I was sorry I had pushed him so hard, but the way he tried to evade the subject at first, the bitterness of his tone, and the excitement into which the allusion threw him, *convinced me that the English neither knew who their real friends in Canada are, nor how to retain their affections.*

"When he returned, I said to him, 'I was only jesting about your having no grievances in Canada, and I regret having agitated you. I agree with you, however, that it is of no *use to remonstrate with the English Public. If you want to be heard, attract their attention in the first instance by talking of their own immediate concerns; and, while they are regarding you with intense interest and anxiety, by a sleight-of-hand shift the dissolving view, and substitute a sketch of your own.* For instance, says you, How is it the army in the Crimea had no tents in the autumn and no *huts* in the winter—the hospitals no fittings, and the doctors no nurses or medicines? How is it disease and neglect have killed more than the enemy? Why is England the laughing-stock of Russia, and the butt of French and Yankee ridicule? And how does it happen this country is filled with grief and humiliation from one end of it to the other?' I will tell you. These affairs were *managed by a branch of the Colonial Office.* The Minister for that department said to the *Army,* as he did to the *distant provinces,* 'Manage your *own affairs, and don't bother us.'* Then pause and say slowly and emphatically, '*You have now a taste of what we have endured in the Colonies. The same incompetency has ruled over both,*'" &c.

This, be it remembered, was written in 1855 by one peculiarly well acquainted with the feelings entertained by our colonists, and possessing a large share of *practical wisdom—the fruit of much deep and grave meditation.*

And what says the *Times'* correspondent from Australia, dating from Sydney, 4th August last, whose very intelligent letter appears in the *Times* of the 16th October, 1877, under the head of "Australian Defences?"

Writing in relation to Sir William Jervoise's recommendation, that "*the Mother-Country should provide an ironclad ship of war for the defence of the colony*, the colony paying all expenses for keeping it," the correspondent says:—

"It is to be hoped that the proposal will receive very *serious consideration*. The arrangement would be to some extent novel, and the study of its details opens up a great many considerations touching the financial relations of the Mother-Country to the colony. The scheme, too, might furnish a precedent, but it seems to many who *look at the matter from a colonial point of view, that it would be a good precedent in more respects than one*. Of course we can understand that the Admiralty would prefer to keep clear of all inconvenient complications with Colonial Governments, which are apt to be touchy and exacting. There is a *beautiful simplicity in the Admiralty minding its own business*, and leaving the Colonial Government to contract for the building and equipment of its own ironclad and the management of it according to its own fancy. But in managing *the affairs of a great empire, something else has to be considered than avoiding difficulties. The matter is* not merely a *Colonial, it is an Imperial one. It is of real importance to the Admiralty that the defence of the Port of Sydney should be thorough and effective."* My Lords cannot wash their hands of us and say, " There ! do as you like. You spend your own money. Please yourselves." *If we do badly for ourselves, we do badly for the British Navy.* If from blundering incapacity, or *from not being properly helped and advised, we let Port Jackson fall into the hands of an enemy, it is not we merely that would suffer, but away will go the depôt of the Imperial Navy in these seas.* Even apart from that consideration, *the Empire is interested in having its Colonies secure,* and in having the money they spend in their defence *wisely and efficiently spent.* It may, perhaps, be argued by those who are strongly influenced by precedent that it is unusual to put an Imperial ship or Imperial officers in any way at the disposal or under the control of a Colonial Government. This objection, however, is rather apparent than real, for the vessel in question would be detailed specially for Colonial service, and would not be at liberty to leave Colonial waters without the leave of the local Government; *it would, so far as discipline was concerned, remain an* INTEGRAL PART *of the Imperial Navy,* and the Governor of the Colony, as the representative of Her Majesty, would be the nominal head of our local navy, just as he is of our local army. It is obvious, also, that if the ships of war to be *maintained by the several Colonies all belonged to Her Majesty's Navy*, co-operation between them, if at any time it should be desirable suddenly to concentrate our one force, would be much more easy, and likely to be much more efficient than if each Colony had its separate ship, with its separate service, and with no supreme officer in any quarter. A spasmodic alliance of Colonial Navies, each navy consisting of one ship, each commander equal in rank to the others, *and each Colony jealous of the rest*, would not be a very formidable combination for a bold, decisive, and dashing enemy to contend with. It would cost the Colonies no more to have their naval defence under Imperial than under local control, while they would get much for their money in the shape of security; *and if such an arrangement would be really the best in the interest of Colonial defence, would it not also be best in the interest of the Empire, which is not unconcerned in having its Colonies well defended?*

The question is deserving of *very serious consideration, because behind it lies the application of the same principle to our land forces.* What is true of ships is true of forts; what is true of blue jackets is true of red jackets. The point has already been mooted in the Colony whether it would not be better to have the whole of our land-force a part of Her Majesty's army, the entire cost of arrangement, of course, to be borne by the Colonial revenues. The men *could be raised and drilled in the Colony;* the officers would be imported and frequently changed."

Few will be disposed to doubt the great good sense and political wisdom that dictated what the *Times'* correspondent has here said. But what says the *Times* itself, in its leader on the subject. It begins:—" The question of Colonial Defence is a very important one. It has its *Imperial* as well as its local aspects, and, as might naturally be supposed, the two are not always identical. *England is vulnerable at many points far away from her own shores,* and were she at war with an active and enterprising foe, he would not be slow to find out the points at which she would be most readily and fatally assailed. *It is England's plain duty, therefore, no less than her paramount interest, to have as few weak points in her armour as possible.* . . . . We quite admit the force of our correspondent's remark, that in managing the affairs of a great empire something else has to be considered than avoiding difficulties. But the worst way of dealing with difficulties is to be blind to their prospect and to be confounded with them when they actually arise. They must be *faced*, not *avoided.*"

Yet, strange to say, the article thus concludes: —" All we can say *at present* is, the question is *not at present ripe for solution.* We doubt if the Colonies have as yet fully realized the obstacles and difficulties inseparable from their scheme.

When they have done so, and show themselves ready to take the consequences, *it will be time* to discuss it more in detail."

Whoever (*pace* Lord Blachford) has read with attention, and in the spirit suggesting *non sibi, sed patriæ*, Sir Julius Vogel's able and interesting article " Greater or Lesser Britain," in the July number of the *Nineteenth Century*, will probably arrive at the conclusion that the proposition of Sir Wm. Jervoise affords a most favourable opportunity, which should not be put aside on account of any difficulties in detail which may exist for carrying it out, but that such difficulties should be at *once* faced, " alike for the interest of the Colonies and the Mother-Country." Delays in legislation have proved dangerous to England on many occasions, and when at last the measures, too long delayed, have been brought forward *and carried*, much of the good that might have resulted from them, if carried at an earlier period, has been lost.

The following passages in Sir Julius Vogel's article are peculiarly deserving of attention:—
" Recent developments, which point to the permanent *loss of foreign markets for many different articles of British manufacture*, have *increased* the hardships of the crowded state of the country, and much enlarged the desire to seek new homes in the Colonies. . . . .

" The *dread* of the producing power, and the

population of the Mother-Country being reduced, is unreasonable, *if the subjects of the nation, their wealth, industries, and resources are merely transferred from one part of the Empire to another. It is otherwise if the Mother-Country has no external possessions, and the wealth and population that she loses pass to other countries, making them proportionally more, and her less, powerful.*"

And let all landed proprietors take especial note of the following :—

"The landed proprietors are generally supposed to feel little interest in the Colonies, and to be opposed to emigration to them. At first sight such a feeling seems natural, *but on reflection its short-sightedness is apparent.* The emigration of agricultural labourers may, it is true, raise the rate of agricultural labour, or, perhaps it is more correct to say, prevent it from falling. The landed proprietors, again, are not likely to be swayed by those sentiments of personal liking for the Colonies so deeply sunk in the minds of the working-classes. A colony may become the home of a working-man and his family. The landed proprietor does not look forward to anything of the kind. Even if some junior members of his family go to the Colonies, their ambition in commencing is to make enough money to be able to live at home, although frequently, as has been said, a residence in the Colonies changes this feeling to one of preference for the new home. But if the *landed proprietors have not the same personal interest* in the Colonies as that possessed by the working-classes, *they have indirectly a very deep interest*, and one with which the *coming years are likely to vividly impress them.* The maintenance of those institutions they most prize, *the safety of their order, of their lands and their family possessions depend upon the Colonies remaining as outlets for surplus home population. If England is to be kept within herself, it cannot be long before the conditions of land tenure are rigidly scrutinized, and the question asked if the nation has not the right to buy up the land for re-division into smaller holdings.* But revolutionists would vainly raise such questions whilst the means to become possessors of estates in the *Empire* is more open to the poorer classes of to-day than it was to those who in times past, from the humblest beginning, founded some of the greatest families in the country. *The landed proprietor should see in the Colonial outlet his best guarantee of safety, and, with the humblest classes, should sturdily resist the decolonizing policy of the international school.* Lord Beaconsfield has at various times vigorously asserted *the common interests that bind together the extreme classes—the landed and the labouring classes.* Probably in no sense is this more remarkably true than in that great interest which the labouring and *landed classes jointly have in upholding the Colonies against the machinations of the politicians who reduce everything to a pounds-shillings-and-*

3 *

pence denomination, and whose chief notion of the future is compound interest."

This passage, from the very able article of Sir Julius Vogel's "Greater or Lesser Britain," is well worthy of the gravest consideration of all—and more especially of the landed proprietors, and members of the aristocracy—who value the present Constitution of England.

At a dinner given so lately as the end of October last, at the Albion Hotel, by the directors of the Colonial Bank of New Zealand, to a few colonial and other friends, Sir Julius Vogel, in responding to the toast "The Colony of New Zealand," coupled with his name, said, in the course of his address:—

. . . "After all what *are* the Colonies but colonies of people from this country, persons who have gone out there *imbued with the spirit of enterprise, and who are on the whole more educated than those who remain behind?* If you come to look at the thing from a *philosophical point of view,* you will arrive at this conclusion, that the community of New Zealand are simply engaged upon *one great task*—that is, of *obtaining from the land* its products, whether animal, vegetable, or mineral. *All other employments in the Colony are subsidiary to that.*" . . . I have been amazed to see public statistics, which have been issued *not from New Zealand,* but from other Colonies, from which it appears that the other six Colonies of Australasia

—that is to say, Western Australia, Victoria, New-South Wales, Queensland, and Tasmania, have under cultivation, including the laying down of land for artificial grass, an extent of 3,480,000 acres; while New Zealand, this small Colony, has 2,377,000 acres. It has been found that in New Zealand you can lay down artificial grasses with the greatest advantage, while in very few parts of the large neighbouring Colonies can this be done. As regards mineral wealth, also, there are few of you who are not aware how much gold the Colony has produced; but you may not *all* be aware of the great field *that has been opened in its coal mines. There are very few parts of New Zealand where coal is not to be obtained, and in some parts it is of the best possible quality.* It has been part of the system of railway construction within the Colony to provide means of *bringing more of the produce of these valuable coal-mines to market*, and there is scarcely a question that in the next two or three years the production of coal within the Colony will be so large as to reduce, if not altogether dispense with, the large quantity of coal hitherto imported."

The nation may well feel indebted to Mr. George Baden Powell for his letter which appeared in the *Times* of the 20th October, 1877, under the head of "The British Empire." What he has there said is worthy indeed of the consideration of all parties in the State, of whatever political party, and the present writer ventures to predict that whatever *Ministry shall first promote and carry out such a policy as will tend to Imperial consolidation, will occupy and justly deserve the brightest page* in the future history of this country.

It must be acknowledged, not without a sense of regret, that many of our important legislative measures have been deferred too long for the nation to derive that full measure of good results which might have followed from them had such measures not been so long postponed, until the people have inferred that the measures introduced have been passed, not from any wisdom or foresight, but rather from a sense of FEAR than from a sense of *simple* JUSTICE.

In a leading article in the *Times* of the 24th September last, in reference to Mr. Brassey's Address to the Trades' Union Congress, the 10th meeting of which took place at Leicester, on Friday, the 21st September, it is said:—

"*Trades-Unionism is now a recognized institution* of modern industrial society. *Whether we like it or not,* we must acknowledge its existence *and its right to exist.* Its operation may be, as we think it is, often blind, often mischievous; its policy may sometimes be, as it certainly has been, rapacious, sometimes even vindictive; but that is only what may be said of many human institutions older and better established than Trades'-Unions. *After all Trades'-Unionism springs from the same motives as* *those which have made human society what it is, and the tendency to combine for common purposes is generally, and rightly, regarded as the first step which mankind takes towards civilization.* . . . It is mere waste of energy to retaliate by blind denunciation of all Trades'-Unions. Certainly, such combinations have not shown themselves commonly to employers in a very amiable light, but, *it may be allowed, have been in most cases a symptom of* INTELLECTUAL ACTIVITY.*

At the 10th Annual Trades'-Union Congress, held the day before at the Temperance Hall, Leicester, it is reported in the *Times* of the 10th September:—

"Mr. Broadhurst, Secretary to the Parliamentary Committee (*i.e.*, of the Trades' Union Congress), read the report for the past year—a valuable

---

* Whilst the nation is so anxious for such "intellectual activity," both in the young as well as adults, let it be remembered—how very important healthy and decent homes are to give such intellectual activity a right direction and a moral tone.

The greatness of our great men even is quite as much a bodily affair as a mental one. It is in the physical man that the moral as well as the intellectual man lies hid; and it is through the bodily organs that the soul itself works. The body, as old Burton says, "is *domicilum animæ*, her home, her abode, and stay; and, as a torch gives a better light, a sweeter smell, according to the matter it is made of, so doth our soul perform all her actions better or worse, as her organs are disposed; or as wine savours of the cask wherein it is kept, the soul receives a tincture from the body, through which it works."

document, which entered with great minuteness of detail into various positions, most of which were to form subjects of discussion during the week." Then are given " extracts which," says the *Times*, " will be read with some interest at the present time."

Now the last of these extracts is the one the most important to which *here* to direct attention, as tending to show what is the ULTIMATE *object of the " Trades'-Union Congress:"*—" Your Committee are fully aware that the *first duty* of a Trade-Union is the *protection and advancement of trade interests*, but it hopes to see the day when our might shall be utilized on *broader lines*, when the influence so beneficially used to amend and adjust the laws by which we are governed shall also be brought to bear on *other imperial matters which intimately affect our every-day life. We confidently look forward* to 'the good time coming,' when our taxation will be more equitably adjusted, *our present enormous expenditure in national affairs greatly curtailed, and when the* LAND *shall be more extensively used for the purpose of providing employment, food, and shelter for the people.* When we can *think out these questions, and discover that reforms of this nature will greatly increase the purchasing power of our wages, we shall* EARNESTLY *set to work to accomplish them."*

* Why should not Parliament take it in hand at once, or as

There was then much wisdom and foresight evinced by Sir Julius Vogel, when he wrote :—
" If England is to be kept *within herself*, it cannot be long before the *conditions of land-tenure are rigidly scrutinized.* . . . . *The landed proprietor* should see in the *Colonial outlets his best guarantee of safety*, and, with the humblest classes, should sturdily resist the *decolonizing policy* of the *international school*."

In the year 1870, a thin octavo volume, *The State, the Poor, and the Country, including Suggestions on the Irish Question*, by R. H. Patterson, Author of the *Science of Finance*, &c., was published by William Blackwood & Sons, and it would be well if our legislators and rulers would bear in mind what the author says in the conclusion of his Preface :—

" Doubtless the recent Reform Act, by which all classes alike have been made partakers in the work and duties of Government, is calculated to give special force to some of the views advocated in this, and also in my larger work. *The masses, on the whole, know best where the shoe pinches;* and, very properly, they will loudly call the attention of Parliament to the matter. But *it is to the* élite *of the nation, the natural leaders of the people,* that I look for *the* INITIATION *and wise framing of the remedial measures.* I have firm faith in the wisdom

early as possible ? Delays are ever dangerous. " Fiat justitia, ruat cœlum."

and virtue of the people; but the people which *I* mean is not the masses alone, but the *complete nation—the whole body-politic—in which the general wants are loudly expressed by the masses, and enforced by their preponderance of votes, but the remedies for which wants must ever come—if they come wisely and well—from the upper and middle classes—the élite of which constitute the head and heart of the body-politic."*

And here, at the present time, it may not be uninteresting or altogether unprofitable to remember what was said by the present Emperor Alexander of Russia to his Nobles, when he had resolved upon the emancipation of the Serfs in 1858.

The following is taken from a Report in the *Times*, of the 9th October, 1858:—

"The Czar and the Nobles of Russia.

"The Emperor Alexander, on his journey to Warsaw, had to pass through the governments of Tver, Kostroma, Jaroslav, Nijnii-Novogorod, Vladimir, and Moscow. In most of these his Majesty addressed the representatives of the Nobility, *speaking chiefly of the topic of the day, the situation of the Peasant Class.* The Moscow correspondent of the *Nord*, transmits some of the Emperor's addresses, which we translate. To the NOBLES of the *government* of Tver the Emperor said:—

"Gentlemen, ...

"I am happy to embrace the opportunity

of expressing to the Nobility of Tver my gratitude for its devotedness and zealous readiness to contribute, like all my other governments, as far as possible, to THE PUBLIC WEAL. This you proved to me during the late war, when you *formed your Militia*. I have now confided to you a work—one of the most important for you and myself—THE IMPROVEMENT OF THE CONDITION OF THE PEASANTS.*
I hope that you will justify my confidence. It is for your delegates to occupy themselves with *this important affair*. *Weigh the matter well*. . . . You know how much I have your welfare at heart; but I hope also that the interest of your peasants is dear to you. I have therefore the conviction that you will strive to have everything regulated in a manner useful to *the common interests of all*."

To the Nobility of Nijnii-Novogorod, the Emperor spoke as follows:—

"I rejoice, gentlemen, at being able to thank you for your *Patriotism;* and I have also again to

---

* Who knows but that the success of the Czar in the later battle with the Turks, notwithstanding serious failures at the commencement of hostilities, may be owing to his noble act of emancipating his serfs, and encouraging his nobles by his own example, to enter upon "improvement of the condition of the peasants, and confiding the work to them as one of the most important?" It is now nearly twenty years since the emancipation took place, and during that interval the peasantry have had time to gain that energy of mind, spirit, and body, which a sense of freedom alone can encourage. They felt more like men fighting *pro aris et focis*. Let not "too late" be ever the bane of our actions.

thank you for having been *the first* to respond to my *expectation in the grave question touching the improvement of the lot of the peasantry.* .... As for me, my object, you know, is the *public good.* Your task in the grave question now pending, is *to balance private interests with the welfare of all.**
Yet I hear, with regret, that egotistic opinions are springing up in your midst. I regret this, gentlemen, SELFISH VIEWS SPOIL EVERYTHING THAT IS GOOD. Abandon them. I depend upon you. I hope they will no longer make their appearance, for then ONLY will the *common cause* make progress."

At Moscow, where the measures proposed by the Emperor had not been very favourably received, his Majesty said:—

"Gentlemen,—I am always happy at being able to address thanks to the nobility, but it is not in my nature to *speak against my conscience.* I always speak the truth, and, to my great regret, *I cannot thank you.* You may remember, two years ago, in this Hall, I spoke to you of the necessity of proceeding, sooner or later, to the reform of those laws

---

* It is due here to insert a letter which appeared in the *Times* of November 10, 1869, from one of our English nobility, and which doubtless expresses the sentiments entertained by our nobility generally:—

"I shall allow no consideration of personal or class interest to stand between me and a satisfactory settlement of the Land Question—feeling, as I do, that my interests must be best secured by the general welfare of the country.

"FINGALL."

which *regulate servitude—a reform that must come from above that it may not come from below.** My words have been ill-understood. Since then this reform has been the object of my constant solicitude, *and having invoked the Divine blessing on my undertaking, I have commenced the work."*

* In the year 1853 a new edition of *Smith's Wealth of Nations* was published by Charles Knight & Co., 22, Ludgate Street; and James Cornish, 1, Middle Row, Holborn. Edited by Edward Gibbon Wakefield, Esq., and in the latter part of his Preface, he enunciates a great truth well worth steadily bearing in mind, so as to influence Statesmen, and more particularly, as nearly a quarter of a century has passed since it was written, and the produce of the country instead of increasing is declining.

"While mere politicians wonder at the rapid progress which democratic opinions have lately made in this country, the economist may account for it by referring to the general discontent which is necessarily produced by low wages and low profits." (Let it be remembered that the Free-Imports Policy had, in 1853, been in operation for seven years.) "A desire of political change is the inevitable result of economical suffering. Urged by the belief that economical suffering has been caused by misgovernment, we are proceeding to establish a virtual democracy. It is a grand but also a fearful experiment. Hitherto there has been but one democracy in the world: and the people of the United States have never suffered the economical evils of low profits and low wages. What will happen here, if popular power should be established with popular discontent? This question alarms rich men, who hate democracy, and some who are not rich, but who love democracy, and wish that it should last, instead of being succeeded, first by Anarchy, and then by a military despotism. There are no means now for stopping the democratic movement. After a halt it only proceeds more rapidly. But the popular discontent may perhaps be removed."

Here the Emperor explained the fundamental principle of the abolition of serfdom, as contained in his rescripts, and continued as follows:—

"I love the Nobility; I regard it as the first support of the Throne. I desire the welfare of the people, *but have no intention that it should be effected to your detriment; but you yourselves in your own interest ought to endeavour to improve the condition of the* PEASANTS."

These are sentiments truly worthy of an Emperor, and may with equal propriety be addressed to all landed proprietors, and happy will it be if they are duly heeded. And the following, which appeared in the *Times* of 10th February, 1858, is of no less interest, nor likely to prove of less value than the extract just given. It shows at least what Russian Political Economists think essential for the best interests of a country.

"RUSSIA.

"A very remarkable banquet was held at Moscow on the 9th of January last. The gentlemen who sat down to dinner numbered 180. The present Emperor has commenced a new chapter in the social history of Russia, by taking the initiative in the emancipation of the serfs. A few quotations from the speeches made on this occasion will illustrate the importance of this event, for such it is, better than any comments.

"The first toast was proposed by M. Katkoff—
'The health of the Emperor.'

"After a few words from M Stankévitch, M. Pauloff made the following *remarkable* speech :—

"Gentlemen,—A new spirit animates us, a new era has commenced—Heaven has allowed us to live long enough to witness the *second regeneration of Russia*. Gentlemen, we may congratulate ourselves, for this movement is one of great importance. *We breathe more like Christians*, our hearts beat more nobly, and *we may look at the light of Heaven with a clearer eye*. We have met to-day to express our deep and sincere sympathy for *a holy and praiseworthy work*, and we meet without any nervousness to mar our rejoicing. Yes, gentlemen, I repeat it, a new spirit animates us—a new era has commenced. One of our social conditions is on the eve of a change. If we consider it in a past light, we may perhaps admit that it was necessary that it should have been allowed to be as it was from the want of a better administrative organization, and of the *concentration in the hands of the Government of the means which have since given so great a development to the power of Russia*. But what was momentarily given to the State was lost to mankind. The advantage cost an enormous price. Order without— anarchy within—and the *condition of the individual cast its shadow over society at large*. The Emperor has struck at the root of this evil. *The glory and prosperity of*

Russia cannot rest upon *institutions based on injustice and falsehood*. No! these blessings are henceforth to be found in the path thrown open by him *whose name Russia pronounces with respect and pride*. The Emperor has ceded this great *reform*, which he might have accomplished by his own powerful will, by ASKING THE NOBLES TO TAKE THE INITIATIVE. Let us then hail this noble idea, *inspired by the sole wish for the welfare of his people*, with that enlightened *heartiness* which may now be expected from Russia. Let us not, however, suppose that *the path traced by history is an avenue of roses without thorns*. This would be sheer ignorance. *When a new, a more moral state of things is about to be established, the obstacles that will have to be encountered must not be taken into consideration*, except with the hope *that the torrent of the new life will sweep them away*. The change in the economical condition of our national existence will arouse our individual energies, the want of which is one of our greatest evils. Let us wish, then, gentlemen, from our *innermost heart* a long life to him who has marshalled his faithful Russia to the conquest of *Truth and Justice*. Let us hope that this great idea will comprise the generous sentiments of the MAN AND THE CHRISTIAN.

"M. Babst, *Professor of Political Economy* at the University of Moscow, then spoke as follows:—

"Gentlemen,— After the eloquent speeches which have been made in honour of our meeting to celebrate a great event in our economical existence, I hope you will allow me to say a few words as an expression of my deep gratitude for him whose thoughts and acts, during the few years we have passed under his reign, *have always responded to the real wants of the people.* We have met here to celebrate an event which will be an epoch in the annals of our history, and *upon which future historians will dwell with pleasure.* Already at the commencement of this century, one of our first manufacturers said to Itrich that trade could never flourish under our system of compulsory labour, or, in other words, of serfage; already, in 1819, the Free Economical Society proved by facts the inconveniences of serfage as regards agriculture. *The development of national wealth has ever gone hand-in-hand with the regular organization of popular labour, which as it gradually emancipates itself from stringent conditions* becomes more active, more progressive, and *consequently more productive.* In proportion, as national labour gradually issues forth free from such disadvantageous conditions, THE LOVE OF WORK INCREASES *among the people.* Emulation and competition arouse the sleeping energies of the nation; they will not allow them to rust, and excite them to healthy activity and continual progress. The day of the primitive forms of the economical condition of the people has now left us for ever. *The wants of a great nation increase daily* and cannot be satisfied with the worse conditions, contrary to all progress, of PRIMITIVE ECONOMY *founded on compulsory labour*—a labour the limits of which are as restricted as its nature is unproductive. Our task is not to double, but to increase tenfold, our *productive* power, our labour, our wealth, unless we wish to see taken away from us *by nations more advanced than ourselves the* MARKETS WHICH ARE OURS BY TRADITION AND BY OUR GEOGRAPHICAL POSITION. And we cannot increase our productive power except by a regular *organization of national labour*, which will then *boldly take in hand and work the treasures now hidden in our land.*"

" The learned Professor concluded with an appeal to all honest men to support the Emperor in this great social reform."

We know that it was ultimately carried, and that since that time Russia has, by " *working the* TREASURES HIDDEN *in her* LAND" *increased in wealth*, and not only *she*, but other nations, *acting on the instinct of self-preservation*, have CONTINUED TO EXCLUDE MORE AND MORE BY FIXED DUTIES OUR STAPLE MANUFACTURES, whilst their *own* have been *growing up to become the* rivals of ours, and hence at last our exports have seriously declined, as our *profits* long have done.

Happily one of our own *patres patriæ*—the Right Hon. Lord Bateman – all honour to him !—

has, after well considering these dangers, been induced to publish a letter* (and a very able one it is), which, he tells us, in the first sentence of his Preface, "is not the result of any sudden impulse, induced by the pressure of the present GROWING commercial *crisis*, but is based on an *earnest and long considered conviction* of the truth or *the reasoning* there attempted to be enunciated." The Noble Lord very modestly says "attempted," but his reasoning is most lucid and sound, and with the facts he gives, must convince every thoughtful and impartial reader that some change in the policy of 1846 is absolutely necessary, for, to suppose that foreign nations will ever give us Free Trade, *i.e.* reciprocity—is only deluding ourselves whilst our own losses go on increasing.

Lord Bateman's letter was first published in the *Times* of the 10th November last, but in rather an obscure position and in small type, and hence probably it was, by the advice of friends, that the author was induced to have his letter printed in a cheap form (6d), though in an excellent type. All will do well to procure a copy of it. His Lordship has truly said—" In any scheme of com-

---

* Lord Bateman's *Plea for Limited Protection, or for Reciprocity in Free Trade*. William Ridgway, 169, Piccadilly, London. 1877. About the same time a Second Edition of a clever and useful pamphlet (6d), *The Effects of Free Trade without Reciprocity*, by Captain Halford Thompson, late Royal Artillery, was published by Henry S. Eland, 261, High Street, Exeter.

mercial policy due consideration should always be given to the *capabilities of production* of the country, on the one hand, and to its *absolute necessities* on the other. . . . We have to deal with many more interests than those exclusively connected with the food *supply* of the people. We have to deal with our own various home manufactures, and with our own skilled (and daily more expensive) general labour question. These latter, quite as important to the well-being of the community, require to be as jealously guarded and protected, exercising, as they undoubtedly do, an equally preponderating influence on the prosperity or otherwise of all classes in the kingdom. It behoves us, therefore, while securing for them the best available market, to be at the same time cautious how we allow them to deteriorate, or permit rival countries *unduly to compete* with our *native industries* to our *own loss* and detriment."* His

---

* The writer of these pages, though perfectly ready to join in "a tribute to the memory of the late Mr. Cobden, Sir George Cornewall Lewis, Mr. Bright, and Mr. Chas. Villiers," for their ability, earnestness, and sincerity of purpose, in bringing about the Free Imports' Policy (for be it ever remembered we have not Free Trade) of 1846, regrets that he cannot think with Lord Bateman that that policy, even as regards a supply of food, " has conferred on the masses a lasting benefit," and this, because it has operated to lessen the home produce, and consequently the power of consumption.

It will no doubt be in the recollection of many that the Right Hon. George Goschen, one of the members for the City of London, has, during the two or three last Sessions, drawn

Lordship also says—" In the case of *Great Britain*, owing to our *area being so much restricted and to the* continual increase in our population, an increase out of proportion to the size and acreage of the kingdom as compared with the relative proportion to the area and extent of foreign countries, it has become virtually imperative upon us to obtain from all nations of the earth the requisite food supply."

It is very possible, as the *Times* has shown, to raise, even in this country, food sufficient for the present amount of our population, by cultivating our waste lands, and by a better management of that already under cultivation. But if, in using the term *Great* Britain, we treat our Colonies as an integral part of the Empire of Great Britain, our area for the production of food is far from restricted, and by so cherishing our Colonies as to be able to obtain a sufficient supply from them they would be able to become better customers for our manufactures, we should encourage emigration, and become less dependent upon foreign countries for our food supply. That we have become so dependent on foreign nations for so large supply of the first necessary of life must be a matter of deep concern to every statesman—indeed, to all of us. It was when we were indebted to foreign countries for little more than a third of what we

the attention of Parliament to the "declining power of consumption."

now are of the main source of our supply of food that the late Sir Robert Peel, in 1842 (impressed *at that time* evidently with the sentiments entertained by Coleridge as to the danger to the country of being dependent upon foreign countries for *necessaries*,* gave the following patriotic reasons

* Those who argue that England may safely depend upon a supply of foreign corn, if it grow none or an insufficient quantity of its own, forget that they are subjugating the necessaries of life itself to the mere luxuries or comforts of society. Is it not certain that the price of corn abroad will be raised upon us soon as it is once known that we must buy?—and when that fact is known, in what sort of a situation shall we be? Besides this, the argument supposes that agriculture is not a positive good to the nation taken in and by itself as a mode of existence for the people, which supposition is false and pernicious, and if we are to become a great horde of manufacturers, shall we not, even more than at present, excite the ill-will of all the manufacturers of other nations? It has been already shown in evidence which is before all the world, that some of our manufacturers have acted upon the accursed principle of deliberately injuring foreign manufactures, if they can, even to the ultimate disgrace of the country and loss to themselves."—*Coleridge's Table Talk in* 1834, 2nd Edit., p. 296.

The following paragraph in the *Times* of the 25th January, 1878, tends to confirm what Coleridge has said, and we seem at least to have induced them to take measures for keeping our manufactures out of their markets :—

SHEFFIELD CHAMBER OF COMMERCE.—The annual meeting of the Sheffield Chamber of Commerce was held yesterday at Sheffield, Mr. W. K. Peace, the President, in the chair. The annual report stated that in consequence of the disturbed state of France, the Commercial Treaty with that country had not yet been signed, and the report suggested that unless some material reductions were made in the proposed tariffs

justifying the maintenance of the sliding scale as a protection to *Home Agriculture*. And certainly nothing he said in his speech on introducing his " great experiment" in 1846 lessened the force of his reasoning in 1842, nor can it be disregarded with impunity.

" I should not, he said, be a friend to the Agricultural class if I asked the House for protection for the purpose of propping up their rents and maintaining high prices for their produce. I disclaim all such intention; my opinion and that of my colleagues is, that it is most important for the country, of *the highest importance* that you should *take every precaution that the main source* of *your supply* of *food should be derived from yourselves,* from home-agriculture—that any additional price which you may be called upon to pay for that purpose cannot be vindicated but as a *boon on Agriculture in this country*—and that to effect this,

the Treaty should not be signed. The new tariff proposed to levy a duty of from 45 to 50 per cent. upon common pocket knives, and 75 per cent. upon common table knives, whereas up to the present time the duty has only been 15 per cent. upon both articles. The Council have been in communication with the Foreign Office with respect to the proposed new tariff for Switzerland, which, it is feared, would shut out Sheffield cutlery manufacturers and Britannia metal and nickel goods manufacturers from the Swiss markets. The resolutions which the Chamber proposes to lay before the autumnal meeting of the Associated Chambers, which will be held in Sheffield, were considered, and Mr. Peace was re-elected president.

you are entitled to place such duty on foreign corn as, by forming an *equivalent* for *special burdens on your own agriculture* may serve to effect this object. But, sir, I consider it is for the *general interests* of all classes,* that by paying *a small sum in advance* upon our own agricultural produce, we can take, as it were, insurance and security on a proper supply, and thus have it in our power to meet the danger of being in seasons of dearth, *altogether or in great part dependent upon foreign countries* for a *supply* of *food.* In my opinion the variation of seasons will occasionally bring a deficient harvest, and I believe also that the deficiency will, on such occasions, be found to exist in other countries as well as our own. If then, you are solely, or *in great part*, dependent upon those countries—if you require a supply of from *four* to *five millions of quarters* of *corn*† in the year, and if the deficiency which you yourself feel should be general in Europe and elsewhere, *what becomes of this country?* You may depend upon it that the *instinct* of *self-preservation* will prevail amongst those who *usually supply us,* you may rest assured that *impediments* of every *description* would be

---

* " Nature, a mother kind alike *to all,*
   Still grants her bliss at labour's earnest call."
THE TRAVELLER.

† What would Sir Robert have thought of " requiring a supply" of thirteen or fourteen million quarters from foreign countries?

thrown in the way of exportation, and you may be satisfied that in the end they would insist on applying their own domestic produce to the maintenance and supply of their own people: and, therefore, I for one most certainly *shall never be a party*—not on account of the *Agricultural interest*, but on *account of the interest of all classes*—to any law or arrangement which will make this country *dependent* upon other countries for any *considerable portion* of its subsistence."*

Who must not regret that the very Statesman who thus spoke, evincing such wisdom and prudence, four years afterwards introduced and passed the unrestricted competition policy, or as he himself termed his measure, " The great experiment" of 1846. Whether he would have maintained that policy much longer had he lived is very doubtful, for in a very interesting volume, *Sketch of the Life of Sir Robert Peel, Bart.:* by his relative Sir Lawrence Peel (the eminent retired Indian Judge, who, till recently, rendered for many years, such good service on Indian Appeals), the following passages occur: " The contests between Free-trade and Protection had *now* [1841] come to be understood as contests between the *many* and the *few*. *Formerly* they had not been *so* regarded. *Protection* to *each* of *many interests had been regarded* as *protection* to the *whole community*, and it was not a *conscious*

* See Appendix.

preference of the *few* to the *many*" (p. 281). "In his posthumous memoirs two minutes were prepared by him and laid before the Cabinet in 1841, which indicate very clearly the course of '*experimental policy*' on which *he was about to enter.*" He entered upon it in 1842, and advanced more boldly in the "great experiment" in 1846, and since his death, *other ministers* have gone *still further* in the same policy, and after twenty-five [now 31] years' experience of *its results*, it would *be surely wise to consider* whether they *have been such as* would *satisfy* Sir Robert were *he now* alive. 'Experience,' said Dr. Johnson, is the great test of *truth*, and is perpetually contradicting the theories of men.'"

It seems clear then from the language here used, that Sir Lawrence himself doubted whether " the results " of the measure of 1846 would have " satisfied " Sir Robert Peel, had he happily lived a few years longer, or at least up to the time Sir Lawrence wrote – 1861.* In order to enable a reader of these pages to judge for himself how far Sir Robert Peel would have been likely to be satisfied with the results of his " great experiment " of 1846 (in other words the Free-Imports Policy, free-*trade* we have not and *cannot* gain)—it is

---

* Sir Robert, it will be remembered, was unfortunately thrown from his horse on riding up "*Constitution* Hill," on the 29th June, 1850, and died a few days after, unhappily for the country, as he might have revised and perhaps reversed or partly modified his policy of 1846.

necessary to remember what *were his* expectations as to results, and then consider how far they correspond with his expectations.*

What his motives and expectations were will be most fairly and best shown by a short quotation from his speech on introducing the measure.

Sir Robert in his exordium said—

"The *great magnitude of the interests which are concerned in the proposal* I am about to make, will insure me the patient and indulgent attention without which it would not be within my power either with satisfaction to myself or to the public interest, to discharge the duties I have undertaken to perform—mainly with a view to our own interests, but partly for the purpose of *encouraging Russia* to proceed in that *liberal* policy of which she has, I trust, given some indication; I propose *without stipulation* that *England shall set the*

---

* In a leading article of the *Times* of the 13th August, 1877, calling attention to the new Tariff of duties on the part of the Spanish Government, in respect of importations from Germany and from several other States, and showing that our productions will be subject to duties in many cases from thirty to fifty per cent. higher than the duties on similar commodities brought from Germany, Belgium, and elsewhere —it is said, "If there is anything approaching 'a favoured nation clause" in these Tariffs, we ought to be preserved from these discriminating duties. Was not Mr. Gladstone wrong in 1845? He made his elaborate speech in answer to Lord Palmerston, who took the opposite view, and *though* the *House of Commons* went with *Mr. Gladstone*, the *judgment of the House of Commons* is not *infallible*." Let this truth be remembered, as regards the measure of 1846.

example by the relaxation of heavy duties, *in the confidence* that that example will *ultimately prevail.*"

In his peroration he said—

"I ask you therefore to give your consent to those measures *not* on any narrow view or principle connected with the *accumulation** *of wealth*, but I ask you to give your consent to them on higher grounds—far higher principles. Encumbered as you are by heavy burdens, solicitous as you are to provide for the public credit, depend upon it the true source of increased revenue is *increased comfort* and *increased taste for luxury*. Thus, I say, are the interests of the revenue promoted by that unseen and voluntary taxation which arises from the large consumption of articles of general use. I ask you to consent to the scheme you have heard on the proof which I have adduced that abundance and cheapness lead to diminished crime and to increased morality." †

* Mark reader, "*accumulation*" in its primary meaning, is "heaping up," and "by heaping up" in our individual capacity, we necessarily take from and thereby diminish diffusion of the general stock. "*Accumulation*" does not therefore necessarily imply *increase* of the general wealth of *the country*, or increase of aggregate wealth, but that the rich have become richer and the poor poorer and by the wealth not being adequately *diffused*. The farmer being the first link in the chain of circulation must be in a thriving condition, in order that there may be a due creation and diffusion of wealth throughout the country in the Home-Market.

† Sir Robert Peel could not have been sufficiently impressed with the very different consequences which would ensue from

Well, it is now more than thirty years since "the great experiment" commenced, and we know that *Russia* has *not* proceeded in that *liberal* policy of which Sir Robert Peel trusted she had given proof, though it was in the full *confidence* that Russia and other nations would do so, that he set the example of taking off heavy duties, trusting that his new policy, or "*great experiment*" would ultimately prevail. Other nations however, have not followed the example, nor are any likely to do so.

In assuming that the interests of the Revenue would be promoted by "that unseen and voluntary "abundance and cheapness" caused by free importation of the produce of the soil and of manufactures of *Foreign* countries, instead of abundance and cheapness arising from the cultivation of *our own soil* and the *manufactures* of *native* industry.

As to "*increased morality*" in trade, let any reader read the article entitled "The Morals of Trade" in the *Westminster Review* for April, 1859," No. xxx. A short extract is here given—

"A still more subtle trick has been described to us by one who himself made use of it when engaged in one of these *wholesale* houses—a trick so successful, that frequently *he was sent for* to sell to customers who could be *induced* to buy by none of the other assistants, and who *ever* afterwards would buy only of him. His policy was to *seem extremely* simple and honest, and during the first *few* purchases to exhibit this *honesty* by *pointing out defects* and inferiority of quality in the things he was selling, and then having *gained the customer's confidence*, he *proceeded to pass off upon him inferior goods* at *superior prices*. These are a few of the various manœuvres in constant practice. *Of course there is a running accompaniment of falsehoods uttered as well as acted.*"

taxation which *arises* from the enlarged consumption of articles of general use," Sir Robert must have forgotten that " *indirect taxation* " (which McCulloch is in favour of) was about to be wholly abolished, and that a very great portion of articles of general use were to be and are the produce and manufacture of foreign countries, and admitted *duty free*. How then could the interests of the *revenue* be promoted by his measure as he said? Each reader will form his own opinion as to whether crime has *diminished* and *morality increased* since 1846. It has been proved however beyond all doubt by the Factory Inspectors and Medical Officers that serious degeneracy of race has set in amongst the Factory operatives, aye! and amongst many of our rural populations too, long fast diminishing.*

* A leading article in the *Times* of the 7th July, 1875, commences thus :—

" The alleged physical *degeneracy of the artisan* classes in our great centres of industry, is a subject of *national importance*, which should receive, both from *statesmen* and from employers, a *greater degree of attention* than has hitherto been given to it. We published yesterday the opinions as stated in evidence before the Royal Commission on the *Factory* Acts, of Dr. Fergusson, who has for *fourteen years* been one of the certifying surgeons at Bolton, and who describes himself as having for forty years taken a deep interest in everything relating to the physical well-being of the population. . . . During the five years which ended with 1873, quite *one-half of the children* brought to him were unfit to work full time, and the *number of this class increased year by year.*" . . . . With great truth the *Times* adds—

Now, although Sir Robert repudiated the idea of asking his hearers to give their consent to his " great experiment "* " on any *narrow* view or

"A community of feeble artisans will not yield a fair *average number* of men who can THINK as well as work, who can *see the defects* of THE MACHINERY among *which they are employed*, who can suggest improvements, or who can lift themselves out of their own class as successful inventors. Such a community, on the contrary, would furnish men who would be *driven by muscular fatigue* to a *craving* for *shorter hours* of *labour* and for the *use of stimulants*, and whose weak brains would be easily led into a fool's paradise by the talk of those who would be for ever on the watch to prey upon them. The manufacturing and commercial pre-eminence of England depends in a degree which it would be difficult to exaggerate, upon the maintenance among the *artisan classes* of a certain sobriety of understanding, as well as of life, with which a *prevailing physical weakness* would be incompatible."

The *Times* does not allude to the Army. When, however, we reflect how large a proportion of recruits are unavoidably obtained from our "great centres of Industry," and how unfit such men are to enter the army after the age of twenty-five years, according to the pathological inquiry made by Dr. Lyons, who was sent out to the Crimea by the Government after the great mortality of the first winter, to procure accurate scientific information on the state of the army, and on the measures necessary then, and for the future, for preserving its health. This Report was published in July 1856, and offers very valuable information. The principle that the Commissioner drew from the facts he ascertained was and is of the highest importance. He took it as proved that English soldiers sent on active service against the enemy ought to have *arrived at perfect manhood*. Yet the Commissioner is against recruiting amongst men of a certain age, particularly those who have led an unhealthy and profligate life in great towns.

* See Appendices.

principle *connected with the accumulation* of wealth," but " on far higher grounds—far higher principles," it will be well to learn whether "accumulation of wealth" in the *hands of the few*, has not been the result, and *that* at the expense of the *National interests*. The *Times*, which has greater credence from the generality of Englishmen than any other authority, shall tell us.

A leading article in the *Times* of 20th February, 1860, commences thus:

" How rich we are! There is the national pass-book just submitted to us by the Board of Trade. These 'Trade and Navigation Accounts,' are to us what the Nilometer is to the Egyptians. We see in them how high the stream of commerce has risen, and we judge from them the quantity of the rich deposit it has spread. We have exported during the past year [1859] a hundred and thirty millions—a greater sum than was before attained by this country, even in exceptional periods of wild and *unsustained* prosperity.

" We are growing *plethorically* rich upon our new Free-Trade discovery. But who are ' We?' There is a tremendous rush of riches somewhere; but, if we look abroad among the intellectual classes we shall find that like the stream of Pactolus, it seeks the lower levels. Those who live among *poets, artists, sculptors, story-spinners, historians, lawyers, physicians, and divines*, see no sudden springs of *wealth* bubbling up among *their friends.** . . . . We throw up our caps and shout for the *general prosperity*, and read

---

* In the *Western Express* of the 23rd October, 1877, there was a report of some speeches made at the luncheon that took place on the opening of a "Fine Art and Industrial Exhibition," at Bideford.

Sir George Stucley occupied the chair, and in the course of his address, said :—

"The town was indebted to some gentlemen for the spirit they had shown in starting the present excellent show. But however artistic one might be, a great deal depended on the soil in the matter of development. Great demands for works of art could be made only in a wealthy country, and the wealthier a country was the greater was the demand for such works."

"Dr. Thompson, in the course of his admirable speech, in proposing 'the Army and Navy,' said. . . . . He had been struck with the philosophical remark of the chairman: Art could not prosper in a community where there was no great wealth, and here it might be added that this country would never have possessed the wealth it now did but for the renowned services of those who had to defend her interests. When they reflected that for 800 years no foreign foe had successfully invaded this country, they had at once the key to the reasons why England has been made the repository of the riches of the civilized world. He was sure if our prosperity were to be maintained it was to be done only by the maintenance of *national independence*, and the assurance that we shall be safe from such revolutions as that which was taking place in the East of Europe. He was a great friend to science and art, but he was afraid they could not be properly cultivated in this country unless we retained the means of protecting *our independence*.† As the poet said :

'Ill fares the land, to hastening ills a prey,
Where wealth accumulates, and men decay.'

† See Appendix.

our own city articles, and swell with pride and glory that we are so rich; but we should be puzzled, if we had not this paper before us, to know where this swarm of golden sovereigns had hived. These columns, however, tell the tale. *There are two classes of citizens in this country who have taken tremendous slices* out of the great sum total from which *the others* have drawn only modest shares. The Ironmasters have got no less than *thirteen millions* of this *foreign* trade, but the Cotton-spinners have, after clothing all the many millions of these islands, succeeded in pocketing from the foreign trade all the profits upon no less a sum than £48,208,444! Here is a pleasant sum to revel and roll in, and to take toll from! We have found then the hive to which all those golden bees have flown. There, *far away in the North*—there in those flats, over which in ancient days *old ocean rose and fell*, sometimes carrying his foray up to the foot of the Cheshire peaks, prostrating the primeval forest and creating by the *waste* he made those coal beds which are now more *precious than gold*" [would that this nation had continued to think so!] "there where the tall chimneys would dwarf the old sylvan giants, *where the sound of the piston-stroke never ceases,*

And thus while wealth accumulates, and they progressed in Science and Art, he hoped the day would never come when there were not stalwart hearts to man the army and navy, to defend the interests of the country and maintain her independence in the world."

and where the frequent square factories gleam from their many windows *all night long* and give appearances of a general illumination—*there it is that all this gold is gone.* It is gathered by an industrious race, with sharp instincts for their special mission, which is to *make calico* and to *amass* gold; *frugal* in their habits, and not too *delicate* in *their tastes;* capable of great efforts of *ostentatious munificence,* but well remembering that *habitual thrift* is the great secret *of growing rich.* Here is *concentrated* all this abounding wealth. Here men reckon each other by what *they save,* and *not* by what they *spend,* by what they have, and not by what they have given away. Here is a community *powerful by their riches,* and *powerful by their intensity of purpose.* Their interests are always propounded as the great interests of the nation : *well paid* and well *well patronized apostles* go forth from them fiercely compelling all men to cry with them ' *There is* but *one commercial* faith, and *Manchester is its prophet.*' We rejoice in the good fortune of the gold-encumbered inhabitants of that wonderful city and bow before their enormous wealth. We feel, in addressing them, that we are venturing to approach busy men, who are *laying up* the *wealth* wherewith to found great families ; to the Rudolphs of succeeding generations, where heralds will be taught to admit that the balls or the coronet of the Baron and the Earl are properly *cotton-balls,* and that the Ducal *Strawberry leaf* is more truly a fossil vegetation of the *coal* measures. We must not venture to ask for any quarter to other *commercial interests.* The *silk* people who import their eight millions and a half of raw material, and who do *not export* £46,000 of *manufactured goods,* must of course, bear their fate, and for the wines of the South African colonist we possess no sympathy. We appear upon this occasion only for those hardly worked people who do not meddle or make in the great floods and ebbs of commercial success. *Manchester is very great,* but *Manchester* is not *quite all.* If she were left alone to-morrow, even with John Bright for her king, there would be something wanting to *make* England what she *now is.* Is there no means by which Manchester may be contented, and and yet we *non-commercial classes may escape sacrifice?* Manchester, and the class whereof Manchester is the metropolis, represents, perhaps, now one-sixth of the population, but still the *rest of the nation form the five-sixths.* We must admit, also, that Manchester and the Manchester class have, very much to their honour, given to us Sir Robert Peel and Mr. Gladstone, who *have been* NOT *unmindful of their origin.* We cannot but accord also that unto those who have much, much shall be given. But *still the Middle class men,* we professional men, we country squires, we *brain-workers,* we *non-millionaires,* would say to them 'Are we *not men and brothers?*' Cannot Manchester *thrive without our im-*

poverishment, and is it absolutely necessary that we should all go up to be taxed 10*d* in the pound, in order that every Manchester gentleman who only made £90,000 last year should make up his £100,000 next year?

Thus then it appears that *National interests have been sacrificed to increase the wealth of the few*,—" an industrious race with sharp instincts for their special mission, which is to make calico and amass gold,—who reckon each other by what they *save*, and not by what they *spend*."

Now here let us remember what our great English philosopher Lord Bacon has said in his Essay *Of Seditions and Troubles:*

" Above *all things*," he says, " *good* policy is to be used that the *treasure and money* in a State *be* NOT *gathered into* FEW *hands*, for otherwise a State may *have a great stock and yet starve*, and money is like muck, *no good except it be spread.* This is done chiefly by suppressing, *or at least keeping a tight hand upon the devouring trades of* USURY, engrossing, *great pastures and the like.*"*

Yet England has abolished her usury-laws, and has encouraged " great pastures, and the wealth arising from the stimulus to foreign trade *has got into few hands.*"

And now let us learn from Mr. William Hoyle, an eminent Cotton-spinner himself, Author of *An Inquiry into the Causes of the long-con-*

* See Appendix.

tinued *Depression in the Cotton Trade*. In the Preface to his later Work, *Our National Resources and How they are Wasted*, 1871, he says, "The attention of the writer of the following pages was first specially directed to the subject treated therein, in the autumn of 1868. During the whole of the years 1867 to 1868, the trade of the United Kingdom, but especially the Cotton Trade, was in a most depressed condition. The year 1869 was ushered in; but instead of there being an improvement, so far at least as the Cotton Trade went, matters grew worse. The belief at that time was almost universal in Lancashire, that the depressed condition of trade arose from the fact that our Continental neighbours were outstripping us in manufacturing, and that they were still more certain to outstrip us in the future; and, *consequently the great Cotton Trade of Lancashire would shortly be a thing of the past*. Having considerable interest at stake, the Author, like other spinners and manufacturers, naturally became anxious about this unpleasant prospect, and therefore, during the winter of 1868 and 1869, he spent his leisure evenings in giving the subject *a careful investigation*.

"In the autumn of 1869 the results of this investigation were embodied and published by him in the work before named, '*An Inquiry*,' &c. The investigation entirely disabused the mind of the Author of all those ideas, as to the falling off of our Foreign trade owing to Continental competition, and the publication of the pamphlet did much to allay the fears of the commercial classes in reference to the matter. An examination of our exports of manufactured goods, alike in cotton, woollen and linen, showed that a continued and enormous *increase* had taken place, AND THE DEPRESSION AROSE FROM THE FALLING OFF IN THE HOME-TRADE." He tells us further, " That this decrease has arisen *mainly, if not entirely,* from the improvident and UNPRODUCTIVE character of our labour and expenditure, especially in reference to the article of intoxicating drinks, and that, *if our labour were properly directed and our expenditure properly applied,* settled pauperism or destitution could not possibly exist." And Mr. Hoyle very wisely in his book says:

" The purpose of all labour is, or ought to be, to secure the *physical comforts of life—good health, good food, warm clothing, and comfortable habitations;* for, although the end of man's existence is not to attend *merely* to the physical or animal, but primarily to *the intellectual and spiritual,* yet inasmuch as the *proper development of these faculties depends upon the healthy condition of the physical organism, it is absolutely necessary,* if we would fully develope the *mental, to attend to the physical.*"*

* There is a great deal of political wisdom conveyed in the following doggerel :

Now, it will be in the recollection of any readers of these pages, that the opposition to Sir Robert Peel's "*great experiment*" of 1846, was on the ground that it WOULD *injure the Home-market* by the effect it would have on the tenant-farmers of the soil of England, and consequently upon the agricultural population and their neighbourhoods, and the tradesmen of many of the provincial towns.

In the Registrar-General's Quarterly return during the Autumn-quarter that ended December 31, 1859, are the following remarks, well worthy of attention: "The increase of births and the decrease of deaths in Wilton, is, in his opinion attributable to the introduction *of a new and superior class of cottages in lieu of the former ill-built and badly ventilated dwellings of the agricultural labourers*. The numerous new cottages which are being built in several parishes of that sub-district by the direction of *Mr. Sidney Herbert* (afterwards Lord Herbert), will no doubt improve the health of the inhabitants."

And the Registrar added—and let this sink deep into the minds of politicians and others—"*The improvement of the health of the labouring population* of the kingdom is one of *the most preg-*

> Oh! a very fine thing is good legislation,
> And a very fine thing is good education;
> But to make people thrive, contented, and *quiet*,
> 'Tis a *sine quâ non* to begin with—*the diet*.

nant measures of defence that can be conceived, and will not (or should not) be overlooked by the GREAT LANDED PROPRIETORS."*

And here whilst reminded of measures of defence let readers remember that although free-traders ever claim Dr. Adam Smith's *Wealth of Nations* as an authority for the policy of the " unrestricted competition" policy of England, that policy has in many respects violated *his* teaching, notably, by the abrogation of the Navigation Laws, for which Sir Robert Peel is not responsible.

" The Act of Navigation," wrote Adam Smith, " is not favourable to foreign commerce, or to the growth of *that* opulence which can arise from it. *As defence, however,* is of *much more* importance than *opulence*, the Act of Navigation is perhaps the *wisest* of all the *commercial* regulations of England." Yet it has been abrogated. The late Sir John Gladstone, Bart. (father of The Right Hon. W. Ewart Gladstone, the eminent statesman and scholar), addressed a letter to his son after having had read to him the speech delivered by his son in

* And Lord Beaconsfield has lately said, when opening " The Victoria Buildings" for Labourers' Dwellings—at Battersea :—" The health of the people is really the FOUNDATION upon which all their happiness and *power as a State* depend."

Much to the honour and credit of the leading Journal of England, it has been for years *repeatedly impressing* this great truth on the mind of the public.

the House of Commons in June, 1848, in favour of the repeal of the *Navigation Laws*, and, in conclusion, Sir John says—

" You are aware that I am at present confined by indisposition, and that I dictate this letter from *my bed* by the pen of a third party. I am conscious you will find it abounds with errors and imperfections, yet notwithstanding, now in my eighty-fourth year, as a last duty, and perhaps *tribute* to the *interests* of my *country*, I give it to the public, and send it for that purpose to the columns of the *Standard*, from whence it may, perhaps, find its way to more general circulation." (It was dated from Fasque, June 6, 1848). See Appendix No. 7.

Sir John Gladstone wrote, no doubt,

" Knowing THAT course is *best* to be observed,
By which a nation LONGEST is *preserved*."

And now let us see what has been shown in the foregoing pages.

1. That whatever amount may have been derived from the policy of 1846 has been confined to " few hands," " concentrated "*—not *generally* " *diffused*."

2. That the health of the factory operatives has for years, more especially since 1846, been declining, until degeneracy of race seems to have set in.

3. We have had it recorded,—in a very valu-

* See Appendix.

able volume by an eminent cotton-spinner, so long since as 1871—"*after a careful investigation*"— that, " during an *enormous increase* in *our exports* of manufactured goods, alike in cotton, woollen, and linen, the *depression*" (in trade, and consequently of the factory-hands) "*arose from the falling off* in the *Home-trade*."

If then in spite of " an enormous increase of our exports" in 1871, depression arose from the *falling off in the home trade*, surely we are only wilfully deceiving ourselves in looking for any further increase of our *exports in order to improve the Home-market;* for the wealth arising therefrom, it seems, would be " accumulated" by " the few," and we shall find, by a still more bitter experience, than we have already had it must be feared that—

> " Wealth in the gross *is death*, but life *diffused;*
> As poison heals in just proportion used;
> In *heaps*, like *ambergris*, a *stink* it lies,
> But, well *dispersed*, is *incense to the* SKIES."

It will doubtless be remembered that one of the arguments used by those opposed to the abrogation of the " sliding-scale" (during the agitation for the total abrogation of the corn-laws) was the periodical disturbance of the " money-market" by *sending* out of the country large sums of gold for the purchase of *corn*. Now the *Times* in a leading article in 1860, said—

" Even at a moment when the whole country is

revelling in *a sense of prosperity*, the *repetition* of the fact, *observable* in 1857, that with all *our wonderful trade*, the tendency *of our bullion returns shows that we are spending more than we earn*— while the advance in the rates of discount has *no perceptible effect in checking the demand*, coupled with the circumstance that the *note-circulation during the* past twelvemonth has been *frequently 10 per cent. in excess of its normal* amount,* are

---

* The writer happens to possess a pamphlet, written in 1812, entitled: *Further Observations on the Increase of Population and High Price of Grain: being an Appendix to Reflections on the Possible Existence, and supposed Expedience, of National Bankruptcy.* By Peter Richard Hoare, Esq. London: printed for T. Cadell and W. Davies, Strand, and Hatchard, Piccadilly, 1812. The pamphlet thus *concludes:* —" Let us not be deluded by this PHANTOM *of an excessive population,* set up against the *reality* of an *excessive currency.* It is this which has augmented the price of the common necessaries of life, as of almost all other commodities of whatsoever kind, though *divers causes may* have operated to reduce the price of some—which has increased the cost of agriculture, as well as almost every other species of labour, the poor's-rates, tithe composition, and rents, but these only in few instances in a like proportion. Reduce the quantity of paper money, you will reduce the price of the necessaries of life, and all other commodities whatsoever, the wages of labour, poor's-rates, tithe composition, and rents: you will enable the *British Farmer, without danger of being undersold by the foreign Trader,* to employ more hands in the cultivation of wheat, and other grain: lands, of late converted *from arable to pasture, may be re-converted, and wastes be broken up,* inclosed, and put into tillage, not only *without loss,* but with *amazing profit, measured* by the real, not *merely nominal* amount. The times are peculiarly fitted for the trial. Humanity and true policy demand it—smarting, as we are, under the severe affliction

signs which *at all events are worthy of our attention.*" And in 1869—nine years later—the *Times* in a leader said, "The question arises on *what terms* has this *trade*" (the export) "*been done?* And it seems probable that it has been *done on losing terms*—that more cotton has been spun and exported than foreign *customers were prepared to buy.* Is there any limit to trade or production at this point? Can *Lancashire capitalists* go on *adding mill to mill* and *factory to factory without exceeding* the *demands of the world?*" (See Letter VII. following.)

Let the correspondent of the *Times* during the late International Exhibition at Philadelphia answer this question. He writes under the title, "Mechanician," and concluded his last communication thus:

"In reckoning up the significance of this

of real or pretended scarcity—looking to *other countries to aid us with supplies,* but *dreading the effects of a stern policy,* which would *mock our sufferings even in the agonies of famished nature* —with a large portion of our population *already a victim to the same policy,* by which, *bereft of its wonted means of livelihood,* and driven from necessity to any other which may offer, *would receive, with eager hands, the plough or mattock—and happily become the means of effectually insuring a sufficient supply, so far at least as* HUMAN *prudence* can provide." Could anything more befitting the present time than the above be written? For, assuredly, all the arguments there used for "insuring a sufficient home supply, so far at least as human " prudence can provide," apply now with tenfold force. The writer of these pages offers no opinion in relation to the Currency.

grand aggregate of *machinery*, and congratulating ourselves on the results, as showing how the toil of men can be mitigated, it is *impossible* not to feel that an *important change* is *approaching*. A century ago no conditions existed which could have enabled *Adam Smith* to anticipate a time when the *producing power*" (it would be more strictly correct to have said the *converting* power, for the earth is the sole producing power) "of automatic machines *would exceed the requirements of the human race. That state of things* is *rapidly approaching*, and it is for the philosopher and *political economist* to consider *carefully beforehand* the *impending revolution*, so that it may all *work for good* to *the family of mankind*."— (*Times* of 18th November, 1876.)

Words of sound wisdom. May philosophers and political economists add " *Domine dirige nos*," —the motto of the City of London, and remembering what Adam Smith has with truth recorded that " *defence* is of much more importance than opulence" let us also ever bear in mind the warning given in a Book, the admonitions of which we should all do the better by following—and which cannot be disregarded with impunity.

" When a strong man armed keepeth his palace, his goods are in peace ; but when a *stronger* than he shall come upon him, and *overcome* him, he taketh from him all his armour *wherein* he trusted and divideth his spoils," (Luke xi. 21-2).

Of this all may rest assured, that the robust cottager and the hardy yeoman will ever be found to be the country's *wealth in peace*—the country's *strength in war*.

"The nerve, support, and glory of the land."

How then can we best provide breeding-grounds for these races. Is it too late to make the attempt? True it is, a poet, who was a deep philosopher also, has long since written:

"A bold peasantry its country's pride,
When once destroyed can never be supplied."

But in endeavouring to render ourselves less dependent upon foreign countries for the *common necessaries* of life, we should at the same time be doing our best to re-animate agricultural industry, cheer the hearts of our agricultural labourers— and by thus *diffusing* wealth, improve the *Home-market*, and cheer also the drooping spirits of our manufacturers and tradesmen. For let it ever be borne in mind, that the *Farmer* is the *first link* in the chain of circulation.

This truth seems to have been recognized by Mr. Bazely (now Sir Thomas, Bart.), when President of the Manchester Chamber of Commerce in 1855. Presiding at a "Morning Meeting" of that Chamber, on the 9th of February in that year, he said:—

"Probably the last year, in *trade and commerce*, had been more disastrous than any we had experienced for a considerable length of time. An *old evil had unfortunately revived* (mark, nine *years after* the policy which was to secure plenty at a low price), for we *had a scarcity of food*, and therefore food had been extraordinarily *dear*, the population had had to live at a greater rate of expenditure for their mere subsistence than for many years previously, and it had become a plain and palpable fact that less had been spent in clothing. *About two years ago* he had called attention to the *earth being cultivated in every possible direction, for the supply not only of food but of raw materials, to employ our industry upon,* and from that moment to the present (1855) he only saw the *increased necessity of less attention being paid to the mechanical element of this country* and *more to the agricultural element*—not only in this, but in *every other country* on the face of the earth. We could not, he believed, *have a sound state of everything until we had food—the first element of our existence—in greater quantity and therefore at a cheaper rate."* At the same meeting, in the course of a long speech by Mr. Bright, after referring to certain *Corn* statistics, he proceeded:—" If we could conceive that in 1854 the *Harvest* had been *no better* than in 1853, and that the supplies from *Russia had been stopped*, there cannot be the slightest doubt that our poor people would have been perishing in our streets, and on our door-steps, and it would have been absolutely impossible to preserve the peace of the country. There are one or two more statements I will allude to with respect to this subject," continued Mr. Bright, " because I know there are people who fancy that as long as people are well employed, it does not much matter what people pay for food; but they *seem to lose sight of the fact that every day somebody is becoming less able to purchase it.*" . . . . Mr. Bright concluded thus :—" I see *no reason* in the world *why such a state of things should not gradually* creep on until it presses with *extreme severity upon every branch of trade,* upon all those persons *whose capital is not super-abundant for everything they have to do, and especially upon all that class of workmen who are the soonest discharged*—soonest plunged into suffering and ruin from disasters of this kind. All I ask is, that we should endeavour *to introduce* to the minds of all *with whom we come in contact a sense of the vast evils which are treading close upon us*—for their *very footsteps you may hear now, if you will only hearken;* and that we should, whenever there be any opportunity, put no obstacle in the course of any Minister who shall endeavour by any rational and moderate policy to put an end to what, I believe, is about to be, *if not soon ended, one of the most disastrous conditions we have seen in this country during our lifetime.*" It is now more than twenty-two years since this was uttered, and let every candid reader faithfully consider whether such a state of things has not, in the interval, been " gradually creeping on, until at last it presses with extreme severity upon every branch of trade," as Mr. Bright foreshadowed. Every one knows that for the last three years general complaints as to the depression in trade have been taking place from all quarters. But let the following extract from the "Money Market and City Intelligence" of the *Times* of the 9th July, 1877, answer the question.*

* A leading article in the *Times* of so far back as *the 8th February*, 1877, begins thus :—" The commercial world has been for *a long time* watching with anxious interest to detect the signs of a general revival of trade; but hitherto, unfortunately, the indications of improvement have been obscure and evanescent. . . . . In January last we imported from foreign countries and British Colonies commodities to the value of nearly *thirty-three millions* sterling—about *two millions and a quarter* more than in the same month of 1876, and half a million more than in the same month of 1875. Among the particulars of importation we look first at the *food supplies*. The wheat imported during the month was *less* in quantity and in value by one-third than that taken in 1876, but a LITTLE greater in *quantity*, and CONSIDERABLY GREATER in VALUE than the imports of 1875, &c. In January, 1875, we imported fresh beef from America to the value of £13,683, but last month (*i.e.*, January, 1877) the imports reached £87,768. The quantities of preserved meat of every kind increased in some cases by one-third, in others by one-half. The same thing is seen in the entries of other *food-*supplies. Fortunately, British industry is founded upon a solid basis of Home-trade [Mr. Hoyle, the great cotton-spinner, tells a different story], and when our commerce meets with a check, our manufacturers can afford to bide their time, and to encounter the slack-tide of fortune with cheerful endurance. At the same time *it must be admitted that the time* has come when a change for the better will be regarded as a welcome deliverance from a *painful* if not a *perilous situation*. The condition of our export trade, as shown by these Returns, is such as to demand all our fortitude and confidence in the *native* resources of the British manufacturer and merchant.

"The Board of Trade returns for *June*, issued to-day, are *again* unfavourable. *The exports have fallen off nearly* 3½ per cent. against June last year; and the imports show an increase of over 5 per cent. As the reduction in the value of the exports is still due to *receding* prices, the actual bulk of the export trade may be said to be well maintained, and that *is so far* satisfactory; but *after making all allowance* for this, the figures *are disheartening.* That the imports should continue to maintain so high a level against ever-receding export values is also unsatisfactory when the source of the increase is examined. *Dearer food* may be said to be the *cause of the whole of it*, wheat and *wheaten flour alone covering more than the excess.* We *have*, therefore, no longer the same large imports of raw materials *for manufacture* which swelled the returns of 1875, and helped to sustain those of 1876. On the contrary, *cotton, hemp,* jute, *and wool* were all *received in much lesser quantities* last *month,* and only *flax and silk in marked excess.* The import totals of value are therefore sustained by the *greater import and*

The total value of the exports for the month of January was £15,946,000, or *considerably less than half the value of the imports of the same period.* Moreover, this amount exhibits a *progressive decline* when compared with the values of the exports in the same month of 1875 and 1876. Since 1875 there has been a *falling off* of more than one million sterling." Is all this written for our learning, and to show us that we are in a painful if not *perilous situation?* It should *so* teach us!

higher prices of corn and sugar, and in lesser measure by that of such articles as silk, tea, wool, and hides. *However rich a country may be*, this state *of things must tell on its prosperity*. We are now *buying* many things *dear* and *selling* most things *cheap*—a state of things *which must pinch the community more and more severely the longer it lasts*.* To sell *cheap* means to *lower* wages, and *low wages* with comparatively *dear* bread can only in the *long* run bring one result. The *evil* is not very *gigantic* yet, however, and an *abundant harvest* would *probably* avert any *alarming consequences*, restoring the two sides of the trade account to *a sounder* footing." After subsequently showing that "the falling off in the principal *woollen* manufactured *staples* has *long* been *continued* and persistent," the report adds—"Demand abroad has *obviously lessened* very considerably, and although the decrease is more visible, perhaps, in June than it was earlier in the year, there *can be no doubt that it is hardly a passing one*. British *India and our own Colonies are in some respects our best customers just now and our steadiest; for even France* has been *buying much less from us than usual*, while the *demand from the United States is of course still declining*. Taking account of these and *such like facts and tendencies*, we can only conclude that *our trade is at present seriously oppressed*, and that *lately* its conditions

* See Appendix.

have in some respects materially altered *for the worse.*"

A leading article in the *Times* of the 10th of July (the following day) admits the truth of the foregoing, and (in endeavouring, judiciously perhaps, to soften the effect it might produce) makes some allusions to the *real* sources of our wealth and comforts, upon which it would be well if our legislators generally would dwell.

" The Board of Trade Returns for the month of June, which we published in our City article yesterday, are still of the kind which financial *authorities are agreed in terming unfavourable.* . . . The more the figures are looked into the *worse does the case appear.* The price of *almost everything* we have to *sell has declined considerably,* while the price of *what we have been buying* has, under some important heads, *been steadily rising.* We send out, in fact, almost as much merchandize as we did last year—in some cases even *more than we did* last year—and we get *less in payment for it,*" &c. " The month's returns are thus proof of a process *even more exhausting* than it would *appear at first sight. They show us in the position of a spendthrift whose expenses tend more and more to advance beyond his returns,* and whose *complete financial collapse is a question merely of time.*"[*]

[*] See introductory part of Letter V. and following: A paragraph in the *Times* of 9th October, 1876, says:—
" The total value of the imports of merchandize into the

The *attempt*, however, the *Times* makes to comfort us under such circumstances is in some respects rather sophistical. The article goes on to say—

"We may remember that the Board of Trade Returns do not profess to show us our entire money relations with the outer world. What they do show is the declared or *calculated value* in passing either way through our ports. What we are sending out will be more *highly paid for when it reaches* its market."* (But it is often frequently United Kingdom in the year was £373,939,577. That total was never before equalled in any year, and the value of the exports of British produce in 1875 was never exceeded or equalled, except in the three years next preceding 1875. The imports of the year comprised articles of the value of £139,047,488, being in a raw state and to be used in manufacture; articles *partially manufactured*, of the value of £28,568,266; articles *wholly manufactured*, of the value of £39,552,176; articles for *food*, of the value of £162,274,950, or *ten millions more* than in the *preceding* year; and other miscellaneous articles, £4,496,697. The total value of the British and Irish produce exported in the year was £223,465,963." Now, if we deduct the amount for the value of *food* alone imported from this amount of our exports, there is a surplus only of £61,191,013; and if we deduct the amount of our exports from the whole amount of imports, it leaves a balance against us of £150,474,614.

* A leader in the *Times* of 27th July, 1862, says:—"How can this falling off in the productions of Sheffield relatively to those of Germany have come about? To give a *practical* answer to this question was the chief object of the meeting to which we have referred. No allusion, however, was made to one cause of *deterioration*, which is alone sufficient to account for the fact. It is *cheapness* which has sustained the vast export trade of Sheffield, and the study of cheapness is *directly antagonistic to excellence.*"

sold for a *less* price, and the *Times* has just before said "that we get less in payment for what we sent out last year than we did for that sent out the year before.") "There are freights and profits to be added," continues the article in the *Times*, "and these together will make a very marked alteration in the Board of Trade's modest figures. We must take account next of the yearly sums which reach us from abroad at no *present* cost to ourselves, and which represent not goods sold during the year, but money permanently and profitably invested. There are *sad deductions* to be *made here.* Foreign *loans count for some hundreds of millions* less *capital* and *for many millions less income* than they did *five years ago.* But we have still a *good property*, untouched for the most part, scattered about here and there all over the habitable globe. If *we were to cease exporting altogether we should still have the means of obtaining large imports without in any degree disturbing the real balance of trade.*" "That we are under no need of paying for what we receive ought not, as far as it goes, to be taken as a sign or a likely cause of financial ruin. Again, as to the general decline of prices in our exported goods, this, so far from alarming, is rather a proof that our trade is in the right way of recovery." [It is difficult to understand why.] "Foreign *trade, moreover, is not the only thing we have to live upon.* CORN, GROWN and EATEN *within the country;* metals from *our own* mines; *wool* from our own sheep, and *woven into* cloth on *our own backs**—all these count for nothing in the Board of Trade Returns; but even in a manufacturing country like this, they count for a very large part of one year's comforts."

May the nation remember this, and act accordingly! Do let us believe the *all-important truth*, that it is only by a great *national effort being made to largely increase the produce* of our *own soil* in *food* for man and *beast* that the *Home*-trade *can be revived*, or that we can maintain the *national status.*

It is not necessary to enumerate the enormous evils resulting from the overcrowding of our large towns,† they are patent to us all, and hourly forced

---

* Only let us take measures for *increasing* the quantity of corn, wool, &c., within *our own* country and our Colonies, and also the number of backs able to purchase the cloth, &c. of *our own manufacture*, and we may yet be a thriving, happy and powerful nation. At present the proportion of wheat and wool, the produce of our own country, is but small, compared with the amount required by our population if every man could afford to provide himself with as much food and as many garments as *his health requires.*

† Presiding at an influential meeting held in Liverpool on the 1st June, 1874, Lord Derby, as President, said in the course of a most able address:—" Well, with all these facts (viz., relating to the wretched effects of overcrowding) before us, and I think I have stated them fairly, we have to ask ourselves—first, what are the *causes* of the excessive disease and mortality? And *next*, *how are we to find a remedy?* The causes, I think, are few and simple. Overcrowding and dirt, drunkenness and immorality, and, among a certain class, *a want of a sufficiency of*

on our attention; but in order to show what is the *only* way to prevent the overcrowding going on and increasing, it is advisable to give an extract from a work of *deep thought and great ability*, entitled, *The Method of the Divine Government, Physical and Moral.* By James M'Cosh, LL.D., Professor of Logic and Metaphysics in the Queen's University for Ireland,—and of which a *fifth edition* was published in 1856. Under the head of *wholesome food.* I say nothing of the temporary mischief produced by epidemics, except so far as they are aggravated by unfavourable physical conditions; nor do I touch upon the subject of drunkenness, because that is not before us, except from this point of view—that if a man or a woman has to live in a hole *where cleanliness and decency are impossible,* you must not wonder if they try to drown—I will not call it their misery—but their discomfort—in drink. There is action and reaction in this matter. Crowded lodgings and poisoned air produce the craving for stimulants, and drunken habits keep the family from ever getting a chance of moving into a more respectable home. I hear many people say, 'Oh! education will do that.' Now, I am as warm a friend to education as any one, but I am *not quite so sanguine. If a man is placed in a position where moderately pure air is unattainable and self-respect almost impossible, it is not being able to read and write that will keep him out of the gin-shop.* (Applause.) I am not arguing in disparagement of either educational teaching, or of that direct preaching of temperance, or rather abstinence, upon which many people rely. It is well that the evil which we have to fight against should be attacked from many points at once; but I believe that if it *were possible that every man, woman, and child in Liverpool should have a clean wholesome, and decent lodging, you would have struck a heavier blow at intemperance than could be struck by all* the School Boards and all the teetotal gatherings in England put together." (Cheers.)—See *Times,* 2nd June, 1871.

"Arrangements *needful* to the *stability* of the *Social System*," the author says—

"All endeavours to elevate the degraded and the fallen, so far as they are not immediately religious, should proceed on the principle of calling in those *aids and restraints* which *Providence* furnishes.* If the *rising members* of our

---

* In *The Life and Times of William IV.*, by John Watkins, LL.B., at pp. 705-6 is the following:—"After the usual Divine Service as used at the Coronation of England's monarchs, the usual offering having been made by the king and queen, &c., the Bishop of London (Dr. Blomfield) preached from 1 Peter ii. 18. The discourse of the learned prelate was impressively eloquent, and free from any political allusion, except the following passage, *reflecting upon the modern doctrine of substituting a flexible morality as the rule of policy, instead of the Divine Rule*, as revealed in the Sacred Oracles. "If the Word of God," continued the Bishop, "be true, and if the history of the past be not deceitful, evil will sooner or later befall *that* nation which loses sight of the *sovereignty of Jehovah, and substitutes other foundations for the duties of public society* than those which have been everlastingly laid by Himself. Evil will befall that nation where the maxims of *a temporary and secular expediency are permitted to supersede the motives and rules which are drawn from the fountain of Eternal Truth*, and where the ruling Providence of God and the supremacy of the Gospel—if they be not in *terms* denied—are *not recognized as influencing the councils of princes*, nor as affecting the welfare of States. It is, we would fain believe, rather to be attributed to the fastidious refinement of modern society, than to a real decay of religious principle amongst us, that even in our own country, *so remarkably favoured and protected by the Most High, His Providence is less frequently referred to, and His glory less ostensibly sought, in our public acts and measures, than it was wont to be.* We fear that it cannot be said of us, *as a nation, that we acknowledge God in*

agricultural labourers, for instance, are degraded in some districts of our land, *by being cast out from the family,* the *cause* is to be *found in restoring them* to the privilege of the *family ordinance.* It will be found too that any effectual means of *reclaiming the abandoned* and the *outcast* must *contain within* it a *method of bringing* the parties anew under the power of *those supports which Providence affords* to *the continuance in virtue.* It may *be doubted,* whether the attempts *at present made to elevate the abandoned* in the *crowded lanes* of our large towns *can be successful,* as *a national measure,* till the *very crowding of human beings as a system contrary to nature,* and until *the population are spread out in* communities in which *the aids to virtue* may again come into force. The *evils* which extended manufactures have brought along with them, must be remedied by the *wealth* which these *manufactures have furnished,* being *taxed to bring about the natural* system which they have *deranged.* In order to secure the *co-operation of Providence,* we must *adopt* the *system of Providence,* and place

all our ways, or 'give unto the Lord the glory due unto His Name.'" And in the "Prayers selected from the services of the Church," given in the *Manual of Family Prayers,* by Dr. Blomfield, the following occurs in the Prayers for Friday Morning: "Increase in us more and more a *lively faith and love, fruitful in all Holy obedience; a spirit of fervent zeal for our Holy religion; grace to forsake all covetous desires, perfectly to know Thy Son Jesus Christ, and steadfastly to walk in the path that leadeth to eternal life.*"

the parties under its influence. *Without this*, all mere secular means will be *found* utterly *useless* in *elevating human* character to a higher *level*. *Human* wisdom is in its *highest* exercise when it is *observing* the *superiority* of *divine wisdom*, and *following* its method of procedure," (p. 240-1.) Sect. iv. (the next). State of Society when the aids to Virtue and the Restraints upon Vice are withdrawn "—commences thus :—

" We have been pointing out some of the *embankments* by which the *turbulent stream* of human life is *kept in its course*, some of the *rocky barriers** by which the waves of this ever agitated sea are *restrained* while they lash upon them. Just as the native power of the stream is seen when the embankments are swept away, and the irresistible strength of the ocean when its opposing barriers are broken down, so there are times and places in which *the usual supports* of *virtue and correctives* of *vice* are *removed*, and we behold the true *tendency* of *inward humanity*. The *character* of *the*

---

* This expression has forced on recollection the concluding lines of Goldsmith's *Deserted Village*, and of his touching invocation to Poetry :—

"Aid slighted truth with thy persuasive strain
Teach erring man to spurn the *rage of gain;*
Teach him that States of *native strength* possest,
Though very poor may still be very blest.
That trade's *proud empire hastes to swift decay,*
As ocean *sweeps the labour'd mole away;*
While *self-dependent power can time defy,*
As rocks resist the billows and the sky."

prisoner is *discovered* when the *keepers* are *absent.* We see the true dispositions of the children at those corners at which the master's eye is not upon them. . . . The difficulty which the philanthropist experiences in dealing with the outcasts of society, on *whom* the *aids* to *virtue** *have lost their power furnishes* another amongst

---

* What was written by Mr. John Simon, the eminent medical officer to the Lords of Her Majesty's Most Honourable Privy Council, at the conclusion of his Report to their Lordships under the Public Health Act, directed to be taken during the year 1870, seems quite in accordance with what is here said by M'Cosh :—

"Having above laid before your Lordships, as the Statute requires, my summary of the work of 1870, I find only one further matter which in my opinion is at once so important and so urgent that, even now, I must submit it for your consideration.

"I refer, namely, to the extremely unsatisfactory state of the laws which concern the general sanitary administration of the country, a subject concerning which I two years ago submitted the chief facts to your Lordships (Eleventh Annual Report), and on which the Royal Sanitary Commission has recently made its final Report.

"I would beg leave to represent to your Lordships that the unamended state of those laws, especially as regards the constitution of local authorities and the powers which they ought to have and exercise for the prevention of disease, is not only an extreme difficulty and discouragement to persons engaged in sanitary administration, but also involves a large and constantly-increasing waste of human life; and that since the resources which might be utilized for the better protection of life are also with the progress of knowledge constantly increasing, so, almost month by month, the contrast becomes more and more glaring between the little which is done and the very much which with amended law might be done to

many illustrations of this truth. It is not because they are not so much *worse* than *others that he finds* his work to be so *difficult*, but because *motives* reform the sanitary circumstances of the masses of our population.

"I believe that your Lordships will deem this matter to be, in various points of view, deserving of the particular notice of Parliament.

"In the first place, there is the largeness of the continuing waste of human life. It seems certain that the deaths which occur in this country are fully a third more numerous than they would be if our existing knowledge of the chief causes of disease were reasonably well applied throughout the country; that of deaths, which in this sense may be called preventable, the average yearly number in England and Wales is now about 120,000; and that, of the 120,000 cases of preventable suffering which thus in every year attain their final place in the death-register, each unit represents a larger or smaller group of other cases in which preventable disease, not ending in death, though often of far-reaching ill-effects on life, has been suffered. And while these vast quantities of needless animal suffering, if regarded merely as such, would be matter for indignant human protest, it further has to be remembered, as of legislative concern, that the physical strength of a people is an essential and main factor of national prosperity; that disease, so far as it affects the workers of the population, is in direct antagonism to industry; and that disease which affects the growing and reproductive parts of a population must also in part be regarded as tending to deterioration of the race.

"Then, my Lords, there is the fact that this terrible continuing tax on human life and welfare falls with immense over-proportion upon the most helpless classes of the community; upon the poor, the ignorant, the subordinate, the immature; upon classes, which in great part through want of knowledge, and in great part because of their dependent position, cannot effectually remonstrate for themselves against the miseries thus brought upon them, and have in this cir-

which operate powerfully on mankind in general, such as pride, vanity, and *a sense of character,* have cumstance the strongest of all claims on a Legislature which can justly measure, and can abate, their sufferings.

"There are also some indirect relations of the subject which seem to me scarcely less important than the direct. For where that grievous excess of physical suffering is bred, large parts of the same soil yield, side by side with it, equal evils of another kind; and your Lordships will often have seen illustrated in my reports that in some of the largest regions of insanitary influence, civilization and morals suffer almost equally with health. At the present time, when popular education (which, indeed, in itself would be some security for better physical conditions of human life) has its importance fully recognized by the Legislature, it may be opportune to remember that, throughout the large area to which these observations apply, education is little likely to penetrate unless with amended sanitary law, nor human life to be morally raised while physically it is so degraded and squandered.

"The above various considerations, taken together, seem to me to invest the subject which I am bringing under your Lordships' particular notice with a degree of national importance to which very few subjects can pretend. Its relative position among such subjects is not a point on which I would presume to speak. But, considering the trust which is reposed in my office with regard to this great national interest, I cannot in too strong terms express my official knowledge that it most urgently needs the attention of the Legislature. And I venture to hope and believe that your Lordships' full cognizance of the case will lead you to accord to that conclusion your authoritative sanction and furtherance.

"I have the honour to be, my Lords,
"Your Lordships' obedient servant,
"JOHN SIMON.
"Medical Department of the Privy Council Office,
"March 31, 1871."

The Times, August 2, 1871.

no influence on them for *good*. It is now generally acknowledged that in *order to the reclaiming of criminals whose term of punishment is expired, it is absolutely necessary to distribute them in* society, and in *localities* in *which their* previous conduct is *unknown*, and *all that* they *may come* once more under the ordinary motives of humanity. Our philanthropists *have thus been brought* to *acknowledge* the wisdom *of the divine method*, and *find that their success depends on their* " *accommodating themselves to it."*

It may be well here to pause and remind readers of the fallacy of the leading maxim of Free-Traders—viz., that it is the *interest* of *nations*, as much as of *individuals*, to buy as *cheap*, and to sell as *dear* as possible. To pay to *home* producers a higher price than foreign producers require, is, according to this theory, to sacrifice a portion of the *national* wealth. Foreign commodities, it is alleged, must be paid for with English commodities,* because foreigners will not be found disposed to give us the produce of their labour for nothing. If, therefore, some branches of home-trade should be abandoned, others, according to the advocates of free-trade, must be proportionately augmented. Free-trade, therefore, we are told, increases our *enjoyments*, and *secures* them at a cheaper rate.

That theory, however, overlooks some *most*

---

* But we find that now the *chief* "*commodity*"—must be our gold.

important facts in the *structure of society*—facts which render the question of *cheapness* a question fraught with very different consequences to different portions of the social body. Society is divided into two great sections. The first section comprehends the classes which produce as well as consume; the second, the classes which consume *without producing*. *Let us bear in mind this all-important distinction*, and test the truth of the Free-trade maxims by it. The supporters of Free-trade, then, tell us that it is for the interest of nations as well as individuals to " buy cheap and to sell dear" (for some time, however, according to a recent paragraph in the City Article of the *Times*, England has been selling cheap and buying dear in foreign markets). Let us apply this maxim to the *productive classes*, and to the *non-productive*, respectively.

Let us begin with the *non-productive* classes. As applied to these classes the Free-trade maxim is undoubtedly true. The *non-productive* classes *have*, beyond question, an *interest in buying as cheap*, and in *selling as dear as possible;* in other words, they have an interest in *getting as large an amount of value as possible for their money:* for, be it observed, that in the case of the *non-productive* classes, the phrases " to buy *cheap* and to *sell dear"* mean precisely *the same thing*. " To buy cheap" means, in their case, to get a large portion of the labour of other men in exchange for their money;

while " to sell dear " means merely, to give little money for a large amount of labour, and of the various products of labour.

Such is the import of the great Free-trade maxim, in reference to the *non-*productive classes. In reference to the *productive* classes, its *import is very different.*

The maxim about " buying cheap and selling dear " is in short, *false,* when applied to the *productive* classes. They have, indeed, a decided interest in " *selling dear*," for they have a decided interest in getting as high a price as possible for their labour. But they have no interest (excepting as shall be shown presently) in " *buying cheap.*" As mere *consumers,* no doubt, they seem to have an interest in buying the produce of other men's labour as cheaply as possible, but then, if each member of the *productive* classes has an interest in getting a high price for his *own* labour, he also has an *interest* in preventing the GENERAL VALUE of *labour from falling.* Now, unless the *general* value of *labour* falls, the labourer cannot hope, PERMANENTLY " to buy cheap ;" whilst if, on the other hand, he succeeds in buying the labour of other men cheap, he cannot in *the long run,* expect to sell his own labour *dear.*

Every member of the *productive* classes, in short, is under the influence af a *double interest—* his interest *as a consumer,* and his interest *as a producer.* But the *labourer's interest as a producer* outweighs, decidedly, his interest as *a consumer;* because, if the labourer did not *produce more* than he is permitted to consume, he would soon find himself without employment. The *non-productive* classes on the other hand, are, it is scarcely necessary to state, under the influence of a *single* interest—their interest as *consumers.*

In a *particular* class of cases, the labourer has an interest in "*buying cheap*" from the *non-productive classes;* in other words, the labourer has a decided *interest in getting as much as possible of the money of the unproductive classes* in exchange for as small a quantity as possible of his labour.

The next maxim in the Free-trade school is, in short, true, only in reference to the interests of the *non-productive classes of society.** It is the in-

---

* It would be amusing if the consequences were not serious, to find how little the leading journal of this country regards the producers' interest, more especially as they must precede mere consumers only, or non-producers.
In a leader of the *Times* of the 14th September, 1858, it was said:—
"The loungers upon the Paris Boulevards pay their money without knowing to whom it goes. If the Press would teach them how much they pay for those ridiculous protections, and to whom the money goes, and in what the difference would consist to each individual bourgeois between protection and Free-trade, Frenchmen would not be long in seeing their own interest in the matter. But the impost is indirect. It takes the form of a difference in the price of a garment or a piece of household furniture. So they pay what they have been wont to pay and feel sympathy with the manufacturers, who are continually crying that, if they fleece Frenchmen, it is in the interest of France."

terest of these classes to buy as cheap and to sell as dear as possible:—it is *their* interest, in short, "to get as much as possible for *their money.*" It is, on the contrary, the interest of the *productive* classes to sell *their labour as dear as possible;* and never to aim at buying anything cheap, excepting the money of the *non-productive* classes.

The interests of these two great sections of society, are, in short, *directly at issue.* It is the interest of the productive classes to sell their labour *dear;* it is the interest of the *non-productive* classes to buy that labour *cheap.* It is the interest of the non-productive classes to sell their money dear: it is the interest of the productive classes to buy that money cheap. Finally, and by consequence, it is the interest of the non-productive classes, to establish a *Free-trade system*, whilst, on the contrary, it is the interest *of all orders* of *producers* to establish a system *protective* of native industry.

To a protective system the Free-traders object, that it must involve general loss. If every man's industry was protected, every man would, according to the philosophers of Free-trade, pay more than the natural price for every article he con-

It would have been well if the loungers and the other unproductive labourers of England had continued "content to pay the indirect impost;" but their great object, and probably sole thought, was to make their limited means go as far as it would, no matter what the ultimate danger to the country or to the permanence of that income itself.

sumed. A protective system would, we are assured, lead to a scramble like that in which the monkeys of Exeter Change engaged when each tried to feed out of his neighbour's pan, rather than out of his own. Every man, say these reasoners, would, under the influence of a protective system, have his hand in his neighbour's pocket; and universal loss would follow this scheme of universal robbery.

Leaving metaphors, however, it is no difficult matter to refute, if not rebuke, these fallacies of the Free-traders.

A system of universal protection would be attended with loss only to the *non*-productive classes of the community—to *the idle consumers*, who should no longer be able to buy labour and its products so cheaply as Free-trade (free imports) now enables them to do. A protective system would leave the productive classes, in relation to each other, exactly as it might find them; whilst it would place the *productive* classes in a position very different from that which they now occupy in relation to the classes of *non-productive* consumers. If, for instance, a protective system should enable one class of consumers to demand—say one-fourth more for the produce of their labour—that very system would enable all other classes of producers to raise their prices in the same proportion.

Under a protective system, be it observed, the baker, the butcher, the brewer, and all the other producers in the community, would still exchange with each other the same quantities, as before, of their respective commodities, *although at a higher price.* That higher price would, however, so far as all the *producers* of the community were concerned, be merely nominal. When, however, we should approach the circle of *non-productive consumers*, the rise in the prices of labour and of all the creation of labour, would be found to be *real.* Every *non-productive* consumer—every idler in society—would be called on to pay a higher price —to give a larger quantity of money—for the commodities which he might consume; and as idlers and *non-*producers carry nothing but money to market, they would not be able, by any conceivable process, to transfer the increase of price to the shoulders of any other class in the community.

Can we not hence plainly discover why *labourers and the productive classes,* in all countries, are averse to Free-trade principles, and why *protective tariffs* are *resolutely maintained?* And does not this tend to prove what Carey, the great statistician of America, has said, in his admirable work, *The Harmony of Interests: Agricultural, Manufacturing, and Commercial,* that " the effect of the English legislation has been that of bringing about an *unnatural division of her population."* " The loom and the anvil," he says, " in that country, instead of *being second to the plough,* have become the *first,* with great *deterioration* in the condition both of *labourers generally and capitalists.* For a long period the *few engaged in manufactures made vast fortunes;* while the owners of land were enabled to obtain high rents, because the *consumers of food* increased more rapidly *than the producers of food.* Land generally consolidated itself into fewer hands,* and *the little occupant of a few acres gradually gave way to the great farmer†* who cultivated hundreds of acres by aid of *hired* labour—

* MR. BRIGHT AND THE LANDOWNERS.—Mr. Alfred Crilly, Assistant-Secretary to the Financial Reform Association, writes to us from 50A, Melville Chambers, Lord Street, Liverpool:—" As frequent reference is being made to Mr. Bright's remarks at Rochdale respecting the list of landowners possessing over 10,000 acres each, published in this month's *Financial Reformer*, will you allow me to correct an error into which the right honourable gentleman fell through a misprint? Instead of holding, as stated, 23,000,000 acres, the 955 persons possess 29,743,402 acres, which is 5,703,415 more than one-third of the entire reported extent of the United Kingdom, exclusive of the metropolis."—*Times*, 15th November, 1877.

† Of this the *Times* seems to approve. Mr. Maguire, in moving on the 14th April, 1858, the second reading of the Tenants' Compensation (Ireland) Bill, observed "that it should be regarded not as an Irish, but an Imperial measure, inasmuch as the question involved not only the happiness and well-being of the people of Ireland, but the interests of England. He contended that the foundation of the social fabric in that country, owing to the condition of its agricultural population, was still insecure, the great social evil being a deficiency of motive in that population for industry." And a leader in the *Times* of the 15th April, 1858, on the debate thus concludes:—" We can see in this annual field-day little else than such a statement of 'sufferings' as a protesting sect or a ruined cause makes once a year on an occasion. These are the sufferings of the Irish tenantry. Do we laugh at

the few became richer, and the many went to the poor-house. The value *of labour in food* was also diminished, because both were, as they still are, *shut out from employment or land, the only employ-*

them in England? We do not, though we might do so; for, as it happens, we have gone through all this before; we have had our sufferings; and, on full consideration, we have given up the class whom Mr. Maguire pleads for, and the idle habit which he wishes to reward with the spoils of industry. The class of small farmers—that is, of those who went on dividing and subdividing farms continually, and descending to a lower and still lower rank of life and scale of cultivation—has long been extinct here. Under our heavily taxed and rated system the petty holdings which Mr. Maguire would fix and perpetuate into virtual freeholds have long since been absorbed into the large farms of the substantial English yeoman, the man with 500 acres and a capital of £5000. We have submitted to the great change which has peopled our cities at the expense of the villages, and swollen this huge metropolis with the near descendants of small farmers and labourers. What is more natural, what is less blameable, than that we should expect from others the same submission to necessity, to public good, and to law, that we have rendered ourselves? Grant that the change has its ill consequences, that our army is not so well recruited from towns as from villages, and that the standard seems to fall; grant that we stand too thick on the ground under the smoke, too thin under the fresh air and bright sun. We bear this in England, and we expect it also from Ireland. Our own peasantry have settled into labourers. They hold nothing except a quarter, or more generally a tenth, of an acre for a few greens and potatoes. We forbid them cows and even pigs. We are jealous of their poultry. They must give us their labour on our own terms. Yet the class that is reduced to this bondage, as it must seem in Irish eyes, is descended from copyholders, from small landowners, and from the same class as that which now calls for fixity of tenure in Ireland. They are not the less comfortable for the loss of

ment *in which both can be used* to an indefinite extent, with constant *increase in the return for labour.*"

In the very valuable and interesting inaugural address of Mr. G. J. Shaw-Lefevre, M.P., as President of the *Statistical Society*, on the 20th November last, the following passage occurs, when speaking of the theory of Free-trade:—

" It is not too much to say *that every year experience* tends to *confirm* the *theory* and to *disprove* and confound all the arguments of those *who opposed* it."

The writer of these pages being a *consumer only*, and enjoying a fixed income arising from the public funds, had every reason (so far as his *own* mere self-indulgence was concerned) to think favourably of a policy that tended to cheapen labour and articles of consumption; but upon reflection, and *dismissing selfishness*, he became

position and independence; but, as they have lost it, and as England accepts this feature of her social condition, she is not likely to advise or maintain another course for Ireland."

How a class could "feel not less comfortable from the loss of position and independence," the writer of these pages can understand as little as he can how the writer of the *Times* article could know that they did not. Whether the results, however, of "giving up the class of small farmers" not a peasant proprietary, has proved beneficial to the country admits of serious doubt. Mr. Shaw-Lefevre's late agricultural statistics tend to increase such a doubt. The real and vital question is, under which system the greatest amount of food for man and beast is produced?

convinced that the effect of the Free-imports system (*i.e.*, unrestricted and unreciprocated free-competition) upon the NATIONAL INTERESTS must, in a short time, prove most injurious to the *permanent* well-being of the country, and therefore it was that he was opposed to the policy, being sufficiently spiced with selfishness, or a *love of self-preservation*, to feel convinced that his own interest, and the interest of each, must be *best secured* by the *general* welfare of the *country*.

Let us, then, reflect how far results, as stated by Mr. Shaw-Lefevre himself in the *latter part* of his address, have tended "to disprove and confound all the arguments of those who *opposed* the 'Free-Imports Policy of 1846.'"

First however, let it be observed, that before *accepting* "the great *increase of trade and prosperity*, GENERALLY, as *a verification*, (by the *results of experience*,) of the Free-trade policy," it would be necessary to show the PROFITS resulting from such increase of trade, either foreign or home, however either may have increased (the latter indeed has rather decreased) and of deterioration, of quality in our manufactures, still more of *degeneracy of our people* has taken place — any "prosperity" resulting from the policy must be sadly alloyed, and it must be feared, *short-lived*.

Mr. Shaw-Lefevre concluded his address thus :—

"Recent statistics tend to show that a *smaller amount of agricultural* produce is being *raised* from the land of the United Kingdom than a few years ago. The extent of corn-crops has *been reduced* since 1870 by no less than 897,000 acres or 8 per cent. and the number of cattle has been reduced since 1874 by 557,000 about 5 per cent. and the number of sheep by 2,606,000, or 8 per cent. What is the cause of this reduction and how far is it likely to be *carried further?* These and many other questions of *no ordinary importance*, as bearing upon *the progress of England and Ireland*,* and *the condition of her cultivators*, arise upon the figures quoted, and *require the careful consideration* of economists and statesmen."

* The Registrar's Returns for Ireland, in May, 1877:— "The birth-rate has been, since 1870, falling steadily to the end of 1875; while the death-rate has been for five years above the average, and the marriage-rate is falling to a lower point. The Irish are generally in these matters compared favourably for themselves with the more provident and prudent Scotchman; but now both the birth-rate and the marriage-rate of Scotland are very much higher than those of Ireland, while the death-rate, though as a matter of fact higher, is gradually diminishing, and was lower last year than it has ever been before during the period accurate observations have been made throughout the kingdom."

The low marriage-rate is an especially ominous symptom of the condition of the Irish people at the present time, for the Registrar-General says of them, "They will marry when they can, and be celibates only when they must." Poverty alone can prevent the Irishman from marrying; and facts, if they indicate a slight increase in the population, do not also indicate an increase of prosperity, which alone will render a fresh rise in numbers a blessing instead of a curse to the country.

They do indeed, Mr. Shaw-Lefevre. But such results were anticipated by those opposed to the abrogation of the Corn-laws and the policy of 1846. And it surely IS *too* much to say that every year's experience tends to *confirm* the theory of unrestricted competition, and to "*dis*prove and confound all the arguments of those who opposed it."

The following extract from a very able article entitled "Free-Trade and Protection in 1844," by the late Sir Archibald Alison, F.R.S. and Historian, will best answer Mr. Shaw-Lefevre's question—" What is the cause of this reduction in tillage and cattle, and how far is it likely to be carried further?"

" If," says Sir Archibald Alison, " capital, machinery, and knowledge, conferred the same *immediate* and *decisive* advantages on *agriculture* that they do on *manufacturing* industry, old and densely peopled states would possess an undue superiority over the ruder and more thinly inhabited ones; the multiplication of the human race would *become excessive* in the seats in which it had first taken root, *and the desert* parts of the world would never, but under the pressure of absolute necessity, be explored. The first command of God to man, ' Be fruitful and multiply, and replenish the earth and subdue it' would be frustrated. The apprehensions of the Malthusians as to an excessive increase of mankind with *its attendant dangers,* would be realized in particular places, while *nineteen-twentieths of the earth lay neglected in a* state of nature. The desert would be left alone in its glory. The world would be covered with huge and densely-peopled excrescences—with Babylons, Romes, and LONDONS—in which wealth, power, and *corruption*, were securely and permanently intrenched, and from which the human race would never diverge but under the pressure of absolute impossibility to wrench a subsistence from their over-peopled vicinities.

"These dangers, threatening alike to the *moral character* and *material* welfare of nations, are completely *prevented by the simple law*, the operation of which we every day see around us, viz., that wealth, civilization, and knowledge, add *rapidly* and *indefinitely to* the POWERS of *manufacturing* and *commercial*, but comparatively *slowly to those of agricultural industry*. This simple circumstance effectually provides for the *dispersion of the human race and the check of an undue growth in particular communities. The old state can always undersell the young ones in manufactures, but it is everlastingly* UNDERSOLD *by them in agriculture*. Thus the equalization of industry is introduced, the *dispersion* of the human race *secured*, and a *limit put to the perilous multiplication of its numbers in particular communities. The old state can never rival the young ones around it in raising subsistence*, the young ones can never rival the old one in manufactured articles.* Either a Free-*trade* takes place between them, or restrictions are established. IF THE COMMERCIAL INTERCOURSE *between them is unrestricted* AGRICULTURE is *destroyed*, and *with it national strength is* UNDERMINED in *the old state*, and *manufactures are nipped in the bud in the young ones. If restrictions prevail and a war of tariffs is introduced, the agriculture of the old state, and with it its national strength, is preserved*, but its export of manufactures to the *adjoining states is checked*, and they *establish growing fabrics* for themselves.† Whichever effect takes place, the *object of nature* in the *equalization of industry*, the limitation of aged communities and the *dispersion of mankind is gained; in the first by the ruin of the old empire from the decay of its agricultural resources;* in the *second*, by the check given to *its manufacturing* progress, and *the transference* of *mercantile* industry to its younger *rivals*. These considerations," continues Sir Archibald " point out an important *limitation* to which *on principle*, the *doctrines* of *Free-trade must be subjected. Perfectly just* in reference to a *single community, or a compact empire*‡ *of reasonable extent, they wholly fail when applied to separate nations in different degrees*

* They have, however. America, at least, and others; and therefore a Free-trade does not take place between them, and restrictions are established.

† Germany, France, and America have long been rivals.

‡ Such as England, with the consolidation of her Colonies, would constitute.

of civilization, or even to different provinces of the same empire when it is of such an extent as to bring such different nations, *in various degrees of progress,* under the *common dominion.*"

How far experience tends to confirm what Sir Archibald Alison has said, the writer of these pages will leave each reader to decide for himself, and should he or others want further confirmation, it will be found abundantly in that most valuable work, *Sophisms of Free-Trade,* by John Barnard Byles, Serjeant-at-Law.* Seeleys, Fleet Street and Hanover Street, London. 8th edition. 1851.

The writer of these pages would most anxiously urge upon statesmen and others to procure, if possible, a copy of that edition—or any later, if there has been one—and ponder over the Preface to it and Chapter IX., headed " What is the good of our Colonies ? So say the Free-Traders."

The chapter thus begins :—

" ' Give me ships, COLONIES, and commerce,' said the greatest administrative genius of modern times.

" Well does it behove the rulers of the British *Empire* to see to it that they commit no mistake in *this matter*. A mistake *here is irreparable*. The world is *now occupied*. No more colonies are to be had. *Repentance and a change of public*

---

* The learned serjeant was elevated to the bench in 1858, and retired in 1873 ; and long may he live to enjoy the *otium cum dignitate* which he so well earned and deserves.

opinon, however soon it may arrive, may yet come too late."

If, then, the " dangers, threatening alike to the *moral and material welfare of the nations,"* have not in this country been prevented by the *simple law referred to* by Sir Archibald Alison,* should not the nation reflect whether it is not owing to a disregard of that simple law? Whether it has not been that we have *persistently pursued an unnatural system, in spite of the very dangers,* moral and material, of which we *have had warning?* And may not the great social evils, long existing, and which are the inevitable *result of overcrowding,* be permitted by Providence in order to warn, and, if possible, *convince* us that human wisdom *is* in its highest exercise when it is observing and *acknowledging* the superiority of Divine wisdom by pursuing the course it dictates? The way it marshals us that we should go is plainly pointed out in that book of Divine wisdom which England was *wont* to accept as the highest authority.

We are *there* told that—

> The profit of the earth is for all ;
> The king himself is served by the field.
> *Ecclesiastes* v. 9.

which is thus expounded by an eminent old commentator:—" Without the field he cannot have supplies for his own house, and *unless agriculture*

---

* See Appendix.

flourish, the necessary expenses of the State cannot well be defrayed. Thus God joins both the head and the feet together; for while the peasant is protected by the king, as executor of the laws, the king himself *is dependent on* the peasant, as the wealth of the nation is the fruit of the labourer's toil."

It has been said "Man's necessity is God's opportunity;" and if we will only make the best use of our land, *both at home and* IN THE COLONIES, may we not have a more reasonable hope that we shall be, in time, relieved from many of the dangers and difficulties that have long been pressing upon us, and from which, *unaided by Providence*, we are utterly unable to escape? Let us, in humility and sincerity, acknowledge this, and not presumptuously think that godless labour and self-trusting adventure will extricate us from the perplexing position into which we are drifting by not duly cultivating God's first gift to man. "The earth is the Lord's, and the *fulness* thereof."

> Omnium rerum ex quibus aliquid acquiritur,
> Nihil est agricultura melius, nihil uberius,
> Nihil dulcius, nihil homine libero dignius.
> *Cicero de Offic.* I. c. 42.

Now the Right Hon. Sir John Sinclair, Bart., who was "Founder of the Board of Agriculture,*

---

* He was also author of the *Statistical Account of Scotland*, and *Historian of the British Revenue.* He was father of Mr. Alexander Sinclair, the eminent Scotch antiquarian, who died in August last, æt. 82.

and so in truth of the Royal Agricultural Society," has, in his invaluable work, *The Code of Agriculture* (printed by Archibald Constable and Co., Edinburgh, in 1817), given a chapter (V.) " On the means of improving the Agricultural State of a Country," and it would be well if that chapter were at the present time printed in a cheap separate form. The work itself has long been out of print and rarely to be met with, and a few of the " Introductory Observations on the Importance of Agriculture" are therefore here given.*

" The prosperity of a nation," says Sir John, " possessing an extent of territory, sufficient for maintaining its inhabitants, *chiefly* depends (1)

---

* The *Times*, however, of the 17th November, 1876, in a leader on the land question in Ireland, said :—" The soundest views of national economy are those which teach us to regard land as differing from a mere chattel in no circumstance save that it is immoveable; and this is a circumstance which has no bearing on the present controversy. But whether the contract be for spinning cotton, for carriage by sea or by land, or for cultivating the soil, whenever we find one class, so to speak, in subjection to another, the State steps in to limit the power of the dominant order."

Our patriotic and loyal ancestors did not so think or teach. In *Froude's History*, Vol. I. p. 10, it is said :—" Turning to the tenure of land —for if we would understand the condition of the people, it is to this point that our first attention must be directed—we find that through the many complicated varieties of it there was one broad principle which bore equally upon every class—that the land of England must provide for the defence of England. The land was to be so administered that the accustomed number of families supported by it should not be diminished, and that the State

upon the quantity of surplus produce derived from the soil after defraying the expenses of cultivation; (2) upon the *surplus produce obtaining such a price at market as will encourage reproduction;* and (3) upon the *cultivator* having *such a command of capital as may enable him to carry on his business with energy.**

should suffer no injury from the carelessness or selfishness of its owners (see especially 2 Hen. VII. cap. 16 and 19). Land never was private property in that personal sense" (a mere "chattel," as the *Times* says), " of property in which we speak of a thing as our own with which we may do as we please; very few things in England were then property in any such sense as that, for duty to the State was at all times and in all things supposed to over-ride private interest or inclination."

Have we then become more selfish? Is "the spirit of selfishness" really, as Mr. A. Froude says, "the canker of English society?"

The Agricultural Statistics of Ireland for 1876, as given by Mr. Shaw-Lefevre, M.P., President of the Statistical Society, in his late address, are, as he said, by no means satisfactory.

* In a recently published well-written pamphlet, *English Land Tenure*, by Mercator (Bemrose and Sons, Paternoster Row, 1877), in speaking of "insufficient capital," the author says :—" On all hands it is admitted, that the want of capital embarked in farming operations is much below the profitable limit. . . . Capitalists will readily invest their money in the wildest imaginable schemes, and even the slowly hoarded gains of the industrial toiler are swept away at one fell swoop to fatten the rapacious promoters of some bubble undertaking; whilst agriculture, one of the most important of all our industrial occupations, is left in struggling penury. . . . If we include the whole of the English counties, I estimate the tenant's capital at £6 per acre; yet double the amount could be profitably employed." (And here let us remember, that this means that the present cultivated lands

8 *

" 1. The surplus produce arises from that inestimable quality possessed by the soil which enables it, *in proportion as it is* SKILFULLY *managed*, to furnish maintenance for a greater number of persons than are required for its cultivation. Thence proceed the profits of the farmer; the rents of the landlord; the *subsistence of the manufacturer and of the merchant;* and *the greater proportion of the income of the State.* That *surplus marketable produce, therefore, is justly considered to be the principal of all* POLITICAL *power, and personal enjoyment.* When that *surplus produce* does *not exist* (unless in circumstances of a very particular nature) there *can be* no *flourishing towns;* no military or naval force; none of the *superior arts; none of the finer manufactures;* no learning; none of the conveniences or luxuries of foreign countries; and *none of that cultivated and polished society* at home, which not only *dignifies the individual*, but also extends its *beneficial influence*

might be made to yield double the produce they now do, and that consequently the national loss sustained by the cultivators not having such a command of capital as would enable them " to carry on their business with energy," is as great as the produce at present yielded by the soil.) "This shows," the author goes on to say, "a great want of confidence either in the industry of the tenants or the probity of the landlords, or why should such sums be unemployed, or only earning the insignificant interest of 2 per cent. per annum. Without better security for the capital employed by the tenant, it is idle to look for any great improvement in the general agriculture of England." See Appendix.

throughout the whole mass of the community. (See Malthus' *Enquiry into Rent,* p. 10.) What exertions ought not, then, to be made, and *what encouragement ought not to be given to preserve or to* INCREASE *so essential a resource, the foundation of our national prosperity?*

" Nor is this subject to be dwelt upon SOLELY in a *financial point* of view. Let it, at the same time, be considered that *it is the land* which furnishes the *raw materials* of the greater part of our manufactures; that *the proprietors and occupiers of land supply the best markets to our manufacturers* and merchants; and that, *through them, the greater part of all other professions gain their livelihood.* Numbers of the *fundholders* are little aware that upon *the prosperity of agriculture the* REGULAR PAYMENT OF THEIR DIVIDENDS MUST PRINCIPALLY DEPEND. For it is to be observed that as the property tax was imposed on all the classes of the community, in proportion to their wealth or income, hence the taxes, payable in every other way, by each class and every individual in each class, who spent his income, must be paid in *nearly the same proportion as the tax on property.*

" It cannot at the same time be doubted, that the agricultural classes are much indebted to those employed in trade and manufactures, for consuming the produce of the soil, and by the skill and industry of those who occupy it, which constitute the REAL *basis of our national prosperity, and exported manufactures are nothing else but so much beef, mutton, wheat, barley, &c. converted into another and more* CONVENIENT *shape*. Where manufactures, however, are maintained *by the productions of foreign industry, and in particular when the articles they manufacture are produced from foreign raw materials, as fine wool*, instead of being an advantage, they have the *effect of depreciating the value of domestic agricultural productions, and bringing foreign articles into competition with them, by* MEANS of BRITISH CAPITAL. The *paltry* PROFITS of the manufacture, *are nothing compared to the mischiefs which are thus occasioned to the real sources of our prosperity.* . . . .

"It is to be hoped," says Sir John Sinclair, "that these statements* will satisfy every impartial individual that the strength and resources of this country principally arise from the productions of the soil—THAT THE LAND IS THE BASIS OF OUR NATIONAL WEALTH†—and that *on the amount, and the value of its productions*, our commerce and manufactures, and the *payment of the public creditors, must* in a great measure depend. The *revenues of the Church;—and by far the largest proportion of the payments to the poor;—and various other public*

---

* Others than what are here set forth are given by Sir John Sinclair in his *Code of Agriculture*.

† "It is," says Sir John Sinclair, "hardly to be credited, how little the superior importance of agriculture was known to the statesmen and ministers of this country, before a Board of Agriculture was established."

charges, are likewise payable from the same source. Hence nothing can be more impolitic than to neglect the adoption of any measure by which the interest of agriculture* can be promoted; or more *hazardous*, than to take any step by which *its prosperity can be impaired, or those who live by it impoverished*, much less brought to ruin.

"The *means* therefore, by which the *agricultural prosperity* of a country can *best be promoted, merit* OUR PECULIAR ATTENTION.

"It has long been considered, as an incontrovertible proposition, and approaching to the nature of an axiom, that whoever could make two ears of corn, or two blades of grass, to grow upon a spot where only one grew before, would deserve better of mankind, and do more essential service to his country, than the whole race of politicians together.

"There never was a greater instance of sophistry than this doctrine of Swift, who seems not to have been at all aware of *the immense benefits* conferred upon agriculture by *a judicious system of* CIVIL POLICY. *In fact,* THE PROSPERITY of *agriculture depends* UPON THE POLITICIAN " (so emphasized *by* Sir John Sinclair himself). " *The better and the*

---

* The *Saturday Review* of 26th March, 1861, on the budget remarked: "The receipt of £800,000 from the 1s duty on corn is convenient to the Treasury, but it represents a loss of many millions incurred by English farmers."

Mr. A. Froude has said, in the first vol. of his *History*, " The spirit of selfishness is the canker of English society."

more EQUITABLE *the civil policy of the country, the more perfect will its agriculture become.** Those

* And Manchester and other manufacturers have long since begun to doubt whether the Policy of 1846 has proved to be wise, as the following leaders from the *Times* show.

Though Mr. Cobden has gone from among us, Mr. Bright still survives to witness a phenomenon which, twenty years ago, would have been rejected from discussion as beyond the very range of possibilities. In the heart of Lancashire, and in the home of the cotton industry, it is now roundly affirmed by spinners and manufacturers that Free Trade is a mistake, that the Anti-Corn Law League promulgated error instead of truth, and that a vast deal more is to be said for the principle of Protection than political economists have been willing to allow. This, as our readers will see elsewhere, is the tale told in Manchester itself, and in that very Chamber of Commerce which represents and expresses the doctrines of the famous " Manchester School." The utmost Mr. Bazley could say for the case is that the heresy had not penetrated within the walls of the actual Chamber; it is somewhat doubtful, as will be presently seen, whether even this limited pretension to orthodoxy can be entirely sustained; but beyond this inner circle both unbelief and apostasy were owned to be rife. Mr. Bazley added, indeed, that he had heard these false doctrines " while he was among his constituents," as if the strange conversion of Lancashire to Conservatism were in some measure due to the collapse of the Free Trade theory; but it was allowed on all hands that Protection had been taken into favour again, and in fact the debates of the meeting were chiefly occupied with this surprising subject. We remarked some time since that the surviving members of the League might advantageously recommence their lectures for the benefit of Trade Unions, but it now appears that manufacturers as well as operatives have lapsed from the faith of the last generation.

It would have been well if Mr. Bazley or some one of his colleagues had explained a little more clearly, for the benefit of the outside world, the origin and tendency of the commercial heresy now infecting the cradle of Free Trade; but it seems

politicians or statesmen therefore, who by *removing every obstacle, and furnishing* EVERY PROPER EN-

as if the source of scepticism were actually nothing less than Mr. Cobden's own darling work—the French Treaty. In a Report circulated with the authority of the Manchester Chamber there occurs this ominous passage:—"A comparison between imports and exports, after deducting the total of raw and manufactured articles on both sides, shows that in the year 1867 the amount of French imports taken as manufactured commodities was, in round numbers, 30 millions, against 13½ millions of English exports of like description—a difference of 16¼ millions in favour of the national industry of France." No wonder the meeting came to words over such a statement, implying, as Mr. Cheetham observed, that England had lost 16½ millions by the operation of the French Treaty. It cannot be denied, indeed, that the language employed, whatever might have been the intentions of those who used it, was "fitted to convey that impression to many minds." Unfortunately, the speakers at the meeting assumed that all the world knew as much of the facts as they did themselves, and omitted to state distinctly what were the arguments of this new Manchester School. We can only gather from words dropped in reply that France is supposed to have the advantage in the interchange of products negotiated by Mr. Cobden. She sends us her wines in ever-increasing quantities, for the obvious reason that we can make no wines like them or produce anything so cheap or so good. But when it comes to her taking our cotton stuffs we have no such decided superiority to rest upon. The French have learnt to spin cotton pretty nearly as well as we can, and they are spinning and likely to spin more and more as time goes on. Mr. Platt was at the pains of arguing that England ought fairly to compete with France in respect of labour and wages, and beat her hollow in respect of machinery; that the instances were few and exceptional in which our fabrics could be undersold by those of the Continental manufactories, and that nothing was to be feared on these grounds for future Lancashire trade. Mr. Cheetham declared, with greater boldness, that "he went

couragement to agriculture, promote *its advancement*, have a higher claim to the gratitude of mankind, further, and said it mattered not a straw on which side the balance might be, for they had the right to purchase wherever they chose, and they would not purchase if they did not want the article purchased." All very sound doctrine; but to what a pass must things have come when such apologies for Free Trade and the French Treaty are required in the Chamber of Commerce at Manchester!—*Times*, 4th February, 1869.

On Monday last, as we yesterday explained, the Liverpool Chamber of Commerce was occupied with a discussion on the present depression of trade, and on the following evening the Manchester Reform Union devoted a sitting to the consideration of the same subject. From these debates we may succeed at last in gathering some definite ideas of the distress reported, the causes assigned for it, and the measures proposed for its removal. Of course, when trade is spoken of in Lancashire, it is the Cotton Trade which is meant, and the Cotton Trade, we are told, is depressed because cotton is dear, because cotton-spinning has been carried to excess, and because foreign nations are competing with us in the cotton-markets of the world. More plainly and specifically, the doctrine of the Lancashire malcontents amounts to this:— That we should be doing better if France would take our cotton as freely and fairly as we take her wines and silks, and that Mr. Cobden's Commercial Treaty has proved a failure in so far as it allows France all the benefits of Free Trade without imposing on her the duty of Reciprocity. Frenchmen are glad enough to send us their silk fabrics and their cheap claret, but, instead of buying our cheap hardware and our cheap calico in return, they persist in manufacturing the articles for themselves.

This is a concise statement of the case advanced for the revival of Protection, and it has been met, of course, by a stout re-assertion of the unimpeachable principles of Free Trade. But Professor Leone Levi, who addressed the Manchester Union at considerable length on this subject, opened an entirely new and by no means flattering view of the ques-

than those who have merely performed *a secondary or practical part, which part they never could have* tion. According to his statistics it is very doubtful if we could, under present circumstances, undersell our neighbours in cotton goods, even if their protective tariff were abolished to-morrow. The French, as we yesterday observed, have made extraordinary progress in manufacturing skill, and if they have not overtaken us already, they are on the very point of doing so. Professor Levi explained to his hearers that in the year 1852 an English cotton mill had for every 1000 spindles an advantage of 1418 francs over a French mill. In other words, an English manufacturer saved £56. in the produce of 1000 spindles by his superiority in all those arts and attainments which render production cheap. Fifteen years afterwards three-fourths of that superiority had been lost. The advantage of the English spinner had been reduced from 1418 francs to 343, and the diminution was still going on. "Yet another effort," observed the Professor, "and France will come up to this country." But who will say that effort has not been already made? The figures we have given relate to the year 1867, and we are now in 1869. There is nothing to show that France is not actually abreast of us, except, indeed, it be her own misgivings as expressed in her protective duties.

Professor Levi, however, proceeded presently to another point of the question. The special merit of our work has hitherto been its cheapness, and yet France has learnt to spin cotton almost as cheaply as we do. But "cheapness is not the only element. Goodness of material and elegance of design are quite as necessary in these days of show and luxury." Exactly so; and what, asked the Professor, "will be the consequence if France can, besides cheapness, best suit the taste and wants of an advancing civilization?" That is a question which our manufacturers should carefully consider, but Professor Levi has already, in our opinion, furnished the reply. If France succeeds in appropriating our best aptitudes, while we make no progress in imitating hers, she must beat us in the commercial race, and it obviously becomes our

performed at all, but under the protection of wise laws, regularly administered, and executed with impartiality and vigour.

interest and duty to do as she has done, and strengthen ourselves at our weakest points. In the combination of capital, enterprise, and industry which makes production cheap we have hitherto been first; in the various tastes and gifts which conduce to elegance of work we have been usually surpassed, and it is here, therefore, that we, in our turn, may gain ground upon our rivals. "What we want," said the Professor, "is greater alacrity and inventiveness, greater power of adaptation, and greater range of industries." If it is asked how these improvements are to be attained, the answer is ready—"by extended education and enlightenment among the whole community." The artisan in France is better educated than the artisan in England. He has, in some respects, greater aptitudes to begin with, but these aptitudes are encouraged and developed by judicious training. This is the chief secret of French progress, though it may be, as Professor Levi thinks, that cheap transport and other economical advantages have helped our neighbours in the race.

It must not be forgotten, in explanation of our present difficulties, that the dearness of the raw material tells heavily against us. It may be that we still retain a certain superiority in the matter of cheapness, but this advantage counts for less when the ultimate price of the manufactured article is so greatly enhanced by the first cost of the material. When cotton is a shilling a pound, instead of sixpence, the cost of workmanship in a yard of calico becomes less perceptible, and thus our special excellence is proportionately eclipsed. Nevertheless, in all these arguments we are met by a strange phenomenon. The fact, incredible as it may appear, is, that we actually do import as much raw cotton as ever, and we actually do export as many yards of manufactured stuffs. We pay, it is true, many millions of pounds more for the material than we did formerly, but still we buy it, and we work it up. Thus the question arises, on what terms is this trade done, and it seems probable that it has been done to

"This *leads to the most important* discussion, perhaps, in *the whole range of political inquiry*, and some extent on losing terms—that is, more cotton has been spun and exported than foreign customers were prepared to buy. Is there, then, any limit to trade or production at this point? Can Lancashire capitalists go on adding mill to mill and factory to factory without exceeding the demands of the world? Professor Levi, though recognizing the fact of over-production at a recent period, is of opinion that, practically speaking, there are no bounds to the world's possible demands. "Millions upon millions of people," he says, "have not yet tasted the benefits of mechanical inventions in articles of clothing," so that there is ample room for both France and England together in the industrial field. Only, these new markets must be sought out and opened, and as cheapness in the goods produced is the very essence of the problem, we must needs endeavour, in the first instance, to get raw cotton at a lower price. It cannot be too often repeated that the groundwork of the whole trade is popular custom. The wearers of calico, whether Europeans, Asiatics, or Americans, are the people who find the money for cotton-growers and cotton-spinners together, and these wearers will never be as numerous as they should be unless we can make calico cheaper and better than any other wear. At present, as the Professor remarked, the high price of cotton has brought wool and linen into the market again.

One thing must needs be clear from these debates, and that is that want of Reciprocity has very little to do with the depression of trade.* The industry of Lancashire could hardly be much benefited by the admission of English cottons into France duty free. If Professor Levi's statistics are accurate, the margin of cheapness still existing in our favour must be very small, whereas in all the elements of recommendation except cheapness we are actually behindhand.

---

* The *Times*, therefore, attaches no value to Reciprocity, and would continue our Free-Imports system at all hazards. See Appendix.

respecting which *the most ill-founded* prejudices are *unfortunately entertained,* viz., ' What public encouragements to agriculture ought a *wise Government* to bestow ?'

" Many able men, *reasoning solely from the* ABUSES to which the *system of encouragement is liable,* have thence been induced to condemn this policy, and to recommend *that of giving to individuals the entire freedom of exercising their industry in their own way, without any legislative interference whatever.* They dwell much on the reply once made by some of the *principal merchants* of France to the celebrated *Colbert* who having asked, ' *What Government would do for them?*' was answered, ' Laissez nous faire ' (Let us alone). On the other hand they *totally repro-*

Instead of crying out for duties on French goods, it would be far better to take a lesson from French manufacturers. We have been accustomed, it must be owned, to make light of our rivals, and to persuade ourselves that nothing could touch us in commercial enterprise. The sooner we undeceive ourselves the better. Such a monopoly as we once enjoyed we enjoy no longer, and shall never, in all probability, enjoy again. There was a time when we had no competitors; we must now look for keen competition. There is not the slightest reason why the national trade should not be as good as ever, but it must be maintained and extended on different terms. We have taught other nations to rival us, and we must now maintain our position by the same arts which have proved so serviceable to our rivals. We must give up the idea of inherent and unapproachable superiority, and condescend at last to avail ourselves of every lesson, and turn every example to account.—*Times,* October 29, 1869.

bate the mercantile *system,* as they call it (or a series of laws which have been enacted in this country for promoting the prosperity of commerce) as in the highest degree impolitic; though *under that* VERY *system the commerce of Great Britain has risen to a height* altogether unexampled in history (1817). *But as our legislature have wisely deemed it expedient, to protect both our manufactures and commerce,* which, *under such a system have so preeminently flourished,* no *good reason* can be assigned why, in a like manner, and on the *same principles, agriculture ought not to be encouraged in Great Britain,* where it produces such a great revenue;—where with a thousand millions of national debt (1817) we still have about *twenty millions of acres, lying in a state comparatively waste and unproductive;* — *where the population is rapidly increasing;—and where it has been found necessary to import no inconsiderable portion of the means of our subsistence.*

"It is certainly better to let agriculture alone, than to establish injudicious regulations respecting it. But if a Government will make such inquiries as may enable it to judge of what can be done *with safety and advantage;* and will promote *agricultural industry,* not only by *removing every obstacle to improvement,* but by *granting* POSITIVE ENCOURAGEMENT; agriculture will *prosper with* a rapidity, and will be *carried on to an extent* which is hardly to *be credited;* and in a much superior degree, than by the 'let alone system' under the torpor of which *ages might pass away** without accomplishing what might be effected in the *course of a few years*, under a judicious system of *encouraging regulations*.

"The principal encouragements which a wise and liberal Government will naturally be anxious to bestow, for the purpose of advancing the Agricultural prosperity of a country, may be classed under the following heads. (1.) Removing all obstacles to improvement; (2.) *Relieving agriculture from any burdens peculiarly affecting it;* (3.) Promoting the *collection and diffusion of useful information;*† (4.) Giving a *preference to domestic*

---

* Well would it have been had our Legislature acted upon the very able Report made by the Commissioners appointed in 1838 (of whom the late Lord Derby, so ably represented by his son, our present most cautious and judicious Foreign Secretary), to consider a general system for railways in Ireland, with a view to the improvement of agriculture and bringing into cultivation large tracts of land lying waste—millions of acres. The Report with great truth said:—"It is a waste of the public available resources to suffer so large a portion of the empire to lie fallow, or to leave it to struggle, by slow degrees, and with defective means, towards its improvement, when the judicious aid of the State might quickly make it a source of common strength and advantage."

† An ancient usage, which dates from the times of Henry IV. (whose great minister the Duke de Sully, used to say tillage and pasturage were the foster mothers (*les deux mammelles* of the State)—that of giving Agricultural Lectures on Sunday after Mass—has lately been revived in some communes in France under government patronage.—*Illustrated London News*, March 24, 1860.

productions in the *Home*-market; (5.) Encouraging the exportation of our surplus produce that might

Of all the pursuits of man, agriculture—the work of production—is the one that most tends to the expansion of intellect. There is none in which so many of the laws of nature must be consulted and understood as in the cultivation of the earth. Every change of the season, every change even of the winds, every fall of rain, must affect some of the manifold operations of the farmer. In the improvement of our various domestic animals, some of the most abstruse principles of physiology must be consulted. Is it to be supposed then that men thus called upon to study, or to observe the laws of nature, and labour in conjunction with its powers, require less of the light of the highest science than the merchant or the manufacturer? It is the science which requires the greatest knowledge, and the one that pays the best for it. For these reasons it has often occurred to the writer of these pages, that it is the want of being instructed, in some degree at least, in this science that renders the ploughman's occupation so dull and insipid to him, and that prevents him from bringing up his sons to agricultural labour, as it is well known he does not, if he can possibly push them into any other occupation. Would it not be well to excite and interest these boys by introducing generally into the National Schools, in agricultural districts at least, the *Catechism of Practical Agriculture*, by Henry Stephens, F.R.S.E., 1857, W. Blackwood and Sons; and also the *Catechism of Agricultural Chemistry and Geology*, by James F. W. Johnston, M.A., F.R.S.L., F.R.S.E., also by Blackwood and Sons, 1873?

The parents of the boys discovering, when the boys are at home, that they are learning something useful to them in their calling, would appreciate the education given all the more, and the more willingly send them to school.

This would be more in accord with what Mr. A. Froude tells us, in the most valuable first volume of his *History of Henry VIII.*, was formerly the course of instruction. He says:—

" Every child, so far as possible, was to be trained in some

remain on hand, after the demands at home are supplied; (6.) *Extending, by every prudent means,* business or calling, idleness being the mother of all sin, and the essential duty of every man being to provide honestly for himself and his family. The Education theory, for such it was, was simple but effective; it was based on the single principle that next to the knowledge of a man's duty to God, and as a means towards doing that duty, the first essential of a worthy life was the ability to maintain it in independence. Varieties of inapplicable knowledge might be good, but they were not essential. Such knowledge might be left to the leisure of after years, or it might be dispensed with without vital injury. Ability to labour could not be dispensed with, and this therefore the State felt it its own duty to see provided; so reaching, I cannot but think, the heart of the whole matter. The children of those who could afford the small entrance fees were apprenticed to trades, the rest were apprenticed to agriculture; and if children were found growing up idle, and their fathers or their friends failed to prove that they were able to secure them an ultimate maintenance, the mayors in towns, and the magistrates in the country, had authority to take possession of such children, and apprentice them as they saw fit, that when they grew up 'they might not be driven by want or incapacity to dishonest courses.'"— *Froude's History,* Vol. I., p. 44.

The late Lord Monteagle speaking in Ireland in relation to Popular Education, in 1857, said:—

"We know that there was great difficulty in securing children's attendance after they had arrived at an age in which they were at all capable of employment, or could be of any use to their parents at home. The withdrawal of the children from the school was therefore owing to causes operating in England as well as in this country; for wherever there was a demand for labour they would find that children who could do any work would be taken from the schools in those districts of the country which were agricultural; and where schools existed in which was added agricultural to intellectual teaching, they found the pupils were allowed to

the cultivation of waste lands, in order that the productive territory may be constantly on the increase; (7.) *Granting public aid to substantial improvements,* such as roads, bridges, canals, &c., on which the agricultural and *general* prosperity of a country so *essentially depend;* and (8.) Countenancing the establishment of corporations to furnish the means of carrying on such improvements as are beyond the power of individual wealth or enterprise."*

The great importance of the matter contained in the above extract, has prompted the present writer to give it at length. And the question is, how far, since Sir John Sinclair's *Code of Agriculture* in 1817 was published, Government *has* afforded such "*principal encouragements*" to the *Agriculture* of England? Without pretending to answer

remain longer, until they grew up and became vigorous plants. This was an agricultural country, and it was necessary that agriculture should be taught in the schools, in order to convince the masses that the instruction which their children were receiving applied to their occupation in after life, and would fit them for it. He considered, therefore, that 'the Agricultural Schools,' which the Commissioners of National Education had established in many districts, were a benefit to the country. In his (Lord Monteagle's) own neighbourhood they had a most excellent Agricultural School, around which there was a cycle of other schools and he could state that the boys, after working in the farm for part of the day, returned to their studies for the remainder of the day with increased activity and with their physical and mental powers greatly invigorated."—*Times*, September 3, 1857.

* See Appendix.

this question, it is sufficient to know that the land does not *produce* (as it might be made to do, more adequately than it does) in *proportion* to the amount of population, and that last year there was a considerable *decline in cereal crops*, in cattle, and in sheep.

The following appeared in the *Times* of Saturday, the 24th September, 1859, "Cause of Discontent in the Tyrol." "An Englishman sometime resident in Germany, writing to one of the Parisian Journals, says, ' Among the lower classes the discontent is great. *The land is not made to produce in proportion to the amount of population, and the peasant is taxed disproportionately to his means.*'

" The result of this misrule is fearful poverty, without a prospect of alleviation, *and the far-famed loyalty* of the Tyrolese peasant has been put to rather a hard *test*. It was with the *greatest difficulty that the sharp-shooters were got together to defend the frontiers during the war*, nor did they come at the first call ; they came when it was better to volunteer than to wait to be called *forcibly*, and the murmurs are long and loud for the promised Tyrolese representation." And in the same *Times* is a report of an Agricultural Meeting at Ledbury, Herefordshire, at which Mr. H. Mildmay, M.P. (in 1859), said, "The *landed interest* was more concerned in the *proper defence of the country than any other*, because while *capital engaged in trade could fly* to any other country, the land was irremoveable!"

Now in a clever article in the *Times* of the 21st of November, 1877, on the increase of population that has taken place in recent years in France, it is said—

"Generation after generation, *all the services, all the trades, look to our villages as the nurseries of strength, endurance,* and those other *natural qualities, which fit man for the most necessary occupations.* Upon the whole, the internal polity of our villages is free. *Preserving a mean between the centrifugal and centripetal forces, it neither* drives away *from,* nor draws too much to, the native soil. It does not hold out the vain hope that by simply clinging to their Parish the humblest men may become Statesmen at home, nor yet does it compel a choice between banishment and starvation. Without *Colonies,* without even a readiness to assimilate and unite with other nations, France is always expelling her progeny from the soil, *with no other result than to accumulate them in the Towns.*

"Here, then, is a *fact* which France *cannot safely overlook,* whatever inference she may please to draw from it. She recognizes *with much complacency* that her population is increasing. Well and good. It would be hard indeed if it did not increase. But it is equally true that the increase *is not in the ranks of agricultural husbandry, in the*

their surplus labour; *so at least* they feel.* If, however, *labour is wealth*, they are *so far the poorer.*" (Let the last truth sink deep into the memory of all who read it). . . . "We are threatened," concludes the article in the *Times*, "*with depopulation and accumulation beyond reason and measure*," and as the *institutions* of this country have been generally framed upon the supposition of an unchangeable state of things *it* IS EVIDENT *they* WILL *have to* UNDERGO SOME ADAPTATION." Do not all these evils and many others—the existence of disease amongst our flocks and herds and the degeneracy of race amongst our people, tend to remind us and warn us that—" A fruitful land maketh He barren for the wickedness of them that dwell therein." And has not God said—" I will be exalted among the heathen and I will be exalted in the earth?" And " The nation that will *not serve Thee*," we are told, " shall perish." Isa. lx. 12.

The philosophy which merely concerns itself with the investigation of the laws and properties of matter and simply deciphers, so to speak, the characters inscribed on the book of nature, has

* On the contrary, they feel greatly the lack of agricultural labourers, as the speeches made at the agricultural gatherings annually announce. One of the most thriving tenant-farmers in Devonshire, about two years ago, told the writer of these pages that "soon they would not be able to find any men to do the rough work of the country." That the strongest of the young men had emigrated, and that only the least strong and aged were left to do the work in agriculture.

taken precedence of that *higher philosophy* which, not content with deciphering these characters, seeks also to *interpret their meaning*, and by a careful study both of mental and physical phenomena and of their *natural adaptations, to rise to a knowledge of the attributes and designs of the Creator.* Hence the tendency so prevalent in our day to construct and adopt such theories of the universe *as either exclude a Creator altogether*, by the assumed sufficiency of natural laws to account for the appearances of design, or, *recognizing the existence of an intelligent First Cause, assign to Him the least possible share of direct agency in the production of creation's wonders,* and nothing beyond the most *general superintendence of the events in creation's history.* When so much of the boasted knowledge of the age is of this description — when the tendency is so general and so strong, to look at the operations and results of *natural law simply as beautiful or striking phenomena in themselves,* or with an eye merely to their subserviency to man's *temporal interests,* while the indications which they give of the character of their divine Author and of His *moral relations to man as his Lawgiver and Judge,* are scarcely, if at all, being *heeded*—it is well that the inquirer should be *arrested* in this too superficial and cursory reading of nature by the significant question—*Understandest thou what thou readest?* That "knowledge is power" is a common saying. The

their surplus labour; *so at least* they feel.* If, however, *labour is wealth,* they are *so far the poorer.*" (Let the last truth sink deep into the memory of all who read it). . . . "We are threatened," concludes the article in the *Times*, "*with depopulation and accumulation beyond reason and measure,*" and as the *institutions* of this *country have been generally framed upon the supposition* of an unchangeable state of things *it* IS EVIDENT *they* WILL *have to* UNDERGO SOME ADAPTATION." Do not all these evils and many others—the existence of disease amongst our flocks and herds and the degeneracy of race amongst our people, tend to remind us and warn us that—" A fruitful land maketh He barren for the wickedness of them that dwell therein." And has not God said—" I will be exalted among the heathen and I will be exalted in the earth?" And " The nation that will *not serve Thee,*" we are told, " shall perish." Isa. lx. 12.

The philosophy which merely concerns itself with the investigation of the laws and properties of matter and simply deciphers, so to speak, the characters inscribed on the book of nature, has

* On the contrary, they feel greatly the lack of agricultural labourers, as the speeches made at the agricultural gatherings annually announce. One of the most thriving tenant-farmers in Devonshire, about two years ago, told the writer of these pages that "soon they would not be able to find any men to do the rough work of the country." That the strongest of the young men had emigrated, and that only the least strong and aged were left to do the work in agriculture.

taken precedence of that *higher philosophy* which, not content with deciphering these characters, seeks also to *interpret their meaning*, and by a careful study both of mental and physical phenomena and of their *natural adaptations, to rise to a knowledge of the attributes and designs of the Creator.* Hence the tendency so prevalent in our day to construct and adopt such theories of the universe *as either exclude a Creator altogether*, by the assumed sufficiency of natural laws to account for the appearances of design, or, *recognizing the existence of an intelligent First Cause, assign to Him the least possible share of direct agency in the production of creation's wonders*, and nothing beyond the most *general superintendence of the events in creation's history.* When so much of the boasted knowledge of the age is of this description — when the tendency is so general and so strong, to look at the operations and results of *natural law simply as beautiful or striking phenomena in themselves,* or with an eye merely to their subserviency to man's *temporal interests,* while the indications which they give of the character of their divine Author and of His *moral relations to man as his Lawgiver and Judge,* are scarcely, if at all, being *heeded*—it is well that the inquirer should be *arrested* in this too superficial and cursory reading of nature by the significant question—*Understandest thou what thou readest?* That " knowledge is power " is a common saying. The objects, however, *within* the range *of man's foresight are placed beyond his power;* while the objects *within his power lie beyond his foresight.* In the one case, man's *knowledge* increases *without an increase* of his *power;* and in the other his *power* is rendered *in*effectual by his *want* of *knowledge.* The *confident* expectations of the *power* accruing from *knowledge* could be *realized* only by the foresight ever *imparting a power of action;* and by the power of action having *provided for it an available foresight.* But there are *limits to the one and to the other;* and where the one is *enlarged,* the *other* is *confirmed;* and where power is given in the one, it is counteracted by a corresponding weakness in the other. No doubt there is great room, as knowledge increases, at once *for foresight and action;* but still there are necessary limits to both; and ALL THAT MAN MAY FEEL *his dependence alike* in the one, as in the other, *on the government of God. Human sagacity* and activity will no doubt both increase as the world grows older; but both the one and the other will find checks *raised to humble them* in their very *extension.** No man

* Therefore, however we may advance in the science of agriculture and in inventions for mechanical aid to the farmer, it will never become the less necessary for the latter to exclaim, as the "Poet of the Seasons" has in his "Spring" so rightly suggested he should do, after the grain has been "thrown into the faithful bosom of the ground," and the harrow "has followed harsh and shut the scene"—

"Be gracious, heaven! for now laborious man
Has done his part."

feels his impotence more than he who knows all the courses of the stars, and yet feels that he cannot *influence them in the least degree*, except it be the person who feels himself surrounded by agents which he can, to some extent, control, but which in a far higher degree control him, and *disappoint by their unexpected movements, his best laid schemes.* The farther *human knowledge* penetrates, it discovers, with a painful sense of weakness, the more objects utterly beyond its control, and moving on in their own independent sphere. The greater human activity becomes, it *complicates* the *more the relations of human society*, and the relations of man to the most capricious of the agents of nature; and the greater the power he exerts, he feels himself the more powerless *in the grasp of a higher power*. Increased knowledge *should* make him bow *in deeper reverence* before *infinite* knowledge; and his own augmented action cause him to acknowledge *in a deeper feeling of helplessness* the IRRESISTIBLE POWER of the action of the Almighty.

This little episode must not run to greater length, but it may help to convince any reader that human wisdom *is* in its *highest* exercise when it is observing *the superiority of Divine Wisdom*, and, so far as it is able, *following its dictates*.

And now let us see how these dictates can best be followed in relation to our Waste Lands, in "Extending" as Sir John Sinclair urges, "by every prudent means the cultivation of waste lands in order that *productive territory may be constantly on the increase.*"

We all know how our present able and excellent Home Secretary has of late been worried as to the *convict* labour in our prisons seriously interfering with *free*-labour—in different branches of trade—mat-makers, basket-makers and others. Now, it is very certain that the waste lands of England, or the greater part of them, will never be brought into cultivation at the expense of employing free-labour; consequently no *injustice could be done* to *free*-labourers by *employing convicts* to bring these waste-lands into such a state of cultivation as that they would ultimately pay for *free* labour, and by so much increase the area for the employment of free labour and consequently increase of produce. But there are many other reasons for so employing convicts. As regards their health and reformation, and particularly with a view to qualify them for such labour as they would be likely to obtain either in England or in our *colonies*, upon gaining their freedom, it is most desirable that they should be employed *out of doors* and in the cultivation of the soil.*

* The Colonization Circular issued a short time since says—
"How we shall provide for our surplus population?" is a question by no means easy to answer. For it is not merely a matter of ships and passage-money ; there is no colony ready to receive human beings of any sort or size, they are all very cautious in bidding for immigrants; each of them is as

Our indefatigable Home Secretary on introducing his "Prisons Bill" last Session, 1st, for promoting economy and efficiency in the management of Prisons; and 2nd, at the same time, for effecting the relief of *local burdens,*" said, " Both of these matters had been brought before his notice not only as a member of Parliament, but as a magistrate of some standing. They were specially brought before his notice in 1874, by a deputation which waited on him at the Home Office, by the Social Science Association. That deputation pointed out that although the Act of 1865, which had done so much to improve not only the discipline of our prisons, but their entire management, had worked well—and in its main features the ministry did not propose to interfere with it, subject to certain exceptions—still there was a

anxious to get a good article as we are to part with a bad one; they will not take off our hands the waste material, the frayed edges of humanity, the sweeping of the shop that so disorder and encumber us. What they want, and all that they will have is capital and its adjuncts, thews and sinews. Poor gentlemen, poor ladies, clerks, shopmen, persons of no particular trade or calling, and unaccustomed to manual labour, they one and all shut their doors against; they want none of these impedimenta, these camp-followers, that hamper the effective strength of a country."

Surely then it is time that we so legislate as to endeavour to divert capital to the rendering of our land more productive in many parts, and also doing our utmost to increase the area for production, not only of the fruits of the earth, but of a breed of men, that will add strength to the mother country, and make any surplus of such acceptable to the Colonies.

great want of *uniformity of discipline in the prisons* throughout the country, a great want of efficiency in many of those prisons, and a great amount of unnecessary expense, owing to the *excessive number* of our prisons. Further, *that there was* a great *mistake* made in *having regard too much to penal labour* as opposed to industrial labour; and perhaps the *result of that* may be traced, and may be *seen very visibly*, not only *financially*, but also *morally* as far as our prisons are concerned."

Now in the employment of convicts on waste lands, not only in England, but in Ireland and other parts of Great Britain (and there are vast natural resources of the country which cannot be turned to account except by State interference and aid) the health, physical and moral, of the convicts would be improved and their reformation promoted at a far less cost to the country.

The following may be taken as a summary of the reasons for recommending the cultivation of land for the employment of prisoners in preference to any other occupation.

1. Cultivating land is the most healthful of all occupations for prisoners.

2. It is the occupation most easily learnt, and practised by able-bodied men, either unskilled, or skilled labourers.

3. It is an employment easily capable in all its branches of being made the subject of task-work,

so as to enable the superintendents of labour to test and record the amount of each man's daily performance.

4. It is best adapted to the circumstances of a mixed body of unskilled labourers of all ages, because its varieties, from the hard labour of deep digging to the light employment of weeding, furnish means of appropriating suitable occupation to each individual according to his age, strength, capabilities, and previous habits and pursuits.

5. It is a pursuit which will enable the discipline officers to maintain order, enforce silence, and prevent intercommunication amongst the prisoners better than any other, because they may pursue their various employments at such distances from each other as with a moderate amount of supervision, will enable the officers to detect breaches of the prison laws.

6. It is *an unfailing pursuit*, and does not, *like employment on public works,* end *with their completion.* It is independent of all external influences, it requires no extra expenses of chargeable labour or materials, both of which *are important elements of cost in all public works* to which auxiliary prison labour can be applied.

7. The system of cultivating land for the *maintenance of the entire prison population, officers and prisoners* (thus combining *production* and *consumption in the same establishment*) is one of *unchange-*

able economy, and *cannot be affected* by a *variation of prices or other external* circumstances.* The money payments by the contractor for rent (if any were required) and labour may be made to adjust themselves to his contract and allowances for the prisoners' diet. His averages of production and consumption being nearly equal, he will (except as to his surplus) be unaffected by market prices, and any loss by friction in bringing and selling will be always saved.

8. Unlike most other productive prison occupations extensively carried out, the cultivation of land by the manual labour of prisoners will not *inflict injustice upon other* classes of the community, even *if adopted to the extreme limit* public *exigencies may require*. The owners and occupiers *of land who are the principal contributors to the County-rate*, though *theoretically affected by the system*, would be practically benefited by the consequent reduction in the rates; besides which the quantity

---

* "Convict Prison Farming.—Our Plymouth correspondent states that the annual sale of stock from the Dartmoor prisons farm having just taken place, it has now been ascertained that, deducting the cost of convict labour, the establishment has gained nearly £1000 as the result of last year's agricultural operations. For some years the convict farm was unremunerative, but now 1000 acres on Dartmoor have been reclaimed, and profits are made. Black-polled heifers from Scotland have been introduced, and more extensive operations are contemplated. The convicts employed are men whose sentences are nearly expired, and who, therefore, have less inducement to escape."—*Pall Mall Gazette*, 6 Sept. 1877.

of agricultural produce raised by prison labour, however important an item in prison charges, would be too small to exercise an appreciable influence over prices, spread as is the supply of prisons, over the entire kingdom, whilst the consumption by prisoners does not amount to one day's average importation of foreign food.

9. The *cultivation of land is an occupation for prisoners*, most *available for* their *future welfare as free-labourers* whether at home *or in the colonies;* and for its effective pursuit no cumbrous or expensive tools or machinery are required; its *natural and invigorating exercise builds up constitutions* in *health and strength*, and it creates and confirms habits and aptitudes for a description of labour which is the *foundation of wealth*, and *is in constant demand in every* quarter of the globe.

To these reasons for employing our criminals in cultivating the soil may be added another not less important—as concerning their *reformation*. Mr. Henry Mayhew in his most valuable publication published some years ago," says—

" We are well aware how difficult it is to give any *pecuniary value* to mere *physical exertion*, *especially* in towns, where field or garden-work, on account of the great value and scarcity of land cannot be adopted on any large scale; nevertheless, if it come to a choice, we boldly declare we prefer idleness itself to making *industry idle* (because *useless*), and *therefore hateful* in every prisoner's eyes. Besides, what necessity is there for *Correctional Prisons being situate in Towns*, where they are as much out of place as Churchyards, and where prisoners must be put to grind the wind, simply because they cannot *be put to till the land?*

" The late Governor of Millbank Prison (and he is a gentleman whose Prison experience extends over nearly a quarter of a century) speaking of Prison labour, told us that it is a great thing to make a prisoner *feel* that he is employed on some *useful work*. Nothing *so disgusts a man*, or makes him so querulous as to let him know that he is labouring, *and yet doing nothing*—as when at the *Tread-wheel*.

" I am of opinion," he said, " that to employ men on work which they *know* and *see is useful*, has the best *possible effect upon their characters*, and *much increases their chance of reformation.**

* " The eighth report of the directors of convict prisons comes opportunely to reassure the public mind and abate the alarm caused by the revival of agrarian crime in Tipperary. The number of convicts in Irish prisons in 1853 was more than 3000. In January, 1861, it was reduced to 1492, and at the beginning of this year it was only 1314. The report states that at the present time Parliament is asked to vote £60,000. per annum less than was required six years ago, though the cost per head is now more than it was then, because there is the same staff of officers over a smaller number. Even now the cost is only £24. 10s per head, while in England it is £35. In the five years preceding 1853 convicts were transported beyond the seas from Ireland at the rate of 1000 a-year. Since that time no person has been transported. In the meantime 6121 convicts have been

Every other kind of work *irritates and hardens them.* After twenty thousand prisoners have passed through one's hands, one must have had some little experience," p. 44, (1856).

Several experienced Governors of Prisons have said that—" The criminal under penal servitude should be made to work *so as to pay up or atone* for the *injury he has done* to the community, and have expressed their belief that if that principle *were carried out,* and if the prisoners were *permitted gradually to partake of an increased portion of their fruits of this industry,** it would *be efficacious*

liberated in this country, and since the establishment of intermediate prisons, six years ago, only 10 per cent. of the liberated have returned to prison, the great majority having been steadily pursuing courses of honest industry. This gratifying fact is ascribed to three causes—the convicts are trained in small numbers, their labour and training are conducted on plans more natural and better calculated to establish good habits, while the appliances for the detection and police supervision of persons who have been once convicted render the pursuit of crime so hazardous that few venture to resume it if they can manage to live otherwise, and the public confidence is so far secured by the reformatory system that employers assist in having the reclaimed convicts absorbed in the labouring population."—*Times' Irish Correspondent,* May 12, 1862.

In the *Cornhill Magazine* for April 1861 there is a most excellent article showing the advantages resulting from " The Irish Convict System."

* This does take place in the treatment of convicts in Ireland.

And the report of a Convict Establishment for 100 men in Ireland, published in the *Irish Quarterly* (1st) in 1858, gives a credit balance of nearly £500 per annum. In America many of the prisons are nearly self-supporting, and in some the

to *their reformation*, and they *might safely be permitted to return to the busy haunts of honest men.*"

And if this could be brought about, surely "*finis coronat opus*" may it not be said! more especially is such a result to be *desired*, when we remember that in many instances the pressure of outward circumstances rather than any inward evil propensity leads to a violation of the law.

It does really seem then that no industrial occupation more beneficial for the convict or advantageous to the country can be found for convicts than on the Waste Lands in the United Kingdom. An immense tract of the central and western area of Ireland, comprising at least a million and a half acres exists at present in the condition of waste.

"As regards the Land," (says Mr. R. H. Patterson in his able and valuable work, *The State, the Poor and the Country*, Blackwood and Sons, Edinburgh, 1870,) "The action of the labour is let out at so much a day. Cannot we make more of our ordinary prisoners?

The present writer would strongly recommend all who would wish to satisfy themselves as to the beneficial results of the employment of convicts, upon themselves as well as financially, to procure a copy of a small work, but of great utility, published by " Simpkin, Marshall and Co., 1862," "*Observations on the Treatment of Convicts in Ireland, with some Remarks on the same in England, by Four Visiting Justices of the West Riding Prison at Wakefield.*"

They pronounce greatly in favour of the Irish system, from results as shown.

State must be of a *more direct kind.* There are *vast natural resources of the country* which cannot be *turned to account save by the direct action of the State.* The works requisite for this purpose are too great to be undertaken by *private* enterprise. They are either so costly, or else the return upon the expenditure would *be so remote,* as to render *their execution impossible* save *by the State*—by the Nation as a whole acting through the Executive."

As in such works as reclamation of land from the sea, or the throwing up barriers to prevent its encroachment—and in many other works in relation to agriculture. Some of the gaols that will be disused by the operation of the New Prisons' Act, and even some of the Union Workhouses, (so *little occupied* except by the staff, since *out*-door relief has become so general) might be made available, in *some* districts, for housing the convicts, when waste lands are found in their neighbourhoods, and thus the expense of moveable iron-huts would be saved.

Not the least important benefit arising from the employment of convicts in cultivating the soil, is the preparing them both in character and health for employment, either in the Mother-Country or the Colonies, on their gaining their liberty.

How we can make the most of our Colonies becomes yearly a more serious consideration of vital importance to the well-being, if not safety of the entire country. A very clever and interesting pamphlet— *England, her Colonies and her Enemies,* by E. G. Hatherly—(Ridgway, Piccadilly, 1848), demonstrated at some length, and *clearly,* that " the distress which prevailed at the time it was written, and *which, more or less,* prevails at *all times* amongst the working classes *of this country,* and *that of almost every other social* evil with which Great Britain is afflicted, proceeded and proceed from *a deficiency,* and a *very large deficiency* in our national supplies of *bread, corn, meat,* and other *articles of food,"* * and he proceeded to

---

* We are most of us well aware that it was an inadequate Land Revenue, resulting from lack of a due cultivation of the soil (not making the most of it), that brought on the financial difficulties of Turkey and perhaps induced the terrible War, still unhappily going on, under an impression of her incapability of long defending herself with vigour. And perhaps many will remember an article that appeared in the *Westminster Review* of October 1870—"The Land Question in England." The writer of it was evidently seriously impressed with the importance of his subject, and well up in his facts. He shows the different forms of tenure of land in different countries, and in writing of that of Turkey he concludes :—

" The last form of land tenure, and that which exists to the smallest extent, is freehold, and is entirely confined to house property in towns and lands in the immediate vicinity."

"In India," he says, "from time immemorial the ownership of the soil has been vested in the State. The Sovereign was the landlord, and the cultivators the tenants. The land was held on the communal system, as in Russia, each community containing within itself all the elements of self-Government. The village community was governed by the

recommend corn colonies as the most *politic* and effectual remedy for our various national maladies.

head man, who collected the rents from the cultivators and paid them to the representative of the Sovereign. And this is the general system of land tenure throughout India at the present day, the Anglo-Indian Government being *de facto* landlord of the whole territory under its sway; but it was long before the English rulers understood the exact nature of the land tenure in that country. The Zemindars who collected the rents in a particular district, were regarded by them as the real owners, corresponding to our landlords. It was not understood that when the Zemindars collected the rents, they did not keep them, but handed them over to their Sovereign, after deducting a per-centage for collection, which enabled them to live in splendour."—*Mill's History of British India*, Vol. i., p. 217.

"The importance of the land revenue to the Government of India may be imagined from the fact that it forms the principal portion of the national income. Even now, notwithstanding the waste and mismanagement inevitable where the rents are assessed and collected by strangers, ignorant of the capabilities of the country and of the customs of its inhabitants, the revenue from land alone, previous to the Mutiny, met all the expenditure of the Empire except military charges, which in a conquered country are necessarily heavy. The expenditure included public works, navy, mint, interest or debt, and pensions; and if we deduct waste and alienated land, the revenue to meet this large expenditure was derived from about one-sixth of the whole territory."

(As the late horrible famine will, it has been said by the correspondent of the *Times*, cost India at least ten millions, let us hope that by prudential measures being taken to prevent, as far as possible, drought, and by bringing into cultivation a far greater portion of the soil, such famines will henceforth be averted).

"So far then," continues the writer of the article in the *Westminster Review*, "we have arrived at the following con-

He proposed that such corn colonies should consist of large quantities of the fine and fertile, but, at present, *waste and useless* lands of our *North American, Australian, and African* possessions, that the Government should cause such lands to be brought into cultivation, that they should be divided into farms of 300 or 400 acres each ; that

clusions : that pauperism has grown with the growth of large estates ; that at the same time our Agricultural labourers have been reduced to a condition incompatible with the maintenance of physical strength, and in many cases to the verge of starvation ; that the poorer classes, driven into the large towns, living in hovels, dens and garrets, in darkness, ignorance and want, constitute a breeding-ground for crime and disease ; that the rent derived from the soil has been diverted from its original purpose, and appropriated by individuals to their own personal gain and advantage, to the great detriment of the public, upon whose shoulders now rests the burden of raising the Revenue ; that the land so appropriated has been negligently cultivated, and the produce therefrom far below the standard of other countries. In a word, the system has benefited neither tenants, nor landowners, producers, or consumers. Whether viewed socially or economically, it has proved disastrous to the country at large.

"These conclusions are still further confirmed," the writer of the article adds, "by the fact that wherever the same system has been tried, it has produced results equally evil,"—and he shows them.

However unpleasant these "facts" may be to any parties in the country, it will be well not to attempt to deny their existence, but to look them steadily in the face and at once do our best to bring about a better state of things though but by slow degrees, for we may rest assured that all such "facts" are impressed upon the great mass of the people who suffer from them. (See Appendix).

suitable farm buildings should be erected on each farm; that a skilful farmer should be placed there; and that *all the corn and other produce* of the *said colonies should be imported into Great Britain and Ireland,* except what might be required for the support of those who should be engaged in the cultivation of the corn colonies. The writer of these pages cannot here enter upon the full merits of this proposition, but whatever be the direct agency employed for the execution of this project, the idea in itself of the founding of *corn colonies* does seem to be a happy one—an idea which meets the exigencies of our age and country *better than any other the writer has heard of.* Such a *substantial increase in our National* or Imperial *wealth* must manifestly bring with it a great gain to *all classes;* employment would then receive the strongest impetus, increased wealth would be followed by an increased demand for labour of every kind; the value of labour would rise therefore in the Home-Market, and so the great problem as to food for the people would be partially solved, on the solution of which depends the happiness and the moral and religious well-being of the working classes, as well as the welfare and safety of the State. But even if this proposition were carried out, it would not supersede the necessity of a *more extended* and better cultivation of *our soil in* the *United Kingdom.*

In turning to *The Memoirs of the Duke of*

Sully, Prime Minister to Henry the Great of France, (*i.e.,* Henry IV.) we find that that great Protestant minister considered tillage and pasturage as the "Foster-Mothers,"—*les deux mamelles* —of the State, and his legislative measures were, fortunately for his country, in accordance with his conviction. At a very critical period in the history of France, when that country had been distracted by the wars of the League, when its finances were in great disorder, and the State on the verge of bankruptcy — Sully, by the encouragement of Agriculture, *re-animated industry* and by *increasing the growth of National wealth*, he in *fifteen years abolished five* millions of direct taxes upon the cultivators of the soil, reduced by one-half the duties levied on the internal trade of the country—and yet the annual income had increased four millions. In the meantime one hundred millions of the State debts had been paid off; thirty-five millions of Royal Domains, alienated by the king's predecessors, had been repurchased, and upwards of forty-one millions of livres were accumulated in the Treasury. Well then does he deserve what a quondam professor of Political Economy at Oxford said of him in one of his lectures. " Sully must not be regarded as a *mere* financier—he did not content himself with *temporary expedients,* or with measures devised solely with a view to the *immediate* replenishment of the State Coffers, but he fully appreciated the truth—which arbitrary power so generally and so strangely overlooks—that, the *best way to enrich the Sovereign* was to *enrich the subjects* of the Sovereign." He advocated *indirect taxation** (as M'Culloch does) saying, "That if he made money to pass through the hands of the people, there would necessarily flow into the public treasury a proportionate quantity *which no one would regret:* if the people have but little money, it can give up but little, and that little must be wrested from it."

If we turn to Frederick II., of Prussia (commonly known as Frederick the Great), we shall find that it was more from his attention to

---

* So long ago as 22nd May, 1856, a leader in the *Times* said:—

"The working classes must be aware by this time that they are not the pure gainers by the substitution of direct for indirect taxes, that they were supposed to be. The Income-tax is paid out of the fund which has to meet the demands of industry, hospitality, benevolence, and other equally pressing applicants. Most of us live up to our incomes, and when the collector has carried off a cheque for £50 or £100 to be spent in gun-boats, ammunition, militia, or subsidies, the signer of that cheque is obliged to contract his expenditure in another direction. He dismisses a servant, or reduces his orders to his tradesman, and denies himself some ordinary expenditure which contributed to the maintenance of a numerous household. Domestic service is one great resource for the children of the working classes; yet, in spite of the general prosperity (?) there is a universal complaint of the difficulty of finding places.

"The working classes therefore are paying much more of the Income-tax than they are aware of." See Appendix.

internal improvement than to foreign conquests, that he earned the title of "the Great." By promoting permanent and *substantial* improvements *in Agriculture* (at the same time not neglecting, but thus cherishing and *advancing other interests*), he raised his dominions, notwithstanding the disadvantages of situation, soil and climate, to such a height of prosperity and power, that he was able to contend single-handed during seven years against the united force of Russia, Saxony, Sweden, France, Austria, and many of the other German States, and in 1763 was left in peaceful possession of all his paternal and acquired dominions. Let us then see and mark well by what measures he made his kingdom, in spite of the disadvantages before named, so powerful and *independent*. His practice was to lay out about £300,000 per annum in the encouragement of Agricultural improvements which he considered as *manure spread upon the ground to secure an abundant harvest;* and instead of being at all impoverished by such liberal grants, he thereby increased his Revenue so much, that he was enabled to leave behind him £12,000,000 sterling —(See *Miscellaneous Essays,* by the Right Hon. Sir John Sinclair).

In the Report made by the Commissioners appointed in 1838 to consider a general system for Railways in Ireland "with a view to promote Agriculture generally, and to aid in bringing into cultivation the *waste lands*, it was said, 'it gave assurance of enormous profits on the greatest possible outlay.' Notwithstanding this assurance such public aid as was required was not given, and consequently ' a large portion of the Empire which might *have been made a source* of common strength and advantage,' was allowed ' to lie fallow.' "

We have a striking example of noble and generous patriotism in the Bishop of Llandaff, Dr. Watson. In his *Essay on Waste Lands* (1782) he explains very forcibly and ably the advantages to be derived from *National encouragement* being given to *Agriculture*. He says—" The agricultural improvements which have hitherto taken place amongst us have been by the expenditure of private wealth; but the country cannot be brought to that perfection of cultivation of which it is capable, unless *individual efforts are aided* and *accelerated* by public wisdom and munificence. I boast not of any particular patriotism, but I would willingly pay my share of twenty or thirty millions of public money to be appropriated by the legislature, to the Agricultural improvement of *Great Britain and Ireland. This appears to me an object of far nearer concern to our independence than any extension of commerce, or any acquisition of distant territory ever can be.* If the time had fully come when *an unproductive acre of land* could *not be* found in *either of these fortunate islands*, we shall then *have food within ourselves* for the annual sustenance of at least 30 millions of people; and with a population of 30 millions, what power in Europe or what combination of powers, would dare to attempt our subjugation?"*

The patriotic Bishop had not contemplated "degeneracy of race" taking place, nor enfeebled millions, making redundancy of people not a source of strength, but rather of weakness.

The Editor of *The principal Speeches and Addresses of the late Prince Consort* (Albert the Good), one who evidently was quite in the confidence of the Prince and knew him thoroughly, after having shown how the Prince devoted himself to Agriculture and how he stimulated the

---

* The Special Correspondent of the "*Times*," writing from Amsterdam on the 30th October, 1876, says: "By the time this letter reaches London the telegraph will, it is to be hoped, have announced the opening by the King of Holland of the great ship canal between Amsterdam and the North Sea— The North Sea Canal."

The gross cost of the Canal is more than £2,000,000. But the net cost in cash will be probably not much more than £1,000,000. . . . The total amount of land reclaimed and to be reclaimed is 12,450 acres. "But the undertaking," says the Correspondent, " was not projected for the sake of immediate gain; and in guaranteeing the interest of the shares for half a century in advance on certain conditions, the Government recognized that the benefit to accrue to the country and the city of Amsterdam was worth purchasing at the National expense." The whole of the Report is interesting and might lead to something profitable.

Why should not miles of land be preserved from the overflowing of the Shannon, in Ireland?

practice of it, says, " That with a large breadth of the land of Great Britain *only partially tilled*, or scarcely *cultivated at all*, the British Nation should not unfrequently have to expend 20 or 30 millions of money in foreign corn, is a *reproach against our practical sagacity*, in which the Prince at least can have no share of blame."

No man can consider the great questions relating to the *social* interests of the country without clearly perceiving that the interests of Agriculture are the interests of *the whole community*. And *great care* should be taken, in fostering any *particular interests*, whether it be that of cotton manufacturing, or any other, not to *hurt the parent stem*, the primary interest—Agriculture. *Nature provides that the stem of the tree shall go on swelling*, as the branch goes on growing, and unless you carefully *follow Nature* and keep strengthening the *parent stem* (or the Mother-Country) as the separate branches (or the Colonies) strengthen, depend upon it, that *both together* will come to grief. Happily for the country the present Prime Minister duly estimates the value and importance of our Colonies. At the great Conservative meeting held in the Crystal Palace on the 24th June, 1872, Mr. Disraeli (now Lord Beaconsfield) said—" If you look to the history of this country since the advent of Liberalism forty years ago, you will find there has been no effort so continuous, so *subtle*, supported with so much energy, and carried on with so much ability and acumen, as the attempts of Liberalism to effect *this* DISINTEGRATION *of the* EMPIRE"—and after making some remarks in relation to self-government, he continued—" Not that I for one object to self-government. I cannot conceive how our *distant Colonies* can have their affairs administered except by self-government. But *self-government, when it was conceded, ought, in my opinion, to have been conceded as part of a great policy of Imperial consolidation.* It ought to have been accompanied by an *Imperial Tariff, by securities to the people of England* for the enjoyment of the *unappropriated lands* which *belonged* to the *sovereign* as the *trustee,* and by a *military* code, which *should have* precisely defined the *means and the responsibilities* by which the Colonies should have *been* DEFENDED, and by which if necessary, *this country* should call *for aid from the Colonies themselves.* It ought further to have been accompanied by the institution of some representative council in the Metropolis, which would have brought the Colonies into constant and continuous relations with the Home Government. . . . . Well, what has been the result of this attempt during the reign of Liberalism for the disintegration of the Empire? It has entirely failed. But how has it failed? By the sympathies of the Colonies with the Mother-Country. THEY have *decided* that the *Empire* shall not be destroyed, and in *my opinion no minister* in this *country will do his duty*, who neglects *an opportunity of reconstructing* as much *as possible our Colonial Empire*, and of *responding to those distant sympathies* which may *become the source of incalculable strength, and happiness to this land.*"

Happily, the present Colonial Secretary, Lord Carnarvon* has proved himself most anxious and able to promote the interest of the Colonies on every occasion that presents itself, entertaining the same *truly statesmanlike* views as his chief; for in the House of Lords, when speaking in relation to the Colonies in 1870, he said—" If there is any lesson which we should draw from the loss of the United States, it is the misfortune of parting from those

* Since the above was written and in print circumstances unhappily occurred which led to Lord Carnarvon's resignation, and on the 6th of March, "A deputation of Merchants and others connected with South Africa," and "the Agent-General of the Australian Colonies, and the Agent-General of New Zealand, also waited on his Lordship at his residence to present to him addresses on his retirement."

In the course of his replying to the first he said in a spirit of generous and true patriotism, "I shall anxiously watch the progress of events, to observe, I trust, before long,*the disappearance of those clouds which now darken your political horizon; *and I need scarcely repeat that whatever little knowledge or influence on Colonial questions I may have acquired during my administration, I hold myself bound by every sense of duty, as well as of personal inclination, to place at the service of my successor in office.*"

We may therefore feel that Lord Carnarvon's successor, Sir Michael Hicks-Beach, will be not less ardent than the Premier and Lord Carnarvon appear to be, for the consolidation of the Colonies with the Mother-Country.

11

Colonies in ill-will and irritation" (and so wrote the retired Colonial Judge Mr. Haliburton). We parted with those great Colonies because we attempted to coerce them; and if we now part with our present Colonies it will be because we expel them from our dominion. The circumstances are different, but the result must be *the bitter alienation and undying enmity of these great countries.* For my own part I see with dismay the course which is now being taken, a part at once cheeseparing in point of economy, *and spendthrift in point of National character. I* will be no party to it, and I beg to enter my humble and earnest protest against a course which I conceive to be ruinous to the honour and *fatal to the best interests of the Empire.*"*

It cannot be doubted that these are sentiments in accordance with those of all capable of due reflection on the present position of this country.

---

* It is due to Sir Julius Vogel, the author of that most important and valuable article, "Greater or Lesser Britain" in the number of the *Nineteenth Century* for *July* last, to state that, although the passage from the speech of the Premier and that from Lord Carnarvon's address in the House of Lords, just given, are also quoted in that article, they had been marked by the present writer long before July last and placed amongst his notes, and he felt highly gratified to find that the same passages had made an impression on the mind of so distinguished a Colonist and able a writer, as Sir Julius Vogel. It would be well if his "Greater or Lesser Britain" were published in a separate and cheap form, for it cannot be too generally read.

It is a somewhat common observation that "*large families often do better than small ones*"—but when is that the case? When all the members of such families have been brought up in harmony and affection, and quit the family circle cherishing *such feelings.* Then as the elder ones go out into the world and succeed, or any one of them, they, or he, as the case may be, help those who may require assistance and rejoice to be able to afford aid to the *parents*, should they, on any occasion require it. For the same reason, the Parent country and her Colonies should cherish feelings of regard towards *each other* beyond what either *can* feel towards foreign countries—but to cherish this regard a mutual INTEREST must exist and be maintained between the Mother-Country and her Colonies—her adult offspring.

Fortunate indeed is it for the country that H. R. Highness the Prince of Wales was inoculated by his late father, the Prince Consort, with the *same ideas as to the importance of a thriving agriculture to the well-being of the State*, as he himself entertained. The Prince of Wales, therefore, as "President of the Royal Agricultural Society," is truly "the right man in the right place." When presiding at the banquet of the Society in Dublin in August, 1871, he expressed in the course of his speech the following sentiment—"I say what will *do more than anything else* towards making a *country prosperous* is the EXTENSION" (mark that term, reader) " of its agriculture." And when presiding at the dinner of the Norfolk Agricultural Society, in June, 1872, H. R. Highness, in proposing the toast of the evening referred at some length to the celebrity of Norfolk Agriculture and Agriculturists,* and went on to say that his father—the Prince Consort—always felt the greatest interest in Agri-

* RECLAMATION OF LAND.—The Earl of Leicester was for two years engaged in a work of some interest and importance—viz., the reclamation from the sea, of 700 acres of the vast tract of low marshy lands near the little port of Wells, Norfolk. For this purpose a great embankment involving an outlay of about £12,000., was carried from the Hookham side of Wells, in a straight line towards the sea, which has been, it is hoped, effectually shut out by this means from the land sought to be reclaimed.

There are similar works required in many parts of the country, by which hundreds of thousands of acres of land that might be made productive, would be secured. Happily Lord Leicester had the capital to enable him to do such work. The Duke of Sutherland too, having capital, is doing a great National work really, though at his own expense. Let us consider what would be the result if such works could be carried into execution wherever required.

There is much wisdom evinced in a letter of the late Emperor Napoleon III., addressed to his Minister of State in 1860—

Sec. 5. "In that which relates to agriculture you must make it share in the benefits of the Institutions of credit, clear the forests, situated in the plains, and replant the hills, devote annually a considerable sum to great works of drainage, irrigation, and clearage. These works transforming the uncultivated districts into cultivated lands, will enrich the districts without impoverishing the State, which will cover its advance by the sale of a portion of these lands restored to agriculture."

culture and used to take his children to inspect his prize animals. For his own part he would support such an EXTENSION of the Society as would enable it to embrace operations with regard to *Cottage accommodation*. He had endeavoured to improve the Cottages on his own estate and he felt *pride and satisfaction* in having his workmen properly housed. In conclusion H. R. Highness strongly supported the idea of having a great County School for Norfolk, and said it would give him the greatest pleasure to support the enterprise." On another occasion, when presiding at an Agricultural gathering, he said, " he felt quite convinced that *Agriculture was the very back-bone of the Army."*

With a Premier and Colonial Secretary holding such strong opinions in regard to the vital importance of the Colonies to the Mother-Country, *let us hope* that early in the next session of Parliament " *a great policy of Imperial consolidation" will be brought forward*. And, in the meantime, let all who feel any interest in their country *and the colonies*, read, mark, learn, and inwardly digest Sir Julius Vogel's reasons for bringing about the *confederation* of the Colonies, for he has shown—

1. The unsatisfactory nature of the relations between the Mother-Country and her Colonies.

2. The urgent necessity for doing something to

Sec. 12. This extraordinary resource will facilitate to us not only the prompt completion of the railways, canals, means of navigation, roads, and ports, but it will also allow us to restore in less time our cathedrals and churches, and worthily to encourage science, literature, and the arts.

arrest the disintegration towards which progress is being made.

3. That a union depending upon the pleasure, for the time being, of the different parts of the Empire, means separation sooner or later.

4. That, under the union-during-pleasure condition, much is being *done to hasten separation.*

5. That, the Mother-Country is *entitled* to retain and consolidate her possessions.

6. That confederation is desirable, and would be fraught with advantage both to the Parent-Country and the Colonies in the shape of *increased trade,* increased value of property, the augmented happiness of the people, and the saving of much misery and disaster.

7. That its accomplishment does not present great difficulties.

Lord Blachford in an article in the October number of the *Nineteenth Century* treats Sir Julius Vogel's suggestion, of preserving the integrity of the British Empire, *as impossible,* and if carried out, as likely to merge the Mother-Country in a general confederacy, where she would be outvoted and ruled by her Colonies. But surely such arguments ought not to deter our Government from endeavouring to carry out what not only Sir Julius Vogel, but the Premier and his Colonial Secretary think so desirable for the welfare, not only of the Mother-Country, but also for the Colonies themselves.

The following extract from a Pamphlet, entitled, *The Perils of England*, 1852, (a copy of which could not be procured a week after it was published) may not be inappropriately given here.

" A few men of the people, of whom the honest and consistent Oastler may be taken as a type, did perceive the real causes of the sufferings of the masses, and various proposals more or less judicious were put forward for their relief. Of the nature of those, the Ten Hours' Bill may be taken as an exponent. The tendency of these measures proved incontestably, that the one thing needful, was to give the people the means of making an equitable bargain with their task-masters, but of the *great opportunity here offered them of coming forward as the champion of the lower classes*, the aristocratic party, less wise than their ancestors at Runnymede, never availed themselves.

In fact, they never perceived that the dangerous *enemies of their order* were *the monied men* of the *manufacturing Towns*, and not the *labouring population.*"

" She (England) is in peril of forfeiting her proud position, and one of the first symptoms of her dangerous state is to be found in the preference which she exhibits to *words* as substitutes *for facts*—' videri' for the ' esse,' and the atmosphere of hypocrisy in which it pleases her to exist with reference to the greatest social questions of the day.

The writer of that pamphlet should not have omitted the name of one member of the aristocracy at least, then Lord Ashley, now Earl of Shaftesbury, who was a fellow-labourer with the late Mr. Oastler, and after many struggles succeeded in carrying the Ten Hours (Factories') Bill through Parliament.

Happily, too, at the present time, there is a nobleman, Lord Bateman, so convinced of the injustice inflicted *on Native Industry*, and of the exhaustive effect produced by the operation of the " unrestricted and *unreciprocated* Free Trade Policy of England that he had the " temerity"— (rather the high moral courage of an unselfish patriot) to send a letter to the *Times* suggesting the necessity of at least " Limited Protection," or for Reciprocity in Free Trade." He has proved himself indeed one of the true " Patres Patriæ." Since his admirable letter appeared in the *Times* of the 12th November, it has been published as a Pamphlet (at 6*d*) by Ridgway, Piccadilly ; and few can read the Preface and the letter without being convinced of the wisdom of Lord Bateman's suggestion and feeling obliged to him for endeavouring to arouse the nation to a sense of the dangers the Policy of 1846 has brought on us, and appealing to the " common sense and patriotism of his countrymen" to correct it.

In 1827, " The Substance of a Charge delivered to the Grand Jury of Wiltshire at the Summer

Assizes, 1827, by the Lord Chief Justice Best" (afterwards created Lord Wynford) was printed for T. Cadell, in the Strand."

It was printed " at the *special request* of the *Grand*-Jury, " in order that observations *so important* may be more generally *circulated*, and that the public may receive the gratification and *advantage* which an acquaintance with such valuable instruction cannot fail to impart."

The Chief Justice thus concluded his charge, "Mutual attachments between masters and servants, and that *respect* of the lower classes for the higher, WHICH IS ESSENTIAL to the peace and good order of Society *must be restored.*

" It may be said, that the times will not allow *of any increase* of wages. *Then the times must be changed.* How *that* is to be done; how the *inexhaustible sources of employment which this great* EMPIRE possesses *can best be opened;* how the productions of each description of labourers are to be made to contribute most to the *comfort and well-being of all labourers;* what is that *just* rule that will afford *equal protection* and *impose equal burthens on all sorts of capital*, and tend to promote *every interest of Great Britain and her* COLONIES, is for the Legislature to determine. This I *will* say, that as the labouring class is *more numerous* than all the others, and yet more HELPLESS, it should be the *first* object of the Nation's care. *Whatever other interests may suffer, the interests of the poor must be maintained. That* nation is most glorious and most flourishing in which the poor are *best fed, and clothed, most orderly, virtuous, and happy."*

If the monied interests of the nation were wise and patriotic enough to be willing to bear a tax that would realize (of course as it might be required) such an amount as the good Bishop of Llandaff said was necessary to bring Agriculture in England to perfection, we might hope to make this nation "most glorious and flourishing," and attain the character given by Virgil to ancient Italy:

"Terra potens armis *atque* ubere glebæ."— Æneid i., 335.*

Laus Deo finitum.

---

* Thus translated,

"For deeds of arms, and *fertile soil renowned.*"

APPENDIX.

STANLEY'S LIFE OF DR. ARNOLD.

Since the foregoing pages were in the hands of the publisher, in the *Times* of the 17th Jan. 1878, appeared the following, being the commencement of the report of what passed at the meeting.

"LIVERPOOL CHAMBER OF COMMERCE. — The annual meeting of the members of the Liverpool Chamber of Commerce was held on Tuesday; Mr. Samuel Smith, President of the Chamber, in the chair. The President adverted to the unsatisfactory state of the commerce of the country, and said he believed that last year was the worst we had yet passed through since the recent commercial depression commenced. He attributed this depression to the competition of foreign countries; protective tariffs abroad; increased cost of production; and wasteful consumption of strong drinks. *In order to prevent strikes* he suggested *that the* education department *should* consider *the desirability* of *providing* for the *teaching* of the rudiments of political economy to boys in elementary schools."

Can it *really* be that a gentleman occupying such a position, or any of those who were present, can think that a want of knowledge of "modern political economy" lies at the ROOT of the present conflict between labour and capital, which has been so fast increasing under the policy of 1846? and that we have only " to provide for the teaching of the rudiments of political economy to boys in elementary schools," to prevent strikes in future?

Perhaps the president of the Liverpool Chamber of Commerce, and many others, will think differently—and throw aside such delusions—upon reading what the late Samuel Taylor Coleridge said so long ago as in "1833," of "Modern Political Economy."

" What *solemn humbug* this modern political economy is! What is there *true* of the *little* that is true in their *dogmatic* books, *which is not a simple* deduction *from* the *moral and religious credenda* and *agenda of* any good man, and with which we were not all previously acquainted, and upon which any man of common sense *instinctively* acted? I know none. But what they *truly* state they do not *truly* understand in its *ultimate grounds* and *causes;* and hence they have sometimes done more mischief by their half-*ignorant*, half-*sophistical* reasonings about, and deductions from, well-founded positions, than they could have done by the promulgation of positive error. This particularly applies to their famous ratios of increase between man and the means of his subsistence.

Political economy *at the highest*, can never be a pure science. You may demonstrate that certain properties inhere in the *arch* which yet no bridge-builder CAN ever reduce into brick and mortar; but an abstract conclusion in a matter of political economy, the premises of which neither exist now, nor ever will exist within the range of the wildest imagination, is not a truth but a *chimera*—a PRACTICAL *falsehood.* For there are no theorems in political economy—but problems only. Certain things being actually so-and-so; the question is, *how* to *do* so-and-so with them. Political *philosophy,* indeed, points to ulterior ends, but even those ends are all *practical;* and if you desert the conditions of reality, or of *common probability,* you may show forth your eloquence or your fancy, but the utmost you can produce will be a Utopia or Oceana."—*Table-Talk,* p. 205.

You talk about making the article cheaper by reducing its price in the market from 8*d* to 6*d*. But suppose in so doing, you have rendered yourself *weaker against a foe;* suppose you have *demoralized thousands of your fellow-countrymen,* and have *sown* discontent *between one* class of society and another, your *article* is tolerably *dear,* I take it, after all. *Is not its real price* enhanced to every *Christian* and *patriot* a hundred-fold?"

If "discontent" had been *then* (1833) "*sown*" and the results such as Coleridge states, can we be surprised, however we may lament, that the crop of discontent has so increased under the Free-Imports policy of 1846, so encroaching upon *native industry*, and rendering *cheapness* in manufacturing (though, alas! at the risk of forfeiting our character for quality), our sole chance of not being superseded in foreign markets by nations who already rival us in manufacturing.

There is reason to fear that it was owing to the teaching of the Political Economists, or at all events the "*unchristian* tone" of some of the works issued antecedent to 1833, viz. in 1831-2, by the "Useful Knowledge Society," that perverted the judgment of many masters perhaps, as well as workmen. No one will accuse the late Dr. Arnold, for so many years the Head-Master of Rugby, with being a bigot in religion, and yet what did he say of the "*unchristian tone* of *Cottage Evenings*," one of that Society's publications? We had about that time and have since admitted the people to a much greater degree of power, and exacted of the people a much greater degree of *endurance* and *self-restraint*. There is nothing so likely to adjust the balance—which, from both these causes—and especially the *concurrence* of *them*—has been deranged—as to enforce on the people a more *lively* sense, in the language of the *world*, of the duties of *imperfect obligation;* in *other and better language*, of *making a conscience of their ways;* and there are no means of doing this half so effectual as by improving,

still improving, their *religious* education, and if the times of strife upon which we have fallen, should give occasion to a blessing so unspeakable, we shall only have another proof of the wisdom of God in overruling events to purposes which their contrivers did not contemplate. For the danger now lies in having substituted *secular* knowledge as the *refining principle* of the country, for the wisdom *which is from above;* or compendiums of *political economy* for the Word of God. But of this all may rest assured that *mere secular* education will not stand, in any rank of life, in the stead of *religious*—that the virtue will not go out of it to improve society, or minister *to the wants of man*, which many persons in these days seem to suppose; and *then*, that if *religious* you *must* have, it *must* be communicated after some *specific form.**
And now what said Dr. Arnold, writing in 1831?

In a letter to W. Tooke, Esq., who was for many years treasurer to the " Useful Knowledge Society," the following passage, deserving certainly of not less consideration at the present time

---

* Let us ever bear in mind that—" They that will be rich fall into temptation and a snare, and into many foolish and hurtful lusts, which drown men in destruction and perdition.

" For the love of money is the root of all evil; which while some coveted after, they have erred from the faith, and pierced themselves through with many sorrows."—1 Tim. vi. 9, 10.

May we all heed the admonition—" Let your moderation be known unto all men."

than when it was written, occurs. See *Stanley's Life of Arnold*, p. 299. The letter is dated " Rugby, June 18, 1831."

" In this day's number of the *Register* there is a letter on the *Cottage Evenings*, condemning very decidedly their UNCHRISTIAN *tone*. It is not written by me, but I confess that I heartily agree with it. You know of old how earnestly I have wished to join your " *Useful Knowledge Society;*" and how heartily on many points I sympathize with them. This very work the *Cottage Evenings*, might be made everything I wish, *if it* were *but decidedly Christian*. I delight in its plain and sensible tone and it might be made the channel of all sorts of information, useful and entertaining ; but *as it is*, so far from co-operating with it *I must feel utterly adverse to it*. To *enter into the deeper matters of conduct* and principle, to talk of our main hopes and fears, and yet *not* to speak of Christ, *is absolutely to my mind, to inculcate poison*. In such points as this, " he who is not with us is against us." It has occurred to me that the circumstance of some of the principal members of the " Useful Knowledge Society" being now in the Government is in itself a *strong reason* why the Society *should take a more decided tone on matters of religion*. Undoubtedly, their support of that Society, as it now stands, is a matter of *deep grief and disapprobation* to a large proportion of the *best men* in this kingdom, while it *encourages* the hopes of some of the *very worst*.

And it would be, I do verily believe, one of the greatest possible blessings, if, as they are honest, fearless, and enlightened against *political corruption*, and as I hope they will prove, against *ecclesiastical abuses also*, so they would be no less honest and fearless, and *truly* WISE, in labouring to *Christianize the people, in spite of the sneers and opposition of those who understand full well, that if men do not worship God they at once, by that very omission, worship most surely the power of evil.*"*

In an earlier letter (Oct. 1, p. 77) to his friend "the Rev. G. Cornish" dated from Laleham, Oct. 18, 1825, Dr. Arnold says:

" I met five Englishmen at the public table at our inn at Milan, who gave *me great matter for cogitation.* One was a clergyman and just returned from Egypt; the rest were young men, *i.e.* between twenty-five and thirty, and apparently of no profession. I may safely say, that since I was an undergraduate, I never heard any conversation so profligate as that which they *all* indulged in, the

---

* The editor of *Dr. Arnold's Life*—the present Dean of Westminster—(to whom the thanks of all old Rugbeans must be due for such an excellent and interesting piece of Biography of a Master who so raised the character of the School and became almost an idol of the boys) adds the following note—

"There is something to me almost awful" he (Arnold) used to say, speaking of *Lord Byron's Cain*, " in meeting suddenly in the words of such a man, so great and solemn a truth as is expressed in that speech of Lucifer—

'He who bows not to God hath bowed to me.' "

clergyman particularly ; indeed, it was not merely gross, but avowed principles of wickedness, such as I do not remember ever to have heard in Oxford. But *what struck me most was*, that with this sensuality there was united some INTELLECTUAL ACTIVITY*—they were not ignorant, but seemed bent on gaining a great variety of *solid information from their travels*. Now this *union* of *vice* and *intellectual power and knowledge seems* to me *rather a sign of the age*, and *if it goes on, it threatens to produce one of the most fearful forms of Anti-Christ which has yet appeared*. I am sure that the great prevalence of travelling fosters this spirit, not that

---

* The late Dr. James, Canon of Peterborough (not long deceased, and therefore, a contemporary of Dr. Arnold) in his admirable *Christian Watchfulness*, has the following remark—

" Surely if ever there was a period in the history of Christianity, when they to whom are afforded opportunities of cultivating their intellectual powers, must be conscious of glaring and open violation of a bounden duty in neglecting the Word of God, it is in these days—days marked by an extension of human learning, and a facility in acquiring it, altogether unparalleled. The experience of the past warns us that as scientific attainments become general there is too much ground to fear lest intellectual pride should elevate itself, and reason should delight to array itself against Revelation (there is a wisdom which "descendeth not from above"). Who sees not then that in proportion as human learning is extended so divine wisdom claims the closer regard ? The wisdom of the world when it stands alone " is foolishness with God" and brings ruin to its votaries by fostering an intellectual pride, which is an especial offence to the Majesty of the Most High. If man fancies his own reason as sufficient guide and trusts to human learning for counsel whereby to guide his ways, either

men learn mischief from the French or Italians, *but because they* are removed from the *check of public opinion,* and are, in fact, *self-constituted outlaws,* neither belonging to the society which they have left, nor taking a place in that of the countries where they are travelling."

In the work before referred to in the body of this volume, *Physical Science compared with the Second Beast, or the False Prophet,* Rivingtons, Waterloo Place, 1845, ch. xiii. 81, under the head of " The Number."

with integrity before men, or holiness before God, he raises in his heart a Babel-tower, whose end is confusion.

"The principle upon which these observations are founded is too clear to be a matter of doubt.

What was man's original offence? Was it not the proud wish to be wise above that which was revealed? " Ye shall be as gods," said the serpent to our first parents, " knowing good and evil." And what pride has worldly pride assumed in this land? Not the pride of wealth mainly, that would lead to a different result, would be productive of carefulness to preserve in quiet what industry had procured in an honest calling. Nor is it the pride of ancestry, that is wont, let us hope, to be the spring of noble feeling and honourable conduct. It is the pride of intellect—striving to supersede as a guide through this life to the next, the Word of God, and the Spirit of God."

"No. viii. of *Nineteenth Century,* September, 1877, contains an article by Mr. W. Malloch " Is Life worth living?" in answer to Mr. Harrison's Article in a former number. Mr. Malloch therein says " Nearly all our great modern unbelievers, the men on whose speculations and discoveries unbelief in our days has based itself, have been men of letters, of research or of science.

"Here is wisdom. Let him that hath understanding count the number of the Beast, and his number is six hundred, three-score and six."—Rev. xiii. 18.

The author says—"When we read, 'It is the number of a man,' I understand by that it is *human*. I will give you my reasons. This Beast is evidently the *embodiment of great power*. He combines the character of the four beasts of Daniel. He is as a lion, a bear, a leopard, and, like Daniel's fourth beast, has ten horns, and is exceeding terrible and strong. He is also of a *very* PERSECUTING *nature, compelling* men to *worship* him. He is the *personification* of *ambition*, obtaining *authority over the nations of the earth*. He puts himself in opposition to God and the servants of God. He seems to be the picture of some great king of men whose mightiness so lifts him up that he *looks upon himself*, and *is looked upon by others*, as at *the summit of human greatness*. To confirm this feeling, he recovers from a blow so deadly that ordinary men could undoubtedly be destroyed by it. The healing of this wound completes the delusion under which the nations of the earth labour, and from henceforth when the Beast issues his commands, they cry, as they did to Herod, 'It is the voice of a god and not of a man.'

"In Scripture language two numbers have been used to signify perfection, *seven* and *three*. Both these numbers are freely applied to God. The perfect Spirit of God is denoted by the seven spirits ; and the perfect Godhead is denoted by the number three, the Trinity. If then it were written, 'Let him that hath understanding count the number of God,' what number would seem so obvious as three sevens—777 ? Here it says, 'Count the number of the Beast, for it is the number of man,' for it seems to me that 'the number of a man' means the number of a man as opposed to the number of God. Now if we examine it in this light, it will seem that this Beast is the representative of the highest development of *human power*. He possesses *great physical authority*, and this is vastly assisted by his compact with the second beast, who is the *representative of human intellect, or science*. If then we have a union between the *greatest material human force*, and the highest development of human intellect, the result is *human perfectibility*. It seems already that science, puffed up by the discoveries in God's physical world, and by the theories of *moral* government, *is, with rapid strides, advancing to the rejection* of the God of science and of morality.*

* In opening the 58th Session of the Leeds Philosophical and Literary Society, at Leeds, on Tuesday evening (the 2nd Oct. 1877), the Archbishop of York delivered an address on "The Worth of Life." In the course of it he said—"That brilliant speaker, Professor Tyndall, lecturing at Birmingham the other day, adopted forcibly the theory of necessity, and in the name of conscience dismissed free will henceforward from all civilized society. . . Of course the neck of this bore is

AMBITION has never allowed divine laws to hinder *its designs, and when these two are combined we shall then have the greatest development of humanity, and the Beast will be revealed.* His number will be 666, for if Divine perfection be fitly represented by three *sevens*, may not HUMAN *perfection* (something just short of absolute perfection) be with equal fitness symbolized by three *sixes?* For these reasons, *I consider the Beast to signify human power in its two natures, physical and intellectual,* and so *conscious of its own greatness* that *it rushes* into *infidelity* and *blasphemy, ignoring* any *higher* power than *itself,* believing its number to be 777, while in reality it is only 666. I think that the *first* beast represents *open practical infidelity.* To a certain degree this has existed from the earliest times. It was exhibited in the first murder. *It is human energy depending on itself, working out its own will, ignoring a superintending Providence.* In the days of Nimrod it excited the admiration of the world: in the person of Nebuchadnezzar men were *drawn* to *worship* it; but it will *not be developed to the fullest extent* till it has the alliance of the second beast - *theoretical infidelity.* Hitherto knowledge, civilization, the arts of peace, have been against the savage persecution of the first beast. Now, science is putting the *revelation of*

safe in the Professor's hands; but logically the right might be asserted—*no responsibility,* no guilt; no guilt, no punishment; punishment without guilt is blind revenge or warfare."

discovery in the place of the revelation of God; and when it has become the 'prophet' of infidelity then we shall see the personification of the number 666."

The little volume contains but 123 pages, and is well worthy the attention of thoughtful readers.

The public journals of the 26th July last, under the heading, *Mr. Bright on Cobden*, at the Unveiling of his Statue, informed us, "The pedestal, of polished Aberdeen granite, bears the inscription, 'Free-trade, peace, and good will among Nations,' encircling the name of Cobden." It was upon reading this, that the thoughts of the present writer recurred to the preceding extract from the little work published by Rivingtons.

Now we read in the Book which in England was wont to stand as the highest authority for Christian morality that at the announcement of the birth of a Saviour, "suddenly there was with the angel a multitude of the heavenly host praising God and saying—

"Glory to God in the highest, and on earth peace, good will towards men."—St. Luke ii. 14.

And the writer of these pages has always been taught, and thoroughly believes that "peace on earth and good will towards men, or men of peace," "or among nations," are more likely to flow from giving "Glory to God in the highest,"

—first, as it stands proclaimed—* than from Free-trade or its maxims. Though doubtless not intended to convey the idea, the motto encircling Mr. Cobden's name, does seem to insinuate that Free-trade doctrines where adopted, would secure to nations and individuals the same results as the due worship of God. If so, the hearers of Mr. Bright's address respecting Mr. Cobden, might almost have exclaimed, "It is the voice of a god and not of a man."

A Short Extract from the Harmony of Interests.

In 1851 was published at Philadelphia, by J. S. Skinner, 79, Walnut Street, a very remarkable work entitled, *The Harmony of Interests, Agricultural, Manufacturing and Commercial*, by the well-known eminent statistical writer of America, Mr. Henry C. Carey. It is indeed a most valuable work, replete with practical information as to the statistics of the Great Western World, and it would be well if all who wish to investigate the

* All may rest assured that the " Gloria in Excelsis," must precede the " Pax in terrâ."

causes of the progress and decline of industrial communities would try to procure it, and read it *with unprejudiced minds.* " To be indifferent" wrote Locke, "which of two opinions is true, is the right temper of the mind that preserves it from being imposed on, and disposes it to *examine.* This is the only safe way to *Truth.*"

That the author of *The Harmony of Interests,* etc., entered upon the examination of the subject therein treated of in such " a right temper of the mind," is manifest from what he has said in the two first pages of his work.

As the Tariffs of foreign countries have been for some time under consideration, and great anxiety is felt as to how far other countries (after upwards of 30 years of the Free-Imports System of England), can be induced to reciprocate with her, it may be well to give the two first pages of Mr. Carey's *Harmony of Interests.* The *Times* has long in vain endeavoured to convince America and other countries of the impolicy of Protective Tariffs, and so lately as the 8th June, 1877, an article on the financial position of the colony of New South Wales thus concludes — "If the Americans are restricted in their range of customers, they have only their own *perversely* Protectionist system to blame for it."

Mr. Carey thus begins his work, *The Harmony of Interests, Agricultural, Manufacturing and Commercial—*

"Why is protection needed? Why cannot trade with foreign nations be carried on without the intervention of custom-house officers? Why is it that that intervention should be needed to enable the loom and the anvil to take their natural places by the side of the plough and the harrow? Such are the questions which *have long occupied* my mind, and to the consideration of which I now invite my readers.

Of the advantage of perfect freedom of trade, theoretically considered, there could be no doubt. The benefit derived from such freedom in the intercourse of the several States, was obvious to all; and it would certainly seem that the same system so extended as to include the Commerce with the various States and Kingdoms of the world could not fail to be attended with similar results. Nevertheless, every attempt at so doing had failed. The low duties on most articles of merchandise in the period between 1816 and 1827, had produced a state of things which induced the establishment of the first really protective Tariff, that of 1828. The approach to almost perfect freedom of trade in 1840, produced a political revolution, and a similar but more moderate measure, led to the resolution of last year (1850). These were curious facts, and such as were deserving of careful examination.

It may be assumed as an universal truth, that every step in the *right* direction will be attended with results so beneficial as to pave the way for further steps in the same direction, and that every one made in the *wrong* direction will be attended with disadvantageous results tending to produce a *necessity* for a retrograde movement. The Compromise Bill, in its final stages was a near approach to perfect freedom of trade, the highest duty being only 20 per cent. Believing it to be a step in the right direction, one of the enthusiastic advocates of perfect freedom of trade proposed, soon after its passage, that, commencing with 1842, there should be a further reduction of one per cent. per annum for twenty years, at the end of which time all necessity for Custom-Houses would have disappeared. With the gradual operation of the earlier stages of the Bill there was, however, produced a state of depression so extraordinary as to lead to a political change before reaching its final stages, and the duties had scarcely touched the point of 20 per cent. before they were raised to 30, 50, 60, or more, by the passage of the Tariff of 1842. With the election of 1844, the friends of Free-trade were restored to power, and two years afterwards was passed the Tariff of 1846—the Free-trade measure—in which the revenue duty on articles to be protected was fixed at *thirty* per cent. Here was a retrograde movement. Instead of passing from twenty downwards, we went up to thirty, and thus was furnished an admission that so near an approach to Free-trade with foreign nations as was to be found in twenty per cent. duties had not answered in practice. Since then it has been admitted even by the most Free-trade advocates, that on certain commodities even 30 per cent. was too low, and within six months of the date of the passage of the Act of 1846, its author proposed to increase a variety of articles to thirty-five and forty per cent. (*Treasury Report*, February 1, 1847). Here was another retrograde movement. It is now admitted that there are other articles the duties of which require to be raised, and daily experience goes to prove that such must be the case, or we must abandon some of the most important branches of industry. The tendency is, therefore, altogether backward. Thirty per cent. duty is now regarded as almost perfect freedom of trade, and instead of proposing a further annual reduction, *each year produces a stronger disposition* for a *considerable increase*. In all this, it is *impossible* to avoid *seeing* that there *is great error somewhere*, and almost equally impossible to avoid feeling a desire to understand why it is that the approaches towards freedom of trade with foreign nations have so frequently failed, and why it is that *every strictly* revenue tariff *is higher* than that which preceded it. With a view to satisfy myself in regard thereto, I have recently made the examination before referred to, of our Commercial Policy during the last twenty-eight years, commencing with 1821, being the earliest in relation to which detailed statements have been published. Before commencing to lay before you the results obtained, it may be well to say a *few words* as to the *merits claimed by the two parties* for their respective systems.

The *one* party insists that Protection is " a war upon labour and capital," and that by compelling the application of both to pursuits that would otherwise be unproductive, the amount of necessaries, comforts, and conveniences of life obtainable by the labourer is diminished. The *other* insists that by protecting the labourer from competition with the ill-fed and worse-clothed workmen of Europe the reward of labour will be increased. *Each has thus his theory*, and each is accustomed to furnish facts to prove its truth, and both can do so whilst limiting themselves to short periods of time, taking at some times years of small crops, and at others those of large ones, and thus it is that the inquirer after truth is embarrassed. No one has yet, to my knowledge, ever undertaken to examine all the facts during any long period of time, with a view to show what have been, under the various systems, the *powers of the labourer to command the necessaries and comforts of life*. One or other of the systems is true, and *that is true under which labour is most largely rewarded; that* under *which the labourer is enabled to consume* most largely of food, fuel, clothing, and all other of those good things for the attainment of which men are willing to labour. If, then, we can ascertain the power of consumption at various periods, and the result be to show that it has *invariably increased* under one course of action, and as invariably diminished under another, it will be equivalent to a *demonstration* of the *truth* of the *one* and the falsehood of the other. To accomplish this, has been the object of the inquiry in which I have recently been engaged.

At page 46, Mr. Carey says, " A great error exists in the impression now very commonly entertained in regard to national division of labour, and which owes its origin to the English school of POLITICAL ECONOMISTS, whose system is throughout based upon the idea of making England 'the workshop of the world,' than which nothing could be *less natural*. By that school it is taught that some nations are fitted for Manufactures and others for the labours of Agriculture, and that the latter are largely benefited by being compelled to employ themselves in the one pursuit, making all *their exchanges at a distance,* thus contributing their share to the maintenance of the system of of ' ships, colonies, and commerce.' The *whole* basis of their system is *conversion* and *exchange*, and not *production,* yet *neither* makes any *addition to the amount of things to be exchanged.* It is the great boast of their system that the EXCHANGERS are so *numerous and the producers* so few,* and the more rapid the increase in the proportion which the former bear to the latter, the more is *supposed to be* the advance towards perfect prosperity. CONVERTERS and *exchangers however* must live out of the *labours of others;* and if three, five or ten persons are to live on the product of one, it must follow that all will obtain but a small allowance of the NECESSARIES or *comforts* of life AS is *seen* to be the case."

PRESENT OPPOSITION ON THE PART OF THE WORKPEOPLE TO THE REDUCTION OF THE AMERICAN TARIFF.

From *The Times*, 23rd February, 1878.

The introduction into Congress of Mr. Fernando Wood's new Tariff Bill has caused quite a flutter among the Protectionists. The Committee of Ways and Means, of which Mr. Wood is chairman, is composed of members, the majority of whom

* Mr. Carey's note in 1851. " Out of 3,400,000 families in Great Britain in 1831, but 960,000 were engaged in agriculture, the work of production Between 1821 and 1831, the number of adult males increased 630,000, but the number of those employed in agriculture diminished 19,000. The Town population, that which lives by the work of conversion and exchange is steadily increasing in its ratio to the producing population, and as a necessary consequence there is a steady increase of poverty, vice and crime."

favour a reduced tariff. For several months, while Congress and the country have been paying attention chiefly to the silver agitation and to the Republican faction fighting over the public patronage, a Sub-Committee of the Ways and Means Committee have been framing, under Mr. Wood's guidance, a new Tariff Bill. A few days ago the Sub-Committee reported it to the full Committee, and it was made public. . . . . . . *The opposition to it in the Middle States, while very strong in the newspapers, also takes the form of indignation meetings and the pouring in upon Congress of almost innumerable anti-tariff reduction petitions.* A prominent feature of this opposition has been the *working men's Protectionist demonstration* at Pittsburg, Pennsylvania, on the 9th inst.

This Pittsburg demonstration was a procession and mass meeting. For several days preparations *were made for it, and all the factories and mills were closed so as to give the workmen opportunity to participate.* The day was damp and the clouds lowering, while a heavy rain the previous day falling upon the remains of the last snowstorm made the not over-clean streets a sea of mud. *But, nothing daunted, at least 15,000 workmen marched in procession, while half a million people gazed upon the pageant, the surrounding country for miles being almost stripped of inhabitants.* Excepting a few coaches containing the city officials, the procession was entirely composed of workmen, marching four and six abreast, and carrying banners displaying mottoes which illustrated the object of the demonstration. The popular belief that England is at the bottom of the proposed reduction of the tariff found expression in a variety of ways. Here are some of the mottoes:— "America first, England afterward;" "The importation of British iron means starvation to American freemen;" "Congress must not reduce Americans to the level of European serfs; we want high tariff and prosperity;" "High tariff guarantees prosperity throughout the country;" "*We want Protection to the last, and nail that to the mast;*" "No British gold for us." Two companion banners were borne, one inscribed "Free Trade with America," and having a picture of John Bull and the British Lion, well-fed and contented; the other inscribed "Free Trade in America," representing a hungry and tattered iron-worker tramping along a road and passing a milestone which said, "One mile to the Poor-house." A banner had on one side an iron mill in ruins, labelled, "Free Trade," while on the other side a mill in prosperous operation was marked "High tariff." Another bore the inscriptions, "This is no time to experiment with Free Trade," and "Put tea and coffee on the free list, but protect home industries." Another large display said, "Free Trade—*foreign countries prosper at our expense.*" The procession showed that the best feeling existed between the employers and workmen, though times have been very bad at Pittsburg, and such expressions as "*Protection to the manufacturer means prosperity to the working man*," were frequent.

The Exposition building in which the mass meeting was held is an enclosure covering several acres, and a vast crowd filled it, listening to Protectionist orations delivered from three platforms at the same time. The speakers were men of local fame only, and came mostly from the ranks of the procession; but the leading people of Pittsburg gave the use of their names as officers of the meeting, the sentiment of the city and its neighbourhood being almost unanimous on the subject. The addresses generally advised that the present tariff be let alone, *denouncing any change in the Protectionist duties*, particularly on iron and steel, the chief Pittsburg industries. *Free Trade was unanimously opposed, and one of the orators declared that "the manufacturing interests of England lie prostrate to-day, the result of Free Trade and open ports."* The meeting adopted resolutions expressive of its sentiments, and determined to send Congress a memorial on the subject. These resolutions represent the Protectionist views in reference to the proposed reduction of the tariff, and I therefore quote them:—

The agriculturists, merchants, manufacturers, and working men of Western Pennsylvania, Eastern Ohio, West Virginia, and Maryland, in mass convention assembled, representing all shades of opinion, having considered the proposed changes in the present tariff laws and their effect upon our industrial interests and the prosperity of the whole country, do hereby declare :—

"That whereas it is especially important at this time, when the country is just emerging from the greatest depression known to our history, that no obstacle be thrown in the way of returning prosperity; and whereas we believe, and experience has shown, that one of the principal causes of business depression in this country has been the frequent and radical changes in the laws bearing upon our material interests, the constant agitation whereof produces a state of uncertainty, which is destructive of business enterprise; and whereas an examination of the provisions of the proposed Tariff Bill shows that its effect will be injurious to many of the industries which we represent, and absolutely fatal to some, and whereas the blighting effect of the agitation of these changes is already apparent in reduced revenues, in the disorganization of business enterprises, and in the check of that returning confidence so necessary to prosperity, therefore,

"Resolved, That, reiterating our abiding faith in Protection and its beneficial effects on the whole country, we protest against any departure from its principles in the framing of our tariff laws.

"Resolved, That, we deem it unwise, inexpedient, and hostile to the best interests of the country to make radical change in a law which an experience of 16 years has shown to be highly advantageous to the welfare of the nation, and to have been the largest factor in the development of our resources.

"Resolved, That a due sense of patriotism and proper regard for the development of the resources of our country and a becoming attention on the part of the Government to the welfare of all its citizens require that the paramount object to be kept in view in all tariff legislation is the protection of the people and their concerns, rather than any concessions to foreign solicitations or interests.

"Resolved, That upon this question the interests of employer and *employé*, of labour and capital, are identical.

"Resolved, That the proposed revision of the tariff must result in the curtailment of the quantity and variety of our products, and imposing burdens thereon which cannot but bear heavily upon the class of men who, by their skill and labour, contribute to the production of these varied articles, and that it is neither wise nor humane to take such a step as shall result either in the enforced idleness of thousands of labouring men or in the necessity of such wages as shall afford only the most meagre subsistence to their families.

"Resolved, That the chairman of this Convention shall appoint a committee of 15, representing the various interests involved, who shall prepare a memorial setting forth the especial hardships that will be entailed by the proposed tariff changes, which shall be forwarded to our members of Congress, with the request that they use all fair and honourable means to prevent any radical change in the existing rates and duty."

AS TO THE POSSIBILITY OF COMBINATION OF FOREIGN NATIONS IN THEIR TARIFFS, AS OPPOSED TO ENGLAND'S FREE-TRADE POLICY.

In 1843, only one year after the 5 and 6 Victoria, c. 47, entitled "An Act to amend the Laws relating to the Customs," 9th July, 1842, the first of Sir Robert Peel's experimental policy, there appeared in the first volume of *The Foreign and Colonial Quarterly Review* (Whittaker and Co., Ave Maria Lane) an able article written in a very fair spirit, "Commercial Policy at Home and Abroad," and looking back through a period of four-and-thirty years and considering foreign tariffs at the present time, the following passage has peculiar interest.

"There is," says the Reviewer, "a supposition which seems to haunt some minds: *that of a combination of Foreign nations against England to exclude her, as a common foe* from the commerce of the world. We do not believe that so preposterous a conception has a place anywhere,* except possibly in the minds of a few among our own countrymen,

---

* We find, however, in a recent number of the *Journal des Débats*, for the 9th of November last (1842) an intimation that such a combination may become necessary. Speaking of the woollen trade of Belgium, the writer says: " Une decroissance analogue, bien que moins sensible, se fait sentir dans ses exportations de tissus de laine. L'avantage pour ses articles passe de plus en plus à l'Angleterre. Ce ne sera pas trop bientôt, que l'union de toutes les forces industrielles de l'ouest du continent contre la puissance productive croissante de cette redoutable rivale!"

With our Home-Trade mainly resting on the safe basis of a more extended and profitable agriculture both in the Mother-Country and her Colonies, however we might regret such a combination we should at least have less reason to care for it. We cannot be surprised that other nations should wish to protect their manufacturers from such a struggle for existence as is named in the following letter which appeared in the *Times* of the 16th January, 1878.

"PAPER MANUFACTURE.—Sir,—Mr. Brook Lambert is incorrect in stating that the extension of paper works now being made is made in the hope of large profits when a revival comes. They are being made in order, if possible, to secure some profit by diminishing the dead weight.

" The chances are that before many years are past (unless the manifest injustice of allowing foreign paper to come in duty free while prohibitive duties are put upon foreign rags is done away with) the paper trade in England will be extinct.

"Your obedient servant,

" January 16, 1878. A PAPER MAKER."

hard pressed by the recent complications of commercial disaster, and predisposed accordingly to the most doleful imaginations. There have been

The Board of Trade returns for June issued to-day are again unfavourable. The exports have fallen off nearly $3\frac{1}{2}$ per cent. against June last year, and the imports show an increase of over 5 per cent. As the reduction in the value of the exports is still due to receding prices, the actual bulk of the export trade may be said to be well maintained, and that is so far satisfactory; but after making all allowance for this the figures are disheartening. That the imports should continue to maintain so high a level against ever-receding export values is also unsatisfactory when the source of the increase is examined. Dearer food may be said to cause the whole of it, wheat and wheaten flour alone covering more than the excess. We have no longer, therefore, the same large import of raw materials for manufacture which swelled the returns of 1875 and helped to sustain those of 1876. On the contrary, cotton, hemp, jute, and wool were all received in much lesser quantities last month, and only flax and silk in marked excess. The import totals of value are therefore sustained by the greater import and higher prices of corn and sugar, and in lesser measure by that of such articles as silk, tea, wood, or hides. However rich a country may be, this state of things must tell on its prosperity. We are now buying many things dear and selling most things cheap—a state of business which must pinch the community more and more severely the longer it lasts. To sell cheap means to lower wages, and low wages with comparatively dear bread can only in the long run bring one result. The evil is not very gigantic yet, however, and an abundant harvest would probably avert any alarming consequences, restoring the two sides of the trade account to a sounder footing.

The export trade is, indeed, in one sense healthy, the quantities in some important instances being larger than they were this time last year, though prices still go downward. Thus, cotton yarns and piece-goods, iron, and steel, linen piece-goods, and several minor articles, continue to be freely

we *must admit*, signs in the course of the last twelve months which might appear to support such an opinion. Within that period France has passed exported. Against this, however, has to be set a heavy falling-off in the export of woollen manufactures, combined with an increased export of raw wool. It is true that for the six months the export of wool has been less than last year and a brief month's demand may mean nothing; but the falling off in the principal woollen manufactured staples has also been long continued and persistent. The exports of refined sugar are also decreasing heavily, and the price of silk has evidently told most materially on the demand for silk tissues. In jute, again, business would appear to very bad, and the falling off in the exports of machinery and mill-work, notwithstanding lower prices, is serious. So with the chemical trade, the copper trade, and the oil trade. Demand abroad has obviously lessened very considerably, and although the decrease is more visible, perhaps, in June than it was earlier in the year, there can be no doubt that it is hardly a passing one. British India and our own colonies are in some respects our best customers just now and our steadiest, for even France has been buying much less from us than usual, while the demand of the United States is, of course, still declining. Taking account of these and such like facts and tendencies, we can only conclude that our trade is at present seriously depressed, and that lately its conditions have in some respects materially altered for the worse. No doubt the outbreak of war has had much to do with the change, the price of corn, to take one example, having been forced up beyond what was justified in the first moments of alarm. This disturbing element is, at the worst, temporary, and we may well believe that the country will soon show signs of surmounting it. As it is, no more signal proof of the wealth and staying power of the community at large could well be given than is to be found in the manner in which it bears its present burdens of depressed trade and low profits.*—*Times*, July 9, 1877.

---

* But is it safe to mistake tranquillity—the result of exhaus-

an ordinance doubling the duty on *linen yarns*, a measure *hostile* enough had it been uniform with its application to all countries, but lest there should

OUR PORTS.—More than nine-tenths (in value) of the exports in the year 1875 of the produce of the United Kingdom was shipped at 12 ports. From London went merchandise of the value of £57,923,927; from Liverpool, £79,460,771; from Hull, £23,273,231; from Grimsby, £10,149,580; from Glasgow, £9,128,372; from Southampton, £8,652,933; from Newcastle, £4,882,433; from Leith, £3,848,466; from Cardiff, £2,837,747; from Harwich, £2,806,149; from Hartlepool, £2,484,648; from Folkestone, £2,253,678. These amounts together exceed £207,000,000 of the £223,465,963 which is the total value of the British and Irish produce exported in the year. Liverpool takes the lead in its vast exports of our cotton, linen, and woollen goods, and the exports of coal materially raise the totals at Newcastle and Cardiff. The twelve principal ports of entry for imports of foreign and colonial merchandise are not exactly the same as the chief ports of departure above named. The imports into the port of London in 1875 reached the value of £135,102,452; Liverpool, £105,095,188; Hull, £18,456,334; Folkestone, £11,822,742; Southampton, £9,236,460; Glasgow, £8,987,005; Leith, £8,084,081; Bristol, £6,911,963; Newhaven, £6,143,741; Greenock, £5,869,987; Dover, £5,409,042; Newcastle, £5,151,115. These sums together exceed £326,000,000, and constitute nearly nine-tenths of the £373,939,577, the total value of the imports of merchandise

---

tion—for content? If we would know how a nation is really progressing we must learn whether her capital of labour is augmenting, and whether the use of it is every day greater and more remunerative; whether her production—that is to say, her additions to her wealth—be annually on the increase. All else is but the filigree-work of our civilization—very interesting to the artist, to the philosopher, and to the philanthropist, but not touching the question of a country's rise or fall.

be any ambiguity about its meaning she has actually left open her Belgian frontier to *that* article at the former duty, on the condition that

into the United Kingdom in the year. That total was never before equalled in any year, and the value of the exports of British produce in 1875 was never exceeded or equalled, except in the three years next preceding 1875. The imports of the year comprised articles of the value of £139,047,488, being in a raw state and to be used in manufacture; articles partially manufactured, of the value of £28,568,266; articles wholly manufactured, of the value of £39,552,176; articles for food, of the value of £162,274,950, or ten millions more than in the preceding year; and other miscellaneous articles, £4,496,697.—*Times*, October 9, 1876.

The above shows that the value of imports in 1875 was £373,930,577; total value of British and Irish exports, £223,465,963; plus imports, £150,473,614.

THE SILK TRADE.— Sir, — Absence from the country prevented my sending you the statistics of the silk trade till somewhat late last month, so that you will have two statements rather close together. The Board of Trade returns to the end of November are as follows :—

	1859.	1861.
Imports in November	(The year before the French Treaty.)	
Broad Stuffs, Silk, or Satin	26,051lbs.	91,909lbs.
Ribbons of all kinds - -	24,483lbs.	50,111lbs.
Imports in the first eleven months of	1859.	1861.
Broad Stuffs - - - -	265,571lbs.	905,463lbs.
Ribbons of all kinds - -	453,709lbs.	746,194lbs.
Exports in the first eleven months of	1859.	1861.
Manufactures of Europe, not British.		
Broad Stuffs, Silk or Satin	6,382lbs.	8,582lbs.
Ribbons of all kinds - -	22,024lbs.	7,873lbs.

Belgium shall levy the high French duty in her own Custom-Houses, so as to *prevent* the *transit* of the British yarns through that country. To

Exports of British Manufactures.

	1859.	1861.
Stuffs, Handkerchiefs, and Ribbons	554,590lbs.	542,616lbs.

From this it will appear that we continue to import of all silk goods largely in excess of what we did before the French Treaty. In ribbons the increase in imports in the eleven months ending 30th of November last year amounted to 292,485 pounds weight, or 64½ per cent. This statement of pounds weight will probably convey to the uninitiated a very vague, if any, idea of the displacement of labour caused by this change in the place where the ribbons have been made for us—that is, in France and Switzerland, instead of Coventry, Derby, and Congleton. But it will be very clear when they are informed that the *increased* imports alone of the first eleven months of 1861 *would have supplied full work to the greatest number of weavers ever employed in Derby at one moment in our most prosperous times for fully three years and four months.* But that is far from being all; for it must be remembered that no weaver can be thrown out of work without those being also so who prepare the silk by throwing, dyeing, winding, and various other processes, and this number cannot be calculated at less than four for each weaver. This perhaps will serve to explain the melancholy fact of the very large number of workpeople now out of employ, and why upwards of twenty—more than half—of the silk mills in the town are now closed entirely, and the rest mostly working short time and with far less than their usual number of hands. I believe we are not worse off than our neighbours in the silk trade. The present condition of Coventry is vividly portrayed in the *Coventry Herald* of last Friday.

Your obedient servant,

Derby Mercury, Jan. 7, 1862.   J. L.

this disreputable and humiliating proposal Belgium has consented. Again, amidst the loudest professions from the Prussian Government of an

THE ASSOCIATED CHAMBERS OF COMMERCE.—The 18th annual meeting of the Associated Chambers of Commerce will be held at the Westminster Palace Hotel on Tuesday, Feb. 26, and the two following days. The notice-paper contains an unusually long list of propositions, Sunderland, Derby, and Sheffield having given notices of motion with reference to free trade, calling attention to the want of reciprocity on the part of several Governments, and requesting the Council to press this question at the Board of Trade. The Dundee Chamber proposes that it is urgently required to enlarge the powers of the present commercial department at the Foreign Office by remodelling it, and placing it in charge of a permanent Under-Secretary of State, and that steps be taken for the formation of an International Free Trade Association. The Leeds Chamber will also propose that Mr. S. S. Lloyd be requested to move in the House of Commons for a Select Committee to inquire into and report upon the manner in which the commercial interests of this country are watched over and furthered by the various departments of the Government. The following proposition will be submitted by the Birmingham Chamber:—"That this Association, after an experience of 35 years of the advantages of Free Trade, expresses its undiminished confidence in its principles, and urges upon the Government the faithful adherence to the same policy, irrespective of the action of foreign nations as regards tariffs and import duties." There are other motions on the French and Anglo-Italian Treaties, and the Spanish Tariff. Among the other subjects discussed will be the necessity of appointing Public Prosecutors, the levying of the Inhabited House Duty, Imperial Taxation, Income-Tax, Post-Office Letter Boxes and Telegrams, the Factory Acts, Board of Trade Statistics, the Australian Mail Service, the Bankruptcy Laws, the Enlargement of County Court Jurisdiction, the Appointment of a Minister of Commerce, the Continuance

anxiety to advance the relaxation of commercial restrictions, that Government has nevertheless adopted a proceeding not less hostile or mischievous than the measure of France with regard to linen yarns. The Congress of Deputies of the Zollverein at Stuttgard have, in a new tariff which is to take effect on the 1st January (1844), besides some minor alterations of an unfavourable kind, decreed, upon the proposal of Prussia, that goods mixed of cotton and wool, if of more than one colour, shall pay fifty thalers the centner instead of thirty ; that is, instead of a very high, shall be liable to an exorbitant and, *as it may prove, a prohibitory duty.* Next, America, as all our readers must be aware, has, after a struggle, passed a tariff subverting altogether the arrangement as established by the Compromise Act of 1833, and imposing upon the various descriptions of manufactured goods rates of duty varying from 30 to 40 and 50 per cent. and upwards, which have had the effect of *stopping a great portion of the shipments of cotton goods to that country from Great Britain* of the Railway Commission, the Indian Famine Commission, the Statute of Frauds, and the Registration of Firms.—*The Times*, Jan. 15, 1878.

Happily, at last, even some of the Chambers of Commerce, have come to doubt the policy of 1844. But the *Times* has told them that the want of " reciprocity " is not the cause of the depression of trade, and Mr. Hoyle has told them that the great falling off in the home trade has caused and ever will cause depression until it is revived by increasing the *power* to purchase more food and clothing.

during the past autumn (*i.e.*, of 1842) and, without doubt, have added greatly to the distresses of our manufacturing population. Besides the greater instances, Russia, according to her wont in such matters, and Spain, have published within the last fifteen months new tariffs, of which it is difficult to say whether they are *still worse* than, or only as *execrably bad* as those which they succeeded; but in the *close rivalry* between the old and the new the latter seem upon the whole entitled to the palm of *prohibitive rigour*. And Portugal, also, has augmented the duties payable upon certain classes of her imports by a measure of the recent date of March 1841, and by another of the present year. In the meantime, Spain has concluded a treaty with Belgium for the admission of her linens, and the King of Prussia has effected an arrangement with the Czar which, in certain particulars, secures upon his own frontier a relaxation of the iron strictness of the Russian system. England has concluded no commercial treaty with any of these powers, and the negotiation with France which the measures of Lord Palmerston interrupted in 1840, at the very period of its ripeness, appears still to slumber."

What is shown by the above extract seems to afford little encouragement to proceed further in such "experimental policy," and yet Sir Robert did in 1846, and other ministers have since gone beyond him in the same policy, and now, in 1878, the struggle and demand for reciprocity with foreign tariffs are being carried on as much as ever. Verily, what Coleridge foretold has, or seems to have, come to pass, viz.—" that, by becoming a great horde of manufacturers, we have, more than at the time he wrote, excited the ill-will of all the manufacturers of other nations." Is there no danger likely to result from the confession that England so requires the maintenance of an extended foreign trade for her prosperity that she is ready to cast herself at the feet of the rest of the world, and acknowledge that we are subject to the liabilities of a dependence which is not reciprocal?

The Christmas Article in the "Times" of 1876.

In the *Times* of the 25th December, (1876), in a well considered and able leader on our Christmas Charities, it is said, " *obligations we all admit* are becoming every year *larger and more difficult.* The chief peril of society consists in *its contrasts* and *its differences.* The *contrasts are growing continually more violent and the differences wider.** The

---

* Which means, in other words, the rich are becoming richer and the poor poorer, and hence unable to clothe and feed themselves as they would and should do, and hence the home-market for our own manufactures, as Mr. Hoyle has shown, is so suffering, and was in 1869 when our exports were so very large.

increasing aggregation of the people in towns, instead of the *more scattered distribution of former days, makes those differences more galling and hard to be borne.*

" These are but homely suggestions—too homely some will think for the season. It is rather a time, they will say, for extraordinary and strictly seasonable hospitalities. *But every year repeats and intensifies a painful impression that sudden gushes and fitful manifestations of benevolence have but a* LIMITED *power to cure the* DEEPER *ills of the social state . . . Perhaps it is possible to improve men upon the Christmas Appeal.* There is *much more to be done than to contribute to charitable Societies, which, after all, cannot go* TO THE ROOT OF THE MATTER." Whilst making these extracts, some beautiful and suggestive lines by one of *the* most elegant female writers of late days, (Mrs. Norton, afterwards Lady Stirling Maxwell), in reference to ' *The* Man of Sorrows,' have been brought to the recollection of the writer of these pages:

> God has built up a bridge 'twixt man and man
> Which mortal strength can never overthrow,
> Over the world it stretches its wide span,
> The key-stone of that mighty arch is Woe!
> Pleasure divides us; the Divine command
> Hath made of sorrow's links a firm connecting band.

Accumulations of Capital.

At the meeting of the Statistical Society held last evening, under the presidency of Mr. Shaw Lefevre, M.P., a paper was read by Mr. *Robert Giffen* on *Recent Accumulations of Capital* in the United Kingdom. *It appeared that the growth of those accumulations had been very rapid.* The Income Tax returns showed that the gross income assessed rose in Great Britain from £115,000,000 at the beginning of the century to £130,000,000 in 1815, £251,000,000 in 1843, and £262,000,000 in 1853; and then, in the United Kingdom, from £308,000,000 in 1855 to £396,000,000 in 1865, and £571,000,000 in 1875.* If the capital of that portion of the income derived from capital had only progressed at the same rate, the annual increase of capital all through, and especially of recent years, must have been enormous. The

* If what Mr. Robert Giffen here states be true, it confirms what the leader in the *Times* of the 20th February, 1860, says, and leaves no doubt as to the wisdom of Lord Bacon in foreseeing and warning that, "above all things, good policy is to be used that the treasure and money in a state be not gathered into few hands; for, otherwise, a state may have a great stock and yet starve," &c.: See p. 15. It will be well for the nation to consider also, whether we CAN violate with IMPUNITY what he has further said in his " Essay on Seditions and Troubles." It was rather unfortunate for Mr. Giffen that the paragraph disavowing the terrible distress in Sheffield should immediately follow."—*Recent Accumulations of Capital in the United Kingdom.*

increase in the income assessed between 1865 and 1875 amounted to £175,000,000, which was equal to 44 per cent. of the income assessed in 1865. Leaving out altogether the capital not yielding income, a similar increase of capital, assuming the present amount to be what he had stated, would give us for 1865 a total capital of about £5,200,000,000, on which the increase at 44 per cent. would be £2,228,000,000; or, in round figures, £230,000,000 per annum. Mr. Giffen observed that if his estimate was moderate, and any cause would justify a higher figure for the present capital, then the increase between 1865 and 1875 would be even more than he had stated. *A question which had been raised of late was whether the nation was now spending its capital.* The figures in his paper might, he thought, be taken to prove that if the nation had begun to spend its capital instead of saving capital, the process was a very new one. *As far as his researches carried him, the fact he had to deal with* was that *the rate of saving had been far greater of late than* at any *previous period during the present century;* that the saving all through had been at an increasing rate. *The figures would also show that the only* fact *alleged in proof* that we were *living on our capital was insufficient to make* out the *case. That allegation was* that the *excess* of imports *was now so great as to show* that we were *calling in our capital from abroad.* There was incidental evidence as to the great amount of lending in former years, *which entitled us to the receipt in each year* of an *enormous income from foreign countries*, so that the *excess of imports would need to be much larger* than it was *to prove any material calling in of capital from abroad.* Apart from this evidence, however, it must also be apparent that if the nation was calling in some fraction of its foreign investment, it was not therefore stopping its savings or diminishing its capital. The foreign investments, though they were very large in the years before 1875, were by no means the chief part of the national accumulations. *Our main savings were at home. Before the nation could be said to be living on its capital, it must be shown that not only was capital being* called in *from abroad,* but that *more was so called in* than was *being simultaneously invested at home.* He had not seen this point considered by any of those who had made the suggestion that the nation was living on its capital. The reading of the paper, which lasted upwards of an hour, was followed by a discussion in which Dr. Guy, F.R.S., Mr. Stephen Bourne, Mr. Newmarch, F.R.S., who expressed his belief that the figures given by Mr. Giffen were considerably below the reality, Mr. C. Walford, Captain Craigie, Mr. Mundella, M.P., and the Chairman took part.

The Distress in Sheffield.

The gentlemen who have been carrying out a tentative arrangement for the relief of sufferers by the distress in Sheffield met the Mayor, Alderman Mappin, yesterday morning, to report the result of their labours. *They stated that the distress was much deeper and more widely spread than was generally supposed, and that to properly grapple with it something more extensive than private* enterprise *was needed.* It was decided to form a committee in each parish, with the vicars as chairmen, assisted by the ministers of the various denominations, and all deserving cases are to be relieved. Among families tickets for groceries and meat will be distributed, and an arrangement is being made by which dinners will be given three days a week in halls in central places to poor children. The Mayor has issued an appeal to the public for contributions, and on Saturday two sheets placed in prominent parts of the town realized £85. 18s 2¾d. The Mayor's fund in addition has already realized over £370.—*16th January,* 1878.

Statistics of Wool Imports.

In 1876, from Australia 263,870,597 lbs.; South Africa, 42,054,712 lbs.; India 24,322,611 lbs.; European Countries, 35,961,694 lbs.; other Countries, 19,793,228 lbs. ; Total 385,987,842 lbs. The Home-supply of *British* grown wool was carefully estimated at 160,000,000 lbs.

A recent number of the *Economist* (Dec. 1877) concluded a paper on the question, " Are we *consuming our capital?*" as follows:—

" While there seems to us no proof that we are living out of our capital, it is yet *obvious that accumulation does not go on in the country at the same rate as previously.* So far as the increased importations, which have been so much discussed of late, have been paid for out of the capital set at liberty by the diversion of trade from one channel to another, we are not necessarily the worse off, *if the imports have been employed in a manner which will be a source of future profit. So far as we are accumulating stocks of manufactured goods in the country for future use,* a source of future profit *may be* merely accumulating unsold, waiting till a demand may, as it doubtless will, in course of time spring up. *So far as our importations of articles of food enable us to support a large population engaged in preparing stocks of manufactured articles drawn from materials found within our own boundaries, this supply of food is the stay also of an industry which may also be classed as productive.* So long as the country is merely fetching back in one shape or another the capital which it formerly exported, no injury is done to its permanent prosperity. But further it cannot safely go. *There are limits in time to the largest accumulated resources, and there are other considerations besides mere movements of capital to be thought of. There may have been, and there probably was, a considerable increase, in the days of our recent prosperity, in the unproductive expenditure of the country, and this must lead to its ultimate impoverishment.* There is the difference in the modes of life started or developed during the recent years of too abundant sunshine to be borne in mind. *There has been much waste of capital in various ways. It is always unpleasant for people, when less well off than they have been, to come down to a lower scale of expenditure; but come down they must, if they would avoid ruin. The prodigality indulged in among the working classes during the time of high wages has been the theme of many a speech and many a statement. The reckless extravagance of those above them in station, who suddenly enriched, thought there was, as the old saying has it, ' no bottom to the money bag,' the sums lavished upon costly buildings, on splendid establishments, on luxuries of every description—all these have to be written off the account, as so much wasted capital.* Yet the business heart of the nation is still thoroughly sound. The evidence is strong in favour of this. The Clearing-house returns, the railway returns, the receipts of the Exchequer, all show that though the great wave of prosperity, which seemed as if it would bear everything so rapidly onwards with it a few years since, is stayed in its course, and has for the moment even receded, *we may well hope to maintain our position by a timely economy. Retrenchment will undoubtedly have to be the order of the day, and when the cloud is removed, it is to be hoped that the lessons of the past will not be forgotten.*"

" *So far*," says this paper, " as our importations of articles of food enable us to support a large population engaged in preparing stocks of manufactured articles DRAWN FROM MATERIALS FOUND WITHIN OUR OWN BOUNDARIES, this supply of food is the stay also of an industry which may also be classed as productive. But *is* the greatest portion of such articles manufactured " from materials found *within our own boundaries?*" The amount of the large increase of imports, though doubtless mainly for food, embraces a great amount of foreign raw materials for our manufactures. Let us ever remember too, that the capital paid for *food* to support our artizans whilst engaged *in these* very manufactures, goes to enrich other nations instead of being circulated amongst our own farmers and agricultural and other labourers in this country, and hence " the *depression*, as Mr. Hoyle tells us, in the *Home-Market* during the very year when *our exports* were the *greatest*. If such an amount of capital were circulated in *this* country, our *Home-trade* would again flourish, but never can till more is done to enable us to feed and provide more food from our own land, for our own people, in proportion to their increase. *Then the power of the people to purchase* would be increased, instead of, as it is under existing circumstances, being *gradually diminished*.

We have in this country tens of thousands of unemployed, half-employed, and mis-employed hands. We have, at the same time, *within this kingdom and its colonies*, hundreds of millions of *uncultivated and half-cultivated* acres of prolific land. The combination of land and labour has ever been, and *must ever be* the foundation of all real wealth. And it really is a scandal to civilization, it is a standing reproach to a Christian Legislature that while within little more than the last half-century, railroads have been invented to traverse the land and steam-boats to over-ride the ocean, so as to be able to convey unemployed hands to uncultivated acres with a degree of speed, cheapness, and safety, utterly unknown to former times, yet the honest poor, the untrained youth, and the mismanaged portion of *our prison population* are shut out from this never-failing source of wealth and happiness, and are left to drag out a miserable existence in involuntary idleness, or in wilful crime.

In a short and interesting paper lately read before the Statistical Society, by Mr. Frederick Martin, author of the *Statesman's Year Book, or Births, Deaths, and Marriages, and the Comparative Progress of Population, in some of the principal countries of Europe*—Mr. Martin said that " as far as could be ascertained from the vital Statistics of the nine States passed under review, and leaving out of view disturbing elements; such as emigration, the average *increase of population is largest in England*, and that it seems probable that at the end of the present century the population of ENGLAND AND WALES will have risen to thirty millions.

OUR ARMY.

In *Blackwood's Edinburgh Magazine* for August, 1871, is an excellent letter from Brigadier-General Adye, on "National Defence and Army Organisation," and his concluding words, setting forth the qualities essential to secure a successful army, are especially worth remembering.

"There are three main principles," he says, "on which all successful armies must be formed—first, *discipline*,* and professional leaders. The first is the *training* of the *body*. Men who aspire to be soldiers must not only be well-drilled to the use of their arms, but they must be *content* to sleep in the *open air*, to live occasionally upon rough, scanty, *badly-cooked food*,† and in every respect to

---

* Can a stronger inducement to discipline be found or suggested than that set forth by the *Wisdom of Solomon*, ch. vi. 17, 18, 19.

† The Club-life of our young men does not tend to promote the qualities here enumerated as essential in a soldier.

submit *cheerfully to exposure and privations.* The second is the *training of the mind*, and is far more *difficult of acquirement.* Soldiers, to be *really such*, must be content to sacrifice their personal and political liberties, and in *silence and cheerfulness* to *submit* to the *superior will* of their *commanding officers.* These *iron rules* are *absolute*, and can never *be relaxed;* they are the *basis* of all success. But above all it is necessary that armed men should be commanded by *experienced professional leaders.* A man who aspires to lead others must *know more*, dare more—aye, have *suffered more*—than they. He must be one to whom his men can look up *with confidence* and with a feeling that he is able to lead them to victory and, what is still more difficult, to save them in defeat. *Armed men without such a leader will rarely gain a victory*, and a *disaster* will render them *a despairing, helpless mob* of men with *muskets.* These principles are *eternal.* They have been the foundation of successful armies *since the creation*, and will continue to be so till the end. Each one can judge for himself *how far they form the basis* of our *present military arrangements*, and how far the *nation generally* is prepared to acquiesce in them. *There are many who fear that a large number of people in this country are gradually giving themselves up* to *luxury* and *pleasure*,* whilst *others are completely absorbed*

---

* Six years after this excellent letter by Brigadier-General Adye appeared in *Blackwood's Magazine*—when he had

in the sordid pursuit of wealth. If this be so in *any great degree our national character will assuredly deteriorate* and the Army cannot be maintained in efficiency. If we continue to be *brave*, simple, en-

become Major-General Sir John Adye, K.C.B., and Governor of the Royal Military Academy, Woolwich, it must have been painful to him, in making his report of the Gentleman Cadets to his Royal Highness, the Commander-in-Chief, to find himself obliged to insert the following passage:—

"The conduct of the Gentlemen Cadets about to be commissioned, has not in *some respects* been so satisfactory during this term, as I could have desired. There have been no *serious* offences committed by them; but a *certain amount of slackness or thoughtlessness has been observable*, and the *officers* of the Company cannot, therefore, have received *that constant support* from the *under* officers to which they were *entitled*. In those circumstances, I regret not being able to make any recommendation to your Royal Highness as to the presentation *of a regulation sword*, which is usually given as a reward for *excellent conduct.*"—*Times*, 25th July, 1877.

It would indeed seem that the passion for gain, the intense *struggle* to keep *up appearances*, the *importance* which is *attached* to mere *physical comfort*, and the *habits of luxury, have sapped the very foundations of the body politic.*

"Sed, per deos immortales, vos ego appello, qui semper domos, villas, signa, tabellas vestras pluris quam rempublicam feestis."—*Sallust, Cataline* i. 11.

In the 4th leading article of the *Times* of March 4th, 1870, will be found the following paragraph:—

"It is said that the *stress of life is growing more intense day by day*. Yet we doubt whether *pleasure was ever pursued with well-intentioned diligence* by a greater proportion of the English-speaking race."

May not dissipation be a more correct word than pleasure, and sought in too many instances in order to induce forgetfulness for a time of the painful consciousness that "the stress of life is growing more intense day by day."

terprising, and *modest, as of yore,* the country is in no danger; but if, on the other hand, we become *lazy, frivolous,* and *effeminate, and if we live chiefly* for the *pleasure of heaping up* MONEY, then it may be relied on that *no army organization, however perfect, will be sufficient* to save *us in the day* of *peril,* should it come." This grave but friendly warning was written and published in 1871.

In a letter which appeared in the *Times* of the 24th December, 1874, from Mr. Edward Walter, Barracks of the Corps of Commissionaires, Dec. 22nd, are the following passages:—

" Previous to the publication of Col. Anson's letter, (which also was given in a previous No. of the *Times*) I had prepared some notes on the *present* as compared with *the former moral and physical state* of the *rank and file.* Circumstances, however, delayed my purpose, and as my views coincide with those expressed by that officer, it is needless now to repeat them. I will, therefore, confine myself chiefly to quotations from official Reports bearing on the controversy, adding a few observations founded on an experience of more than thirty years, acquired, during half that time, among discharged soldiers and sailors of every rank and branch in her Majesty's service, of whom nearly 3000 have presented themselves for admission into this corps from its foundation to the present time.

" The first official document I quote from is that

of Major Du Cane, R.E., on 'Military Prisons,' dated 1873; in this, Col. Wellesley, writing from Gosport, says:—

"Desertion would appear to have been on the *increase*, and assumes, with *insubordination, a prominent place* in the list of offences for which imprisonment was awarded."

Surgeon-Major Tuffnell, Dublin, says, "The *physical development* of the prisoners admitted during the past year has not been in any way an improvement. There are a large number of men, or RATHER LADS, now in the service who must break down, if *put to hard work and heavy exertion, as inseparable from war*. Many of those who have been under confinement during the past twelvemonths, have been *weakly and ill-framed*, without *muscle, bone, or courage, crying* LIKE WOMEN *in their cells*. An inspection of every regiment, each man stripped naked, as they are upon admission into prison, would, I feel assured, exhibit many individuals as in the ranks *who are never likely to become efficient soldiers*."

The medical officer at Millbank, Mr. Gower, says:—

"A large proportion of the *military prisoners*, amounting to fully 13 per cent. were found to be unfit for hard labour on *medical* grounds. This unfitness arose in some cases from *organic disease*, but in most cases it was due *either to feebleness of constitution, tenuity of muscle, or defective bodily development.* *It is to be hoped, therefore,* that although drawn in tolerably equal proportions from the regiments quartered in England and Wales, they do not fairly represent the British Army."

" The next witness I intend," says Mr. Walter, " to produce, is Surgeon-Major Leith Adams, whose paper on the Recruiting Question, read last Spring at the Royal United Service Institution, ought to be carefully studied by all who WISH to make *themselves acquainted* with the *facts* of the present *physique* of the *army.* He says, p. 10:

" Now, *I must candidly* assert *that the* PHYSIQUE *of our infantry is not at present* up to *the standard of our race,* and I cannot conceal from myself a feeling, that *unless remedial measures are adopted,* it will become *lower and lower.* This conclusion has been arrived at mainly from my personal inspection of about 25,000 recruits, over 17,000 of whom have been passed into the army."

After quoting other statistics, one of which is, that out of 1812 enlistments in *Scotland* during 1872 *only* 746 men *finally* reached *their regiments,"* he adds—

" I now venture to assert, as the *result of my experience,* that *the army has deteriorated in a moral and physical sense to a deplorable extent; a gradual change has been going on for many years, but in an increasing* RATIO OF LATE."

All who remember the Report on the Pathology

of the Diseases of the Army by Dr. Lyons, the physician to whom the inquiry as to the cause of the great mortality of the first winter in the Crimea was intrusted, and who went out at the end of April, 1855, and made his Report in July of the same year, will be inclined to agree with Mr. Walter as to *deterioration* taking place at least in the physique of our raw material for the army.

"The British army suffered fearfully from dysentery, which assumed at length the scorbutic type, and the question arose what were the causes which produced so violent a form of sickness in so fine an army? The Crimea, it was stated, has by no means an unhealthy climate. Dr. Lyons told us that "the soldier was ill-clothed, ill-fed, and ill-housed during the winter months, while exposed to harassing and excessive duties. These things were the direct cause of disease, but the Report attributes much to the *physical character* of the *men themselves.* Among the *predisposing* causes of sickness were counted, as they must be, the *youth* and *immature condition* of a great part of the army. Another class of men, says Dr. Lyons's Report, ill-fitted for a military life, are the recruits gathered at a somewhat advanced age from the large towns. Those who have passed 25 or 30 years of life in the close streets and impure atmosphere of a manufacturing or *seaport* town are generally found to have *passed* the *meri-*

dian *of their physical development.* The testimony of the medical officers is unanimous that such men are early and constant applicants for admission into hospital. The effects of a campaign on the appearance of the soldiers is strikingly described *in the Report,* and causes us to understand how those *whom* YOUTH or *social antecedents* may have *rendered unsuitable should have so early sunk under the toils of the siege.* Some of those effects were visible to the eye. A marked *characteristic* of the *Crimean soldier* was a *premature appearance of age.* With the HAGGARD FEATURES *of disease,* especially that of a *chronic kind,* these appearances became still more exaggerated, often to a most marked degree."

" The *principle* that the Commissioner has drawn from these facts is of the *highest importance.* He takes it *as proved* that English soldiers sent on active service against the enemy, ought to have arrived at *perfect manhood.* Many will remember that great numbers of mere *boys* were sent to replenish our army in the Crimea, and provoked Lord Raglan, then Commander-in-Chief there, to say, in one of his despatches home, " We don't want *mere gristle* sent out to us, we want bone and sinew."

It is not the artizan class only that look prematurely old, as many members of the bar, and, the writer of these pages doubts not, the judges also, would state that when agricultural *labourers have been placed in the dock at the assizes* for trial, their personal appearance and their ages given in the Assize Calendar so little *coincide* that all in court have been astounded. The writer of these pages has often heard the presiding judge question such prisoners as to whether they were *really not older* than was stated in the calendar. The *Times* article, 28th July, 1856, continues :—" Yet he (Dr. Lyons) is against recruiting amongst men of *a certain* age, particularly those who have led an unhealthy and profligate life in great towns. He advises early enlistment, and a system of training. . . . . Some singular facts are mentioned in the Report in connection with the surgical operations practised in the various hospitals. *A tolerance of the effects* of injury and of greater surgical operations has been observed among the Russian prisoners, both in the French and English hospitals, *far superior* to that exhibited by the wounded *among the allied troops*, with the exception, perhaps, of the Sardinians. Our men, though stalwart and healthy looking, were found *too soft and inflated* for a safe endurance of *wounds* or the surgeon's knife. The report refers to a *fact* which, it will be remembered, was warmly *contradicted*. " It was with regret," says Dr. Lyons, "that I noticed *subsequently* to the month of May that the *increased facilities* for procuring *malt and other intoxicating* liquors became a means of great and general *abuse*." The Report condemns the issue of porter as a ration, even in moderate quantities, and states that, immoderately used, as it often was, the consequence was "an inflation of the system and plethoric state not consistent with *firm and vigorous health.*" The document, as a whole, confirms many of the views that have been taken by former observers of the condition of our army, and will, no doubt, *furnish suggestions* for the conduct of any future campaign."

So ends the article in the *Times* of 28th July, 1856, more than twenty years since; and it is, indeed *an all-important consideration* whether the increase of our population during that period has added to the strength of the country or contributed only redundancy without strength.*

And, as regards our Volunteers, the official report on the last Easter Monday Field Day, from the General Commanding Home District to the Adjutant-General of the Forces, dated from "Home District Office, Horse Guards," is not very satisfactory or assuring. Lord Elcho who, with becoming zeal on behalf of the Volunteers, questioned some parts of the Adjutant-General's re-

---

* The *Times* of the 24th December, 1874, in an article relating to our army, truly said:—"We have to keep in the front line of the most powerful States in the world by making one man do duty for several, and this can only be done by a liberal and judicious expenditure. But peace in these days is as expensive in its requirements as war, and we that stay at home are bound to try to live healthily, strongly and long, as in that way only can we spare to send out the men who are to protect our commerce and shores."

port, says in his letter which appeared in the *Times* of the 2nd July, 1877, under the heading "Volunteer Officers," "if its *general tenour be correct, enough remains to fill with well-founded alarm not only the general public* and Parliament, who annually vote £500,000 for the maintenance of the Volunteer Force, but also all those who, whether as ministers or Volunteers, have for the last eighteen years, been labouring to create, establish, and improve it, in *the belief* that, even as at present constituted or organized, our Volunteer army may be relied on in time of need as a material and efficient element of national defence."

We may some time or other be compelled to take our part in the European struggle, to defend and keep down by the parade of an imposing force possible *disaffection in India*, to hold with strong garrisons imperial strongholds in the Mediterranean and beyond the seas. The spirit of the nation may be as bold and determined as ever, but *moral determinations* cannot compensate for the *shortcomings of physical force*. Compared with legions at the beck of other states, our armies are but a mere handful—some 50,000 bayonets at home, 15,000 in our colonies, and in India 60,000 more, making up the sum total really under arms. Nor can we lay the flattering unction to our souls that *quality* makes up for *quantity* as heretofore.*

* In a late review of the troops at Aldershot the *Times* commented on "*the youthfulness of too many.*"

Our *boy* battalions have too recently been tried and found wanting.

It was a wise saying (and might well be taken as a warning) of the late Lord Ellenborough on the late Lord Lyndhurst's motion relative to national defences (*Times*, 6th July, 1859)—"When *one* nation determines to apply *all her energies to making* MONEY, and another to making preparations for war, it is obvious enough with which of the two nations ALL the money *will* ULTIMATELY *be*."

An able letter of the late Sir Chas. Napier upon the defenceless condition of the British people which appeared in the *Times* of Oct. 11th, 1850, and was inserted in the appendix to "The Defenceless State of Great Britain," by Sir Francis Head, Bart., 1850, thus concludes:—

"Napoleon said Cherbourg was an eye to see and an arm to strike. We had better take care, or some day it will strike with a vengeance. We have Russia on our left in the Baltic, and France with a harbour capable of holding a large fleet in our front waiting only a railroad from Paris to make it complete. Should these two powers at any time fall out with us, I do not think they will pay much attention to Cobden's Peace Congress. *One* wants to go *to* CONSTANTINOPLE, the *other* wants to go to the *Rhine*, and we want to prevent both; and when the pear is riper, *Cobden's preaching at Frankfort* will not prevent them.

"Your obedient servant,
"*Merchistown*, 1st Oct.   CHAS. NAPIER."

A correspondent with the Mediterranean Fleet in Besika Bay writes as follows, under date Aug. 22, 1877:—

"I am sorry to mention that on Friday last some very *serious acts of insubordination were committed on board Her Majesty's ship* 'Achilles,' *recently arrived on this station.* It appears that on that day, after the customary exercise of general quarters, the ropes were ordered to be coiled up for the better clearing up of the decks, and, owing to some slackness in the manner in which this duty was performed, the watch were ordered to have only one hour for their dinner-time instead of two, which they are allowed during the hot months. At one o'clock they were piped to fall in, and afterwards employed in coiling up and down ropes as a punishment until two, when the bugle sounded 'Quarters, clean guns.' The men not moving as smartly as it was considered they ought, were piped to fall in, and told that they were to double to their quarters when dismissed, which order seems to have been greeted with murmurs and exclamations of 'Stop where you are,' and it was *not until an order had been given to a ship's corporal to take the names of the men who did not move that they commenced to go to their guns.* The same evening *it was discovered that a number of tangent sights and some other gear connected with the guns had been thrown overboard; also a quantity of brass belaying pins.* The ship's company were then, at about twelve o'clock at night, mustered at quarters, and severely admonished by the captain, Sir William Hewett. The Admiral has since given them a certain time to discover the men who are guilty of throwing the gun gear overboard, *and in case of their not being discovered has determined upon disrating the whole of the petty officers in the ship and replacing them by others from the different ships in the fleet. It is certainly very discreditable that such proceedings should occur in our finest ships, but I think it is not difficult to find where the fault lies. In the first place, in all newly commissioned ships there is far too large a proportion of young ordinary seamen and boys just out of the training-ships, who are not accustomed to the hard work and strict discipline of a sea-going man-of-war.* The 'Achilles' has, I hear, of this class *some* 400 *lads out of a complement of* 700 *all told,* of which a great many are marines, stokers, and artificers, *so that the seaman class is principally composed of these young hands. The mistake is not having more old and well-seasoned men, who, in conjunction with the petty officers, would steady and control the young blood. The fact, unfortunately, is that the best men at the end of their ten years' service go into the Coastguard or else are lost to us altogether.* In the second place, I am afraid *the cause of these outbreaks* is too often to be found in the want of tact and judgment of those in command, who, being old hands themselves, forget that they have unbroken youngsters to deal with, who require careful management and judicious handling. The system employed in the harbour training-ships, perhaps, requires investigation; *but the greatest evil we suffer from is the want in newly-commissioned ships of a proper proportion of thoroughly trained seamen, and until this is rectified we must expect to hear of these acts of insubordination, which throw discredit on the navy, and also on the country.* The Achilles will leave this evening for a cruise, calling at Salonica, and will be picked up by the fleet next week. The Agincourt, carrying the flag of Sir J. E. Commerell, K.C.B., arrived on Sunday last from Malta. The fleet went out on the 7th, 8th, and 9th, returning the same evenings, to practise at evolutions under steam."

The Army Strength of Europe.

A special lecture on this subject was given on Friday afternoon at the Royal United Service Institution, Whitehall, under the presidency of General Sir William Codrington, *by Mr. C. E. Howard Vincent, F.R.G.S., late of the 23rd Royal Welsh Fusiliers.* The lecturer, after a few words of apology for the amount of statistics which his subject necessarily involved, and also for other circumstances which he trusted would entitle him to the consideration of his audience,—he having but recently left the ranks of the Army for those of the Law,—proceeded to review various nations of Europe and their strength both on land and sea, premising, however, that, by the rules of the Institution, all lecturers are responsible for what they utter in the theatre, and that, therefore, all conclusions he might deduce from the facts he should advance were to be taken as purely personal, and in no way ratified by the Council or any other official. With regard to the manner in which he was to treat his subject—a subject which was peculiarly appropriate to the day, inasmuch as just sixty years ago the fate of Europe was at stake on the field of Waterloo—he had been advised by some to take the major states separately and group the minor; by others to consider Europe collectively. He, however, preferred to "personally conduct" his audience round Europe. Beginning, then, with Holland, it appears that the military forces which can be assembled for the defence of that country consist of 68 battalions of Infantry, of five companies; 111 companies of Engineers, Transport Corps, &c.; 24 squadrons of Cavalry, four to a regiment; 18 batteries of Artillery, of six guns, with a "combatant" strength of 90,260 Infantry, armed with the Snider and Beaumont breech-loaders; 3850 Cavalry, with 108 bronze breech-loading rifled guns; while the Dutch Navy consists of 113 ships, of which 17 are armour-plated, with 981 guns, and

7250 men—all exclusively recruited by enlistment; for, although conscription is allowable, it is never enforced. To Belgium belong 84 battalions (mostly of four companies) of Infantry, armed with Albini, Braendlin, and Comblain breech-loaders; 16 companies of Engineers; 45 squadrons (14 to a regiment) of Cavalry; 20 batteries (of six guns) of Artillery; with a "combatant" total of 130,000 Infantry, 7500 Cavalry, and 152 guns, on the Prussian system; and since October, 1874, the kingdom has been divided into two military conscriptions, the one embracing the provinces of Antwerp and of East and West Flanders, the other Brabant, Hainault, Liége, Limbourg, Luxembourg, and Namur. To Norway and Sweden, 122 battalions, mostly armed with the Remington; 15 companies of Engineers, 58 squadrons of Cavalry, 40 batteries of Artillery, with 152,800 Infantry, 10,540 Cavalry, and 322 guns, *plus* 20,000 Volunteers; while their Navies, recruited partly by voluntary enlistment, partly by conscription among the seafaring population, consist of 65 vessels, of which five are armour-plated, with 491 guns and 5100 men. The combatant strength of the Danish Army may be set down at 5 territorial brigades, 42 battalions of Infantry, armed with the Snider and Remington rifles, 28 companies of Engineers, 21 squadrons of Cavalry, 12 batteries of Artillery, with 36,050 foot, 2100 horse, and 96 guns. In time of peace the German Army, including that of

Bavaria, numbers 18,079 officers, 401,659 men, 97,379 horses, which are in times of war increased to 31,195 officers, 1,273,346 men, with about one million combatants, 270,920 horses, and 2472 field-guns. Besides these there is the Landsturm, which is divided into two classes. The first, including all able-bodied men not already in the Army, is calculated to produce 175,800 men; while the second, which is not yet organized, will include every other available male. The German Navy, which is yet comparatively in its childhood, is manned by some 9000 officers and men, the latter drawn by conscription from the seafaring population estimated at 80,000, who on that account are exempted from military service. The Russian Army, which three years ago formed a subject for the same lecturer in this theatre, now consists of 752,000 combatant Infantry, 172,000 Cavalry, with 2768 guns, including 400 mitrailleuses, and in about 10 or 15 years will probably consist of 2,000,000 men, of whom about three-fourths will be combatant. The Navy, which every day is increasing in importance, consists of some 300 vessels, including 25 ironclads, with an armament of over 1500 guns. Turkey claims 350,000 combatant Infantry, 21,000 Cavalry, with 648 guns, with an ironclad Navy, perhaps one of the finest in the world, and commanded by an Englishman of no less ability than experience. Passing by Greece, with the 100,000 men and 50 guns, the 20 ships, and 2 ironclads that the Government of Athens is reputed to have at command, Austria and Hungary next claim our attention, with 798,172 Infantry, 62,746 Cavalry, and 1616 guns, and a fleet of eight or ten ironclads in the Adriatic. Italy, with an Army of 447,264 Infantry, armed mostly with the Remington breech-loader, 15,850 Cavalry, and 1240 guns; Portugal —Spain in the present deplorable state of affairs being necessarily set aside—with 50,000 combatants and 100 guns and 50 ships, of which, however, probably not more than half are seaworthy; Switzerland, with 174,000 Infantry, 5000 Cavalry, and 294 guns, brings us to France. *With a recuperative power peculiar to Gaul*, said the lecturer, *Frenchmen have been unremittingly devoting themselves to remedy the evils in their military administration which the last war laid bare in so terrible a manner.* Those, however, who know France best, who have resided there of late, will need no telling of how much there is yet to do, in what a transition state is the whole mechanism of the Army, how wholly unfit it is at present for revenge. The new laws are but imperfectly understood by the local officials, and *years must elapse before the eagle of France can again be borne against a foe.* Not half a million combatants is it possible for France to put into the field, and before even this, it may almost be said, paltry number could be brought to bear on any one spot, could be available for the defence of one frontier, could be concentrated for any attack, months of preparation would be essential. *But in her Navy France is strong.* The Tricolor is hoisted by hand upon 350 ships of war, with an ironclad fleet of 50 strong, and all are manned partly by conscription and partly by enlistment. With regard to Great Britain, the lecturer said that it is the inherent delight of Englishmen to depreciate themselves and to condemn their own institutions. *Nevertheless, though the* services *might be in many points defective, he maintained* that *an Army Corps of* 30,000 *regular troops complete in all its branches, could within a week set sail from our shores.* Both the Militia and the Volunteers he considered to be not only at present of a certain degree of efficiency, but easily to be made far more so; while as for the English Navy, he held that the figures would speak for themselves—those figures being 586 vessels afloat, including ironclads; 29 building, also inclusive of ironclads; 6250 guns and 60,000 men. *In conclusion,* the lecturer considered that, looking at the Armies of Europe from every point of view, the rapidity with which they can be mobilized, fed from reserves, concentrated on any point, maintained in the field, they may be ranged in the following precedence:— First class — 1, Germany; 2, Austria; 3, Russia; 4, France. Second class—5, Italy; 6, England. Third class —7, Belgium; 8, Turkey; 9, Sweden and Norway;

10, Holland; 11, Denmark; 12, Spain; 13, Portugal; 14, Switzerland; 15, Greece. *Altogether four Armies* of the *first class*, *two Armies* of the *second*, *and nine Armies* of the *third*, *with, in round numbers*, a *paper strength* of *seven and a half millions* and a *combatant strength* of *five millions*, with 15,000 guns, and a million and a quarter of horses. In Navies, Great Britain is supreme; then come in their order—France, Russia, Turkey, Austria, Germany, Italy, Spain, Holland, Denmark, Sweden and Norway, and Portugal, with an aggregate total of 2039 vessels, of which 209 are ironclad, the whole being manned by some 280,000 men, and armed with 15,000 cannon. One hundred and ten ships of war are building in European dockyards, and of these 56 will be armour-plated, and the expenses incidental to these forces exceed £112,000,000 sterling per annum, of which fully three-fifths are devoted to the land forces. Of all these armaments, those of Turkey and Austria are maintained at the least cost—viz., at about £29 a year per man; that of Great Britain at the most—close upon £100 a year.—21*st June*, 1875.

Recruiting.

The Report by Major-General R. C. H. Taylor, Inspector-General of Recruiting, upon recruiting for the Regular Army for the year 1875 has been presented to Parliament. It states that the establishment of the Regular Army for the year 1875-6, as voted by Parliament, was 178,423 men, exclusive of officers, being very nearly the same strength as for the previous year 1874-5, but slightly in excess. As during the past twelve months the country has enjoyed peace, and there have been no exceptional circumstances to affect the condition of the Army, *a number of recruits equal to that raised in* 1874 *would have been sufficient to meet all requirements.* Such *number*, however, *has not been raised.* The number of men who have joined the service during the year 1875 is 18,494, as against 20,640 in 1874, and 17,194 in 1873. *There has consequently been a falling off* in the *numbers raised in the past year to the amount of* 2146 *recruits, as compared with* 1874 ; and the Army in the aggregate *is now* 897 *men below the establishment. No special reason can be assigned for this falling off, except* that *there was a good demand for labour,* and *that the rate of wages obtainable was high in comparison with the pay of a soldier.* The consequence is that the deficiency is noticeable in the Brigade of Guards and in the Royal Artillery for gunners, *both these arms of the service demanding men of a higher standard and of superior physique generally to the ordinary recruits.* The great care taken to insure a proper description of recruits, *upwards of* 5000 *of those offering for enlistment having been rejected* as ineligible, may also in some degree account for the diminution in numbers. The numbers raised for the Cavalry and Infantry of the Line have been sufficient to keep the regiments and brigades of those arms of the service up to the authorized establishments, the Cavalry of the Line having, on the 1st of January, 1876, supernumeraries to the amount of 356, and the Infantry 634. *The Colonial corps are in the aggregate 237 men below their establishments.* The Army Service Corps is complete to within four men, while the *Army Hospital Corps,* for *which special qualifications are required, is deficient* 61 *men.* No changes had been made in the system of recruiting, an account of which was given in the report submitted last year. *It only remains therefore to be stated* that whereas on the 1st of *January,* 1875, *there were* 33 Brigade Dépôts "formed" and *in full operation,* the number up to the present date has *been increased to* 37, showing an addition of four during the last twelve months. In the course of the present year it is anticipitated that in 11 more sub-districts the necessary buildings will be completed, making up the number of these establishments to 48 by the beginning of next year. The scheme *for carrying out the principle of local organization is thus annually becoming nearer completion,* and in the year 1878 the period will arrive when the system may receive a full and fair trial. *In analyzing the returns from the several sub-districts of the number* of the recruits raised within their respective limits, the results will be found to be very variable. In some sub-districts a number has been obtained considerably in excess of what was required to keep the linked battalions of the brigade up to their establishment, the surplus in such cases passing to other brigades in want of men. In certain others the supply has been about equal to the demand, *but in several sub-districts the deficiency has been very apparent, notably in counties on the seaboard and in remote parts of the United Kingdom.*

The degree in which localization has promoted recruiting is not easy to ascertain; but in one respect there has been a good result, inasmuch that in nearly all cases the Militia corps of the sub-districts have provided during or after the annual training a fair number of volunteers for the affiliated battalions of the Line. *Thus the men who have lately joined the Army have been procured in a greater proportion from the large towns and the great centres of population.* The recruits obtained *in towns and manufacturing districts may not be on the whole physically such eligible men as those raised from among the agricultural classes, yet they are stated be intellectually, and as regards educational attainments, superior.* It may be asserted that the recruits who have joined the Army during the past year, are, on the whole, of *a fairly good type, and of a somewhat better description than those raised in the previous two years.* It may be taken for granted that no system of conscription or compulsory service is likely to find favour in this country, and that, therefore, the principle of voluntary enlistment must continue in force; but, *in the present prosperous condition of the country as regards the rate of wages,* the existing advantages, direct and indirect, which together form the remuneration offered to a soldier, are evidently insufficient to attract to the ranks *men physically and intellectually suitable for service in sufficient numbers to supply our requirements. It is probable that as the system of localization becomes more perfect the Militia may be made one of the chief feeders of the Regular Army.* Already many excellent recruits are obtained from that source during or at the end of the annual training; and if a regular quota from each Militia regiment could be supplied for its affiliated Infantry Brigade, a great step in advance would be taken towards furnishing the number of recruits required under the short service system of enlistment. *It must be remembered, however, that the Militia force throughout the country is at present much below its authorized strength, and that recruits are enrolled in it at an earlier age and of a lower standard than the regulations for the Regular Army require.* It is consequently apparent that, *in order to carry out such measures as are here proposed, it would be necessary to alter or amend* the system upon which the Militia is now raised, so as to insure at every annual training a full complement on the rolls of each corps. The regiments of Militia Artillery might in like manner supply the requirements of the Royal Artillery.

As an additional means of furnishing the increased supply of recruits which it has been shown will in future be required, *it has been strongly urged that the practice of enlisting boys from the several industrial, district, union, and other schools shall be still further extended.* If authority were given for the enlistment of a larger number of boys in *excess of the establishment*, to be *retained* at the depôts or at their *present schools until they reached* the age of 17 or 18 years, *during which time they should attend to study, be instructed in trades, and thoroughly drilled, besides being put through a course of gymnastics, it is believed that a very valuable element would be introduced into the Army*, and that from this source many good non-commissioned officers especially would be obtainable, supplying thus a want from which many corps are now reported to suffer. *In order* to induce a *higher class of the community to* enter the service, *and to remain in it, it is suggested the prizes* of the profession *should be made more alluring;* and with this view it is very desirable that the dignity and emoluments of non-commissioned officers should be increased, and that all

16

ranks of that valuable and deserving class, from the Regimental Sergeant-Major downwards, including those holding lance rank, should receive more pay while serving, and possibly for those who complete their full term of 21 years a corresponding addition to pension on discharge. As regards desertion, the returns for the past year show a decided improvement, the number, which amounted in 1874 to 5,572, having fallen in 1875 to 4,382.—*7th March*, 1876.

DESERTION.—*Our soldiers desert at the rate of a strong company per week*, and *less than half surrender* or are *recaptured*. This *is a crying evil*, and the cause of its existence, as well as the best means of diminishing it, ought to be carefully inquired into. The obvious mode of procedure is, in the first place, to try and remove the causes. What the causes are could easily be ascertained by taking the evidence of private soldiers and referring to the reports of the Chaplain at Millbank.—*Army and Navy Gazette*, 4th February, 1878.

THE GREEKS IN THE TIME OF ARISTIDES. WHAT LED TO THEIR DEGENERACY?

Perhaps there never has been, making the necessary allowances for the age, so prosperous a nation as Greece at the time of Aristides. After becoming free from outward dangers, their energies were turned upon their interior advancement.

What, then, overthrew *that nation?* The cause could not be in the Government; no Government, however bad, could possibly have ruined, or even degraded, a people such as were the Aristidean Greeks. The cause of all the evils *lay in themselves.*

As *gains accumulated,* commerce was turned from its employment of *mutual support,* and followed chiefly as a means of procuring unlimited *prodigality* and *refined voluptuousness* of body *and intellect.* Acts that before had tended to gratify that thirst for the *beautiful* which so largely dwells *in every healthy mind,* in the course of time were prostituted before *growing sensuality* and *glittering depravity,* and were made the instruments for satiating the newly-kindling, fast-extending thirst for *costly superfluities* and all the *effeminate* luxuries *of the senses.* From *manly men,* the Greeks sank swiftly into *elegant machines,* the *mind gradually adopted a tone* of *bland oiliness,* and *Truth* was in every instance *sacrificed* to *conventional smoothness,* until a century after the heroic age of Miltiades and Aristides, we find them sunk so low as to fully warrant the remark that they had "become *a degenerate race; levity* and *indolence* had taken the place of *patriotism* and *honourable* ambition." See Dr. Vaughan's *Age of Great Cities,* page 32.

" Let that word *levity* be noted particularly," says another able writer, " it is of itself the key to the fall of Greece, and of every other empire, ancient, mediæval, or modern."

Soon this luxuriousness and levity began to show itself in their *literature.* Instead of revelling in the child-like *Samsonism* of the *Homeric* poetry, and the severe sublimity of the drama—*comicalities, personalities, buffooneries,* and even *obscenities,* formed the staple part of their popular compositions. The nation that could tamely submit to—nay, eagerly applaud—a man like Socrates being openly ridiculed on the stage, was already fast advancing towards its period of visible decay. But that was not all ; the very gods were *laughed* at. The stern old deities became legitimate subjects for wit and frivolous jestings. A *scepticism took possession of the people,* and the gods were *rendered nullities.* This did *not proceed from a conviction* of the *falsity* of *such gods;* had it done so, it would have been well (though surely a *cast-off faith of any kind, however unworthy,* should produce another tone of memory than that); on the contrary, they *were still, professedly, worshippers of their* old *deities.* Socrates was poisoned for *denying them,* and hecatombs were offered to the omnipotent powers, at the *very time when* half the city was *enjoying* the *ridicule* of their *peccadilloes and extravagant adventures.* A nation of men thus so *degenerate* from all *real manliness* required no evil government to accelerate its fall. It had the *sure* seeds of that fall deep sown and far-scattered *within itself.** That no Solon, no Lycurgus, no

---

* Here one is reminded of Byron's lines in " The Giaour— a Fragment of a Turkish Tale " :—

" 'Twere long to tell, and sad to trace
Each step from splendour to disgrace ;
Enough—no foreign foe could quell
Thy soul, till *from itself it fell ;*
Yes ! self-abasement paved the way
To villain-bonds and despot sway."

In the *Times* review, 2nd September, 1859, of Senior's *Turkey and Greece,* commencing thus :—

"We have to thank Mr. Senior for the most suggestive work that has yet appeared on the great Eastern Question. It is a question which the Crimean War rather opened than settled, and which is the *rock ahead* of European politics."

The following passages occur, worth heeding, at the present time especially :—

" Nearly all the violent crimes of Constantinople are due to the wine-shops and spirit-shops which *exist*, it is said, *only* because the English Government forces the Turks to submit to them. The Turkish law is something like the Maine Liquor Law ; it prohibits the sale of wine and spirits in retail. But, by the Treaty of Commerce negotiated by Lord Ponsonby, English subjects are entitled to full liberty of trade in Turkey, and *we* have interpreted this as giving them full liberty to trade in any manner whatever—let it even be in defiance of Turkish laws. Englishmen, for example, claim a right to open shops as tailors and shoemakers, though these trades in Constantinople are incorporated, and no *Turk, not* a member of the Corporation, can exercise them." " When we gave to you full liberty to trade in any manner whatever," say the Turks, " we meant *commerce,* not *retail* trade. We meant that you might bring us cloth or leather—not that you might be our tailors or shoemakers. We meant you to bring us wine and gin in barrels—not to open spirit-shops in breach of

lawgiver *earnestly bent* upon producing a code *intrinsically true,* and not *vitiated into conformity* with *the evil demands* of *the time*—that no such appeared, and that the State was corrupt, discordant, and *paralyzed* from *its imbecility* and *dividedness,* was but the natural result, and not in any way the *cause* of such degeneracy.

Every prodigal voluptuary, then—every elegant and *flippant conventionalist,* as he plunged deeper into his prodigality and BRILLIANT hollowness, added his share to the *final extinction* of the *prosperity of his race and nation.* This is not a new theory; it finds a place among others in many histories and essays, *but it is a* NEGLECTED *one.* Smothered and concealed too often by the *sensational solutions,* it is nevertheless one that *should not be neglected*—that should not be allowed to lie unnoticed, but perpetually *should be brought forward* prominently as the one great all-explaining fact; in no time so particularly as the present, when the root of all our errors and disasters is our

our religion and our laws, and to *corrupt and poison* our people."

* * * * * * *

"If it be true," says the reviewer, further on, " that *the love of money* is the *root of all evil,* it is in the corruption of the Turkish Government that one must seek the *true* source of the evils which afflict the empire. This corruption is universal among the holders of office, and is bad not only as *a cause,* but as *a sign of evil.* It shows that the *higher classes have lost their self-respect, despair of the future,* and grasp only at immediate and monetary advantages."

regarding *Government* as the cause of *all good and all evil*—as a *power*, as it were, *out of the nation* and working upon it; and not, on the contrary, as *the mere surface* of the great *social stream*, which flows on beneath its wave-broken gas-coloured breast, the *surface not influencing the waters underneath it*, but, *true* or *false*, *substance or shadow*, as the ceaseless *under-current* varies. Let us then ever remember that

   'Tis EDUCATION forms the common mind,
   Just as the *twig is bent the tree's inclined.*

Dr. Schimtz, in his *History of Rome* (p. 94), thus paints the character of the early Romans:— "Their character was more severe, and *warlike*, and *practical*, and *domestic duties* had more charms for them than the VOLATILE Greeks" (that is, the Greeks of the same age, then beginning to degenerate.) "Their domestic life was of the simplest kind." And Gibbon speaks thus of some characteristics of the *beginning* of their fall:— "They diligently practised the *ceremonies* of their fathers, devoutly *frequented the temples of their gods*. . . . They concealed the sentiments of an *atheist* under the *sacerdotal robes*. . . . Tacitus indulges an honest pleasure in the contrast of *barbarian* virtue with the *dissolute conduct* of the *Roman ladies*.

But the fall of empires is fast becoming an unknown thing, because empires have well-nigh ceased to be great in the ancient sense. If there be now one pre-eminent power answering in any way to Rome or Greece it is perhaps England. But hers is not a supremacy over enslaved tributary nations—a feudal domination. It is, or was, a power of a *moral* rather than a *physical description* —of the conquest of common sense and commercial skill, and not of belligerent aggression. Her supremacy consists in the *moral* weight she possesses, or did possess, among the other nations of the world. Instead of nations falling from their pride of place into the tributary subjects of a newer and more powerful race, crises—ruinous, terrible, prostrating, political, commercial, and social crises—are the forms in which such falls will for the proximate future be experienced."

LETTER BY AN OLD TORY, TO SIR HENRY PARNELL, AFTERWARDS LORD CONGLETON.

" A Letter to Sir Henry Parnell [afterwards Lord Congleton], showing the unsoundness of the doctrines laid down in his work on *Financial Reform*, and *proving* that *Free-trade will inevitably produce the ruin of the country*,' by ' an Old Tory'— was published in 1830, by ' Thomas Cadell, Strand,' and as experience is said to be the test of truth (to arrive at which is the sole object of the writer of these pages), it may be well to give the conclusion of the said letter.

"Now, Sir Henry Parnell, I ask you as a gentleman, have I not proved, *beyond the possibility of controversy*, that a *free-trade in corn would inevitably ruin the country*, and I expect, as a matter of course, you will admit, *that if our artizan* is obliged to *purchase his bread from the British farmer*, so also, *he* is entitled to demand that the British farmer shall be *obliged* to purchase *his manufactures*. No person with the slightest pretence to just feeling, can for a moment hesitate at making such an admission. But supposing that your belief in the tenets of free-trade be shaken, you will immediately say, what must we do? To make laws one year upon the principles of Free-trade, and in another upon those of prohibition, will unhinge all common transactions, and render us the scorn of our neighbours. My *answer is that if our rulers refuse to retrace their steps, when satisfied they are leading the country to certain destruction, they deserve to lose their heads for their vanity or their cowardice.* The truth is, this kingdom, for the last ten or twelve years ' (*i. e.* prior to 1830),' has been governed by no fixed principles. A succession of ephemeral ministers have appeared and vanished with unheard-of rapidity. It was the policy of former governments to foster *rising talent,* give it a proper bias, and thereby afford *permanence to their principles.* But during the long time Mr. Peel has been in power, whom has he brought into notice? He has acted upon the principle, that if the country is properly governed during this time, it is of no consequence what becomes of it afterwards; she may become a prey to any political adventurer, when he can no longer taste the sweets of power and office.

"We were just beginning to recover from that depressed state of commerce which was inevitable on the transition from war to peace, when every political quack insisted that his nostrum would more speedily recover us. There was Mr. Peel with his *Currency Bill*,* Mr. Huskisson with Free-trade, and poor Wilmot Horton with his Emigration panacea. I cannot but think this latter gentleman has been unfairly treated by his scheming brethren. While Mr. Peel was allowed to try the effect of his *Currency Bill, which has depreciated property from £20 to £30 per cent.;* while Mr. Huskisson was allowed to try his Free-trade theory upon the manufacturing population of the country, driving thousands to want and beggary; Mr. Horton only wanted a few millions to transport his fellow-citizens to other countries; only desired, in fact, to make this country a breeding-place for our colonies. His was by far the most innocent remedy, and therefore left untried.

"That retracing our steps will be productive of

---

* See Miscellanies, Nos. 1, 2.

confusion, and some injustice, is doubtless; but I firmly believe the country will suffer much less of both, by reverting to the ancient order of things than by continuing the present system. Something must be done. That those plans may be adopted which will best *uphold the real welfare of the country, is the sincere wish* of one who glories in the name and principles of an Ultra Tory, and remains, your most obedient servant,

"The Author."

Read by the light of the experience of the forty-six years since it was written, the letter is worthy of grave consideration, and the writer of these pages thinks himself fortunate in coming upon it, bound up with others on a variety of subjects.

THE FRENCH STATESMAN, BARON DUPIN, ALLUDES TO SIR R. PEEL IN REFERENCE TO HIS MEASURE OF 1846.

On the 5th March, 1859, that eminent French Statesman, Baron Dupin, read to the Senate the Report of the Commission in support of the Petitioners praying for the maintenance of the protecting Corn Laws. The Baron said—

"Sir Robert Peel, the celebrated Statesman, is deservedly noted as one of the most enlightened on the alliance of economic science with the prudent practice of Government. We must therefore take into great consideration the system he defended *so long as he remained master of himself*" (*sic* in original), "the system which he patronized in 1828, and which he maintained with so much eloquence when he was Prime Minister from 1842 to 1845. Sir Robert, gentlemen, defended the sliding scale. He proclaimed that system to be the only one applicable by turns, and without detriment to years of abundance and scarcity, when the figures are fixed with moderation. He denounced another combination which Lord John (now Earl) Russell particularly supported, that of a fixed duty—a duty raising with unintelligence, the price of bread in times of abundance as in times of scarcity, while the sliding scale then reduced to zero the protection which ceases to be necessary, and which when prolonged becomes odious.

Baron Dupin thinks that the British Constitution itself is endangered by the repeal of the Corn Law, of which the present (1859) cry for Reform is the *first* symptom. The Report concludes as follows:—

" We have the honour to propose for the petitions in question, the following recommendations which are required by *the greatness of the interests endangered.*

1. To the Minister of Commerce, because this

minister is also the Minister of Agriculture, and because he ought to cherish by the same title these two Breasts of the State *(les deux mamelles de l'état)*, as Henry the Great and his sage friend Sully used to call them.

2. To the Minister of War, because France has for its right arm Agriculture, and in *defending the labour of the soil he defends the force of the country*.

3. To the Minister of Marine, that he may tell us what perils, in case of a struggle at sea, might occur to the quarter or a third of France with foreign corn, if substituted for our unprotected and discouraged Agriculture.

4. To the Minister of the Interior, because the surety, the security, the affections of Agriculture form the security of the State; they are France and its life.

5. To the Minister of Finance, the necessary friend of Agriculture, and of the taxes it pays so well when it is happy, and even now (1859) " in spite of its sufferings, to him that he may defend the *primary* and *principal source* of all revenues, and the interesting legion of tax-payers, who are called in France 25,000,000 of men, women, and children disseminated in our rural districts."

In the year before this Report was read, the *Times* (1858) said:—

" France and Wheat Growing.

" The Minister of Commerce in a Report to the Emperor some time since, stated that not only had arable land become more fruitful from the better system of manuring employed, but that the extent of land sown with wheat had increased since 1846 a million of hectares (1,250,000 acres), and the yield gave an average augmentation of from ten to eighteen hectolitres."

The late Emperor, Napoleon III., who throughout his reign proved that he considered tillage and pasturage as the Foster-Mothers of the State, in a letter to the Minister of State dated " Palace of the Tuileries, January 5th, 1860," said :

5. Sec. " In that which relates to Agriculture you must make it share in the benefits of the Institutions of Credit, clear the forests situated in the plains, and replant the hills, devote annually a considerable sum to great works of drainage, irrigation and clearage. These works transforming the *uncultivated districts* into *cultivated lands will* enrich the *districts without impoverishing the State*, which *will cover* its *advance by the sale of a portion* of those *lands restored to Agriculture.*"

12. Sec. in letter:

" This extraordinary resource will facilitate to us not only the prompt completion of the railways, but it will also allow us to restore in less time our cathedrals, our churches, and WORTHILY to *encourage science, literature,* and *the arts.*"

Napoleon III. was doubtless well acquainted with Edmund Burke's works and remembered what he had written.

Statesmen before they valued themselves on the relief given to the people, by the destruction of their revenue, ought first to carefully attend to the solution of the problem—whether it be more advantageous to the people to pay considerably and to *gain in proportion*, or to gain *little* or *nothing* and to be disburdened of all contribution? My mind is made up to decide in favour of the first proposition. Experience is with me and I believe the best opinions also. To keep *a balance between* the *power of acquisition* on *the part* of the *subject*, and the demands he is to answer on the part of the State is a *fundamental* part of the skill of a true politician" (Burke's *Reflections on the French Revolution*).

From what was said in a leader in the *Times* of the 4th January, 1877, there is reason to fear that this "fundamental part of the skill of a true politician" was not duly heeded when the Free Imports Policy was introduced.

" The experience of the last quarter," says the *Times*, " was the natural sequel of the quarters which preceded it. We have been passing through a year of sluggish trade, of limited productions, and of *diminished profits*. There has been no elasticity in the Revenue, and the Christmas quarter has even shown *a decline.*" . . . . Will the receipts between this time and the end of March be sufficient to satisfy the necessities of Sir Stafford Northcote and give a promise of equilibrium in the next year? There is at least one significant fact that makes us hesitate to answer this question as we could wish. The yield from the Income Tax in the last nine months has been £1,273,000. against £1,287,000. in the corresponding months of the preceding year—a decline of £11,000. . . . An examination of the returns of the several quarters leads to the conclusion that there has been *more difficulty in collecting arrears in* 1876 than there was in 1875; and a larger proportion will be abandoned, while the effect of the increase from 2*d* to 3*d* has not been sufficient to counterbalance this loss. This conclusion is important in its bearing on our prospects in the present quarter. A greater difficulty in collecting arrears means a diminished productiveness in the Income Tax in the current year, and the Chancellor of the Exchequer cannot rely with any confidence on getting in the four millions which he requires between this and the 1st of April to make up the estimated Revenue under this head. The returns thus confirm the lesson of every-day experience, that 1876 has been a year of straitened incomes. Is not the same lesson taught by the figures of Customs and Excise receipts? Diminished receipts from the Income Tax imply *diminished profits* for Manufacturers and Traders, and where profits are diminished wages are almost certain to be diminished also."

What wrote the late Canon (the Rev. Charles) Kingsley?

"We have sold ourselves to a system which is its own punishment. And yet the last place in which a man will look for the cause of his misery is in that new money-mongering to which he now clings as frantically as ever. But so it is throughout the world. Only look down over that bridge-parapet, at that huge black-mouthed sewer vomiting its pestilential riches across the mud. There it runs and will run, hurrying to the sea vast stores of wealth *elaborated by Nature's chemistry* into the ready materials of food—there it runs, turning them all into the seeds of pestilence, filth, and *drunkenness*. How can it be wondered, if the appetites of those who live in the midst of such scenes, sickened with filth and *self-disgust*, crave after the gin-shop for temporary strength and then for temporary forgetfulness? Every London doctor knows this—would that every *Preacher* would tell that truth from his pulpit!

"But are not pestilences a judgment on the rich in the truest sense of the word? Are they not the broad unmistakeable seal to God's opinion of a state of society which confesses its economic relations to be so utterly rotten and confused that it actually cannot afford to save yearly millions of pounds-worth of materials of food, not to mention thousands of human lives? Is not every man who allows such things *hastening* the ruin of the society in which he lives by helping to foster the indignation and fury of its victims? Look at that group of stunted haggard artizans—what if one day they should call to account the landlords whose covetousness and ignorance make their dwellings hells on earth?"

So wrote the late Rector of Eversley, to whose widow thanks are due for the two very interesting volumes she has given us of "his Letters and Memories of his Life."

An Extract, not uninteresting, read in relation to "The Eastern Question."

The following, which appeared in the *Times* of the 14th September, 1859, under the head of "The Ionian Islands, from our special Correspondent," acquires, at the present time, renewed and perhaps greater interest than at the time it first appeared.

"The alarming state of the Ottoman Empire, which country seems going through a *succession of financial summersaults*, from which however, somehow or other, it manages to alight with only *an additional confusion*, renders the accounts from *the Provinces truly deplorable;* extra taxes have been levied on the unfortunate population, to be redeemed by the *imports of future years*, while hoardes of Albanian Irregulars render the province bordering on Greece insecure, and expose the *poor* inhabitants to *every species of extortion* and injustice. It is not to be wondered at that the old feeling of hatred to the Turkish yoke, which dates from the day that Mahomet II. took possession of Byzantium, should be as much alive as ever. The Christians are replacing everywhere in the East, by a constant and unperceived effort, the Mahomedans, who are disappearing, and under these circumstances, those of the Christian elements which offer some guarantee for *the future*, must naturally attract the attention of Europe. Owing to their religion, the Christian population of the East consider themselves specially placed *under the protection of Russia, and the influence of that power with the Greeks* has been *generally considered all-powerful*. This feeling *was confirmed in* 1854; when, at the commencement of the Crimean war, the Greeks crossed the Turkish frontiers and invaded Epirus, *espousing the cause of Russia,* and attacking Turkey, the ally of England and France—a movement which led to the occupation of Greece by the Western powers. The later demonstration of Athens in favour of France, consequent upon the successes in the cause of Italian nationality, however, go far to show that the sympathies of the Greek people are, in reality, ever strongest with that power from which they at the time hope for more aid towards the emancipation of their countrymen from the Turkish yoke."

Mr. Bright at the Rochdale Working Men's Club, on 2nd January, 1877, and The Origin of the Corn Laws.

In an address delivered by Mr. Bright at the "Rochdale Working Men's Club," on the 2nd January last (see *Times* of the 3rd) in eulogizing the "Unrestricted Competition Policy," he seems to allude to the Corn-Law of 1815, as the *first* ever enacted. He said, "he (Ebenezer Elliott, the Corn-Law Reformer) knew, everybody knew, who comprehended the character and operation of that law, that if it should have continued to afflict the people as it did through *thirty years of its existence*, there was no institution in the country, not even its venerable monarchy, that could stand the strain that law would bring to bear upon it." Had Mr. Bright possessed a copy of Dirom's excellent but little known work on the Corn-Laws, he would have known that the origin of the Corn-Laws dates back *to* 1393, and the following extract will show that they have operated favourably for *national* prosperity.

"We find that the origin of the Corn-Laws dates back to 1393. This law, confirmed in 1413, reserves to the King in Council, a power to restrain exportation. In 1463, from *grievous damage to farmers and occupiers by import* of foreign grain, it was *prohibited until prices exceeded certain* rates. [This was just what the law of 1815, called the Sliding Scale, did]. In 1562, exportation was allowed in ships *owned by English-born subjects.* This *Act was the dawn* of the *Navigation Laws.**

"The encouragement given by Protection, made England and its agriculture flourish to such a degree as to *cheapen* food, so as to enable much surplus corn to be exported. In 1750, no less than 1,667,776 *quarters were exported,* and in ten preceding years 8486 quarters.

"In 1773-4, the system was revised and improved as to export, *regulating it by average prices;* and the capability of England to increase growth to any degree—if *duly protected*—was satisfactorily proved. The *direct contrary must arise from improper laws.*

"During that prosperous period of Agriculture, the result was that labourers and manufacturers, &c., had their bread at a very cheap rate.

"The reverse was the case when the country was opened to foreign grain by injudicious duties or restrictions on our produce. Our farmers were dispirited—very much soil lay uncultivated—*the prices rose very high,* and *population was restrained.*

"But when not only restrictions were removed but bounties were given on the export of surplus by the Acts of 1668 and 1700, the happiest effects

---

* See "Defence of the Navigation Laws," p. 271.

were immediately experienced; these laws acted like magic; our agriculture immediately arose as from the dead. Population increased, and instead of eating *foreign* bread, *people were maintained at a lower rate than ever before known*—the kingdom increased in riches and *strength*—our shipping increased—and a state of prosperity continued for above half a century after the Union of England and Scotland.

"No sooner, however, was importation again encouraged, than our agriculture languished, and exportation declined. Prices again rose, and the nation became dependent on foreign grain, *raised by foreign capital and untaxed industry*, to the detriment of the Industrial classes of the British Nation.

"From the experience of several hundred years we have found that the *principle of protective* Corn-Laws is *calculated to promote the improvement of our land*, and to raise all the *produce our soil and climate admit* of. This is only attainable through securing a certain and steady market to the farmers — both by preventing importation and encouraging export, giving bounties when abundance affords a surplus above our requirement— thus ensuring a ready vent for our superabundant stock in foreign countries."

"It is not enough to raise sufficient food for national consumption—*more* should be raised so as to afford plenty in *bad* seasons; and the annals of the country ought to be distinguished by a greater or less exportation, *but on no account ought we* to be *reduced to apply to foreign countries* for an *expensive* and *precarious* relief. (So thought Sir Robert Peel in 1842)."

" The effect of lowering duties on Barilla has been ruinous to the Scotch islanders, who, by the manufacture of Kelp, in a great measure supplied the soap manufactures of this country."

The Real Sinews of War.

In a work of great ability and evincing deep reflection, entitled, *The Strength of Nations*,* it is said:—

" Since the publication in 1776, of Adam Smith's immortal work on the ' Wealth of Nations,' the *wealth* of nations has, in this country at least, *engaged so much attention*, that but little has been left for another quality of nations—their *strength;* without which their wealth, with all its advantages may be of little use, *since it may be destroyed* at *any time* with *fearful rapidity.* There appears to be a time in the history of all powerful nations at which, while *their wealth* goes on increasing, their *strength begins to decline*, till—to use the words of Bacon—it comes to that, that not the

* *On the Strength of Nations*, by Andrew Bissett, M.A., and of Lincoln's Inn, Barrister-at-law. London : Smith, Elder & Co, 65, Cornhill, 1859."

hundredth poll will be fit for a helmet; and so there will be great population and *little strength.*" *

And it is also well to bear in mind another remark of Bacon in the same Essay: " Neither is money the sinews of war (as it is trivially said), where the *sinews of men, arms* in *base* and *effeminate* people are failing; for Solon said well to Crœsus (when in ostentation he showed him his gold): 'Sir, if any other comes that hath *better iron* than you, he will be master of this gold.' As soon as this current has fairly set in, unless its course can be arrested—which is a difficult if not an impossible operation—the decay of that nation has commenced, and will continue till the time arrives when its strength is made greater for its defence, and its wealth becomes the prey of an invader."

Dr. Russell who was the *Times'* " own correspondent " during the Civil War in America in 1862 (and was also during H.R.H. the Prince of Wales's late tour through India, and which he has happily published), writing from " New York, Jan. 14, 1862," said:—

" I am, I may be permitted to say, by no means a believer in the omnipotence of gold or credit *in war*. The sinews of War cannot be of much avail unless there is *heart, brain,* and *bone* to give them force, direction and leverage. France has

---

* *Essay on the True Greatness of Kingdoms and Estates.*

proved it, old Fritz demonstrated it long ago, England in the midst of her millionnaire extravagance showed it, the history of all nations fighting for honour, liberty and life, has recorded it. But there is a time, when the *saying* is true, and *that time may arrive when the love of gain is greater than the love of country*, and *when the only army that lives* and moves *and has its being* in the field when the *country* calls for *help*, is the whole *army* of contractors."

This was written probably in relation to America, but other nations may well take warning from it.

Lord Overstone on the Results of Invasion.

16 *June*, 1860.

The following extract from the replies of Lord Overstone to queries put to him by the Commissioners of National Defences will have much interest for our readers:—

"2. Question 2 asks my opinion of the probable effects of the occupation of London by an invading army, — books, security, and public property having been previously removed, and private property being respected by the invader.

"I cannot contemplate or trace to its consequences such a supposition. My only answer is, it must never be. In proportion as a country has advanced in civilization, and in commercial and manufacturing prosperity, the metropolis of that country becomes more and more intimately connected with all the operations and interests of the whole community; it becomes the centre, the heart of the entire social and industrial system. The movements of the central city become connected by an indefinite number of the most delicate links with the daily transactions of every town in the empire. *Ruere illa non possunt et non hæc eodem labefactata motu concidant.*

"An invading army occupying London will be in possession of the centre of our Governmental system, the centre of internal communication, the centre in which a large proportion of the transactions of the whole country is daily adjusted, the centre of our financial system; and, as Woolwich must of course be included in the fate of London, the enemy will hold the great dépôt of our military resources. Can any doubt exist as to the effects of this?

"But the enemy will respect private property, and will endeavour to allay alarm, to restore confidence, to obviate confusion, and to give to his presence the character of a purely military occupation. What, it is asked in question 5, will be the results of this?

"I believe that in the case supposed there would exist a prevalent feeling that the fatal blow had been struck; that the deep humiliation had been sustained; that the means of satisfying his exactions are under the command of the enemy; that the means of further and effectual resistance are doubtful, while the calamities attending it are certain and overwhelming. Under these circumstances, many, no doubt with a noble spirit, would counsel determined and persevering resistance at all hazards and under any sacrifice; but many would deem such courage to be recklessness, and would think the time come for bending under the blow, and that no rational alternative remains but that of purchasing the withdrawal of the enemy upon the best terms that could be obtained. Which of these conflicting views would prevail I cannot undertake to determine.

"The efforts, however, of a country thus humiliated, paralyzed, dispirited, and divided in opinion, would not, I fear, lead to any satisfactory result.

"The *safety of the country*, as much *as its honour*, requires that the *integrity of the empire be defended on the* sea *principally*, and in *the first instance;* and *in case* of any serious mishap *there, we* must be *prepared to* fight the battle upon *the first inch of ground upon which* a foreign foe sets his hostile foot. *Our riches, the complicated nature of our social and monetary system, the limited extent of our country, the necessity of internal order and confidence for the maintenance of our manufacturing population, would I fear be found to* render *a prolonged conflict upon our own soil perhaps impracticable*, at all events fatal to all that constitutes the power, the wellbeing, and the happiness of the country.

"3. A *serious apprehension of invasion*, still more the actual landing of an invading army in force, would, I apprehend, *necessitate the immediate suspension of specie payments by the Bank of England;* this *would be followed by* the *prevalence of monetary alarm, partaking more or less, according to circumstances, of the* character *of panic. Money* would *be withdrawn from savings banks, from country banks, from all parties holding money at call. To meet* these *demands Government securities* must *be brought* to *market in unusual quantities* at a *time when the credit* of the *Government would be shaken,* and the *disposition to* invest *in Government securities* would *from the same cause* be *seriously checked.* The *consequence is obvious;* a *heavy* fall in *the price of public securities,* a *prostration of public credit,* and grievous inconvenience, *amounting not improbably to the absolute* suspension *of the usual course* of *monetary operations.*

" In *this country the use of money is economized by various complicated expedients to an extent infinitely greater than in any other country.* The *efficiency of these* expedients *depends upon the undisturbed state of* social order and public *confidence;* they would be *at once paralyzed* by any serious *invasion of the country. More money would be required for the purposes of circulation when more money could not be had; and the existing amount of money would* be *rapidly secreted for safety. Money, and the substitute* for *money, credit,* would *disappear simultaneously.* To what extent would this go? No man can say beforehand. *But these results would be more disastrous in England than* in *any other country,* on *account of the complicated character of our monetary arrangements, which renders* the whole *system peculiarly sensitive to any movement tending* to *produce disorder or discredit.*

4. The fourth question directs attention to the effect which an invasion of England may be expected to produce upon the prosperity of other countries, and the strong reaction which it is supposed this might cause against the author of the aggression.

"I cannot doubt that the consequences of any blow inflicted upon the prosperity of England would be felt, and seriously felt, through every quarter of the globe to which trade and commerce have penetrated. A large portion of the productive energies of the world are sustained by British capital and British credit. *Look at our annual exports amounting* to *about* 100,000,000 *of sterling value.* This *indicates the* extent *to which other countries* derive the supply *of their necessaries or their luxuries* from *British industry. Look again at our annual imports, swelling to the same amount, and thus showing the extent to which other countries find a market for their products in British prosperity.* The country from which these gigantic transactions emanate cannot be seriously injured without disastrous consequences to every country which directly or indirectly has held intercourse with her. Such is the beneficent law of international commercial intercourse; all trading countries have a common interest in the progressive prosperity of their neighbours, and no doubt can be entertained that the effects of a blow which an invasion of England would inflict upon our commercial prosperity must vibrate through the whole trading world. But these effects will be very slightly estimated by anticipation; it is only after the fatal occurrence other nations will fully recognize the extent to which their interests are involved in the well-being of this country. *Our safety must in no degree be left dependent upon the precarious and tardy sympathy of other countries.* The *aid to be derived from this source* will *arise after the evil has been consummated.* With ourselves alone must rest the defence of our country.

" We have every *inducement to* make our system of national defence complete and effectual, because the calamities and misery which a successful invasion of England must produce would be far more serious than any of which the world has yet had experience."

Defence of the Navigation Laws.

To the Right Hon. Wm. Ewart Gladstone, M.P.

Forfar, *June* 6, 1848.

My dear Son, William—

Last evening I had read to me the speech you delivered in the House of Commons on Friday last, in favour of the repeal of the Navigation Laws. I think your facts are fairly stated, but your *conclusions*, drawn from them, I cannot admit to be generally *just* in *principle* or well-founded.

It appears to me that in your attempt to justify and defend a general principle founded on the *modern* notions of free trade—which implies a desire to *concede* existing *rights*, because it is in the present day *called liberal* to do so—you work yourself into a labyrinth from which you can only escape by the undue *sacrifice* of certain rights and privileges which are possessed by and belong to us, and for which, if given up, I cannot discover that we are to receive in return any due and just consideration. Hitherto the discussion of those interests has *been confined to national treaties*, and those *founded* on *Reciprocity*, where there was to be a *quid pro quo* to be the principle, that an *equitable consideration* was to be *conceded* to us *in lieu of it;* but you propose to abandon rights *which have been* proved by *experience to be natural, and nationally important* and valuable. When the Governments of two countries meet to decide these interesting subjects, the one proposes to the other to relinquish certain branches of their trade by laying them open under treaty, *with the understanding* that those with whom they treat possess *similar advantages* which they are to relinquish. Thus let us suppose that the United States propose that if we will consent to admit the produce of the Brazils or of France to be imported into this country in American bottoms, subject only to such conditions as are required when these importations are made in British bottoms, to make us in return similar concessions in favour of British shipping employed in carrying on a similar trade between the Brazils and France and the ports of the United States.

Here then is a clear principle of reciprocity adopted, a *quid pro quo*, which being acted upon, draws nearer, and into closer intercourse and connection, those countries that agree *to make* such *concessions to each other*, and is, therefore, likely to prove for their mutual benefit; but such concessions can only be special and founded on Treaty—they cannot, without the risk of great sacrifices, be admitted or acted upon under such general principles and practice as you propose to adopt. Thus for instance we have very *extensive Colonies* and foreign possessions (many of them earned at a cost of British blood and treasure and thus considered to be achieved by conquest, though now, I lament to think, *likely to be rendered valueless to us* by the present measure of our rulers) with which an intimate and constant intercourse is maintained and carried out in British shipping, productive of *important advantages* to Britain and British ship owners. If I understand you right, you propose to lay open this carrying trade to the shipping of other countries—for instance to *the United States.* Now it does happen that the United States possess neither Colonies nor Foreign possessions, and therefore have no such privileges to offer to us in return or to concede. It therefore follows *there can be no reciprocity* in such a course of conduct no *quid pro quo*, but *all the advantages*, whatever they may be, to be given up by us *without a consideration.* You contend that, in such a case, our *Colonists* have a choice of conveyance, some of them, perhaps, on lower terms than by *British* shipping, are willing to adopt them, and would reap the advantage. If this *principle* is to be *recognized* and acted upon, do *you not* at once *lay* the axe to *the root* of the tree *out of which have grown the sources of our Commerce,* our wealth, and our *maritime greatness?* By laying them open, you propose to abandon to others the sources which support the superiority we have hitherto possessed in our ships, our colonies, and commerce, the sources of envy and jealousy to other countries. You say, that if you do so, in return we shall confer advantages on our colonies; as, for instance, you suppose a German ship carries emigrants from Germany to Australia, and on her arrival there the Colonists should have the power of loading their wool or other produce and through such foreign channel conveying it to a British market. If such a concession were to be made, the benefit to the *Colonist* would only be incidental and unimportant. But whilst the transport of their produce is restricted to British shipping the certainty of their finding employment secures the necessary supply on which the Colonist may depend ; but if laid equally open to the foreigner, they with such competition, can have no dependence on finding employment; thus, between the two stools, whilst you propose to benefit the Colonist, you risk his being left without the means of sending his wool to market.

But this is only a secondary consideration. We have at a great expense established and settled our *Colonies;* we have given them privileges, protection, and admission to our markets of consumption for their produce, on conditions advantageous to them—concessions all calculated to promote an union and intercourse alike *beneficial to both*, but which, under your propositions, are to be *abandoned and thrown open to the world*, whilst that *world*, caring *only for itself*, makes no *optional contribution* in *return towards raising our enormous* revenue—defraying or providing for our sources of taxation, local and general, or supporting our systems, institutions, or *habits of industry*, labour, expenditure, and consumption. These are wholly local and depend upon ourselves; whilst you propose, with a *hand of vast and liberal profusion*, to lay open every source we possess, or advantage we enjoy, to the free and open competition of others, who, so far as I can discover, while we are to part with *substantial* good, have nothing to give, or even to offer us in return.

If I understand you right, you are also disposed to lay open our coasting-trade to the foreigner, which certainly, in many instances, would be not only gratuitous, but without *pretence* to reciprocity. The principle of reciprocity might be urged by the United States, if she proposed to us to admit British shipping to participate in carrying on their coasting-trade, provided the same privileges were conceded by us to American shipping in the coasting-trade of the United Kingdom. If such an uncalled-for, unnatural, and inconvenient concession, with a sacrifice of local feeling, was to be made, I can discover no serious advantage it would be productive of to the interests of either party, whilst it would be found to prove a source of great *jealousy* and risk of misunderstanding.

But come nearer home, and let us suppose that the excess of shipping belonging to the ports of Hamburgh and Bremen, built and fitted equally well with British shipping, though at a *much lower cost*, navigated and provisioned on more favourable terms, and now spread over the ocean and advantageously employed in the *commerce of the world*, which seems rather a favourite object of yours. I say that if these bottoms from the opposite coast were to be employed in our coasting trade—let us suppose that great branch of it, carrying the supply of coals from Newcastle and its neighbourhood to supply the consumption of fuel by near two millions of our population residing in London and its vicinity, employing many hundred sail of British ships, and many thousand of British seamen; suppose the trade laid equally open to the shipping of Hamburgh and Bremen, what have they to give us in return? I answer nothing, literally nothing; for they have neither coast nor coasting-trade of any kind or description. Yet in this *mania* of liberality you, with others, appear disposed to make such *vast and uncalled-for sacrifices*. You may say that what we give up is to be occupied by others, but that the general trade and commerce of the country is to be extended and increased by it. That may be true, but the concessions and sacrifices are to be ours— *the gains and advantages are to be given to others;* whilst this country, raised to power and eminence by the advantages of situation, united with *well-regulated* liberality in our intercourse with others, but *with a due regard* to our own interests, supported by the wisdom of laws and institutions, has gained a pre-eminence in the affairs of the world, which these *new-fangled doctrines* and theories are calculated to undermine and ultimately to overthrow, but which I would fain hope, by hastening a change of both men and measures, may be preserved to us unchanged.

These novel theories and *dangerous experiments* with which our legislation now teems bring to my recollection a favourite toast of a very old and respected, but a too liberal friend of mine, now no more, Mr. Thomas Booth, a well-known merchant in Liverpool. His toast was, " May the world be our country, and doing good our religion "— *sentiments beautiful in the abstract*, but totally incapable of application to the conduct and habits of mankind in their relations with each other. But in the proposed mode of re-casting and liberalizing our Navigation Laws, I think I see an attempt to introduce and act upon such impracticable doctrines. God in His wisdom instilled into the breast of man *self-preservation* as *the first* law in his nature ; but our rulers, in the present day, seem disposed to give it only the *second* place. Once lay open our colonial possessions and coasting-trade to the shipping and seamen of other powers, I ask, where is your *boasted nursery* that has hitherto manned your navy and *protected your shores?* If they are to be laid open, and passed into the hands of foreigners, who, in place of being our *friends*, may prove to be our inveterate enemies, and if we shall thus be *cultivating the means and engines for* our *future destruction,* what then is to become of your justly-boasted wooden walls?

You are aware that I am at present confined by indisposition, and that I dictate this letter from my bed by the pen of a third party. I am conscious you will find it abounds with errors and imperfections, yet, notwithstanding now in my eighty-fourth year, as a last duty, and perhaps tribute to the interests of my country, I give it to the public, and send it for that purpose to the columns of the *Standard,* from whence it may perhaps find its way to more general circulation.

I am, ever your affectionate Father,
JOHN GLADSTONE.

SIR STAFFORD NORTHCOTE ON THE CONSOLIDATION OF THE EMPIRE.

Since the foregoing pages were sent to the press the writer of them was greatly rejoiced to read in the *Times* of Friday the 7th December, the following in a speech singularly happy and able for the occasion, made by the Chancellor of the Exchequer at a dinner given to him by the County of Devon at Exeter, at which both Liberals and Conservatives united to do him honour.

Sir Stafford Northcote said: " At the present

time I need not say to you that England requires in *every possible way* to *strengthen herself* and to consolidate her power. I am not one of those who take a gloomy view of the *possible* future; at the same time it is impossible for any man who is in any way or degree charged with the conduct of public affairs *not* to take a somewhat anxious view, and I believe myself that the true safety of England, the true line to follow for the *preservation of the Empire* which *has been bequeathed* to us, and for its *strengthening* and *development, is not so much fear and jealousy* of others, as a determination to *strengthen and consolidate power within ourselves* . . I do not say that we are to *extend* the *physical limits* of our Empire to a great extent beyond the point at which they already stand, but *I say this*, that for the *consolidation of our power*, for the *knitting together of our great Colonial and Indian Empire with the Mother-Country at home*, there is an *enormous amount of work to be done,* and it is to the doing of the work and doing it *fairly,* that I look for the *salvation* of the greatness and continued prosperity of this Empire."

The excellent and hard-worked Chancellor of the Exchequer, who

"Smiles without art, and wins without a bribe,"

having wisely reminded us of the "*enormous amount of work to be done* in *knitting together* our great *Colonial and Indian Empire*," it has occurred to the writer of these pages that the carrying out of the scheme, or something like it, named in a printed letter sent to him by a friend a year or two since, might perhaps well be allowed to form part of that "enormous work." Such a scheme, if wisely worked, and judiciously extended from time to time in the Colonies, might aid alike the material and spiritual interests of the people. It would, too, afford strong proof (at present rather deficient) on the part of the Mother-Country, that she *does* " respond " to the requirements and the " distant sympathies of her Colonies," and the scheme, viewed in this light, would lead to a stronger bond of union between them than the pursuit of *mere material interests alone could do*. At all events, the letter deserves as wide a circulation as can be given to it.

> Benevolence is like the generous sun,
> Whose free *impartial splendour fosters all* :
> It is the radiance of the human soul,
> The proof and sign of ITS *Celestial Birth*.

MISSIONARY COLLEGES.

" HENFIELD, *August* 1, 1873.

" Dear Sir,—The large and rapidly increasing number of boys, from all stations in society, now under training in the several Schools of St. Nicholas College has directed the mind of the Society to the enquiry whether it would not be possible for such a body, to contribute an important instalment to the cause of Missions both at home and abroad.

"The Missionary labour of the world has fallen chiefly upon this small island, and I believe, in point of money, we of the Church of England have contributed more to this cause, than the whole of the rest of Christendom. But no exertions hitherto made are at all equal to the necessities of the case, and it will be obvious to those who have considered the subject, that other means, besides those already existing, must be used, if we are to meet the wants of our times. When we consider the extent of the field, and the thousands of labourers required at this moment to occupy it, we are at a loss to conceive how it can be dealt with. If we looked to man only we should despair, but to faith all things are possible. The greatest obstacle can be removed by an earnest and never-flagging faith, and we may not question the ability of the Church of England to occupy that place, which God, in His providence has assigned her.

"I have no intention at this time of writing in favour of Missions, but I wish to ask you if you do not think that our Society could largely help the general cause by some such scheme as the following, viz.:—That we should have attached to St. Saviour's School, Ardingly, a College for Missionaries, as we have at St. John's, Hurstpierpoint—a College for Commercial Schoolmasters, and

"1. That boys from any of our Schools should

be eligible as candidates for this department, removing when approved to the Mission College.

"2. That the diet table at the Mission College should be the same as the one used for the St. Saviour's School.

"3. That the College should be made nearly or quite self-supporting, and that the general scale of payments should be as follows:—

"Accepted Candidates from St. Saviour's, Ardingly, and other schools of that grade—£15 per annum.

"Accepted Candidates from St. John's, Hurst, and other schools of that grade—£20 per annum.

"Accepted Candidates from St. Nicholas, Lancing, and other schools of that grade—£25 per annum. And that a few exhibitions be founded to relieve the needy among them.

"4. That persons on becoming members of the Mission College engage to place themselves in the hands of the College as to their future destination and employment.

"5. That the object of their joining shall be to promote the spread of the Gospel at home and abroad, either as Clergymen, Catechists, and Schoolmasters; or as Scholars devoted to literary pursuits; or if need be, as Architects, Builders, and Mechanics.

"6. That for the sake of the latter class of persons, the College should have attached to it workshops, and teach the candidates trades.

" 7. That no candidate be received who has not been, for one year at least, a pupil in some school belonging to the Society, nor then until he shall have reached fifteen years of age.

" 8. On being accepted, he shall remain one year as a probationer, and then if approved, continue three years or more a student, so as in no case to pass his final examination before he is twenty.

" 9. Having passed, he shall be considered as an Associate of the College, and his payments to the College shall cease; and where he can be employed, he shall receive a stipend.

" 10. Associates thus prepared and qualified, shall be eligible and bound, either to teach at home in the schools of the Society, at a fixed and sufficient salary, or to go out to the colonies or other dependencies of the British Crown or elsewhere as Missionaries, Schoolmasters, Catechists, or in any other capacity which the Society may determine for them.

" 11*. That the *Society shall purchase land*, and otherwise make arrangements for settling such Associates in the colonies, or in places to which it shall send them; and that their place of settlement shall be called and shall be a College. That is to say, it shall be a Society, with an authorized, and

* This rule might in necessary cases be applied at home, and bodies formed as precursors of our large centres of education.

responsible head, holding the lands and other property in trust for the common good.

" 12. That the Principal shall be a clergyman, and that all the fellows and members of the Society shall be in communion with the Church of England, and that the Bishop of the Diocese shall, if he be willing, be visitor.

" We believe that by a scheme of this sort, much might be done for our colonies, and for India—much for the emigrants, especially for those who have been educated at our schools, and generally for the spread of the Gospel, by teaching, direct and indirect.

" Our plan of settling Societies would bear some resemblance to that adopted by the Moravians. We should purchase land where it could be had cheap, but as near to the large towns as possible. The lay members of the Society might cultivate this for the general good—others would keep schools or work on trades, and others again would be clergymen, and place themselves in the hands of the Bishop. The architects and mechanics might build the College with their own hands, and would above all things provide a fit chapel in which the services might be daily said, as in our cathedrals at home. If they settled near a town how great a help would it be to the ordinary missionary, while to young men from England, the brothers or friends of the members of the College, the good would be inestimable, and tend to keep our emigrants from being a disgrace to the mother country. This would certainly be one of the special advantages of having a large portion of the members of the College of the same class as the emigrants themselves,—and moreover, as these Colleges would, from time to time, be replenished with new members from home, and also from among the natives or colonists who may be educated by them, they would form nurseries to supply regular missionaries, and afford retreats for the worn and exhausted missionary when he needed a rest or a change.

" I confine this paper to as few lines as possible, and it is only put out as a feeler, to discover how far it may prove acceptable to those whom God has blessed with a missionary spirit, and also to ascertain the opinions of parents on the subject in case any of them should entertain the hope of giving a son to the service of religion. It may be as well to add an explanation on one or two points.

" 1. I propose the St. Saviour dietary because, if people are to be of any use as missionaries they must start with, and retain afterwards plain and inexpensive habits. They must lay aside, too, all pride of birth and station, and seek only to surpass others in goodness and learning. And because, if they will content themselves with this diet table of abundant and wholesome food, we may train missionaries by thousands instead of hundreds, and give them many more years education without calling for any large amount of public charity, as most of the parents can find such a sum as £15 or £20 a year; especially if aided in necessary cases with small exhibitions, say of from £2 to £5 a year.

"2. It must however be remembered that a Mission Fund would be needed for several purposes such as for the purchase of land; outfit, perhaps, and passage money; a professor or two beyond the ordinary masters of the school; scholarships, and exhibitions; a foreman to workshops, &c. But all this would be a mere trifle compared with the usual cost of missions.

"This opportunity appears to me a great opening, and my belief is that we shall find the boys from St. Saviour's School—many of whom have relations and friends in the colonies—glad to devote themselves to this work, and that they will prove, in not a few instances, the fittest agents we could get. Will you, therefore, be so kind as seriously to think this matter over, and to let me have a letter from you, stating your opinion on the subject?

"Believe me, dear Sir,
"Faithfully yours,
"N. Woodard,
"*Provost of St. Nicholas College, Lancing.*"

To the Editor of the " Times."

Sir,—My attention has been drawn to a letter in the *Times* of Wednesday, under the above heading, which very properly emphasizes afresh the evidence of the genuine British feeling of our Colonies afforded by the subscription of South Australia to the Indian Famine Fund.

Allow me, however, to protest against the latter part of this same letter. *There is a large and widening circle of the home public taking a vivid interest in matters colonial. The Royal Colonial Institute is but the outward* sign of the fact *that the rapid growth of our Colonies is inevitably thrusting to the front their importance as integral parts of the Empire;* and, considering their far distance, and the fact that they are creations of yesterday, with no past to be set out in histories, with a present in "perpetual flux," and a future of probable surprises, *it is matter of congratulation that so much definite public interest should be centred in so puzzling a subject.*

But to those numerous Englishmen, both in England and in the Colonies, who are regarding our fast-growing Empire with feelings of sanguine hope or puzzled apprehension, it is distressing to read the remarks of " B. L.," put forward with all the apparent emphasis of well-founded authority. Australasia, he remarks, " is generally spoken of as Australia, whereas Australasia is nearly as large as Europe, and is divided into separate States, with laws almost as distinct, with feelings and tastes certainly as different as those of Spain and Russia." Were this the case, farewell once and for all to every hope, or, indeed, rational prospect of a continuance of *the integrity of the Empire*. But to say of the different Colonies of Australasia that in laws, feelings and tastes they differ as much as Russia from Spain, is to put forward an interpretation of actual facts which is totally inadmissible, and, moreover, damaging to the intelligent treatment of the Colonial Question.

So far as there is any type in a nationality, it is a type entirely the resultant of antecedents, Spain and Russia have developed their respective national types; their laws, and feelings, and tastes have grown to what they are out of widely different and entirely distinct antecedents; *they inherit no one point in common, because their ancestors were ever unknown to each other. But can this be said of English Colonies?* Is it not rather a notorious fact that wherever Englishmen congregate there they promptly reproduce in every detail the national idea that they left behind them in the British Isles? And above all is this true of the Colonies in Australasia. *They are pure reproductions of English communities, unmixed by the presence of the large "servile" elements of our "Tropical" Colonies,* unmixed by the presence of the large native and alien populations of South Africa and North America.

Another correspondent, giving an able American view of the Eastern Question, has asked " Shall people of distinct nationalities, races, religions, languages, manners, and customs . . . be bound to each other in political servitude? Yet this question would almost fit to the English Colonies *if the description of* " B. L." *were actually correct.* In our *Colonies, above all in those of Australasia, I, for one, have found nothing but genuine English feeling.* Pervading the whole Colonial Empire there exist the essential characteristics of one distinct nationality, one race, one religion, one language, and one system of manners and customs. And, *remembering their historical origin, as offshoots of the British race, it is difficult to see how there could be other than a distinct unity of* " laws, feelings, and tastes " *pervading all British communities.*

These remarks of " B. L." do call for earnest correction, and urge us to hope with " B. L." that all things may " lead many people who write and speak about Australia to acquaint themselves a little with its history."

I am, Sir, &c.,
GEORGE BADEN-POWELL.
20*th October*, 1877.

CULTIVATION OF WASTE LANDS BY AID OF GOVERNMENT.

On February 21st the House of Commons was occupied with the discussion of a Bill, introduced by Mr. MacCarthy, for the reclamation of Waste Lands in Ireland. Had the purpose of the Bill been accurately and adequately described in its title, it would be difficult to understand why it should have been refused a second reading. No opponent of the Bill attempted to deny the evils which it proposed to remedy. Ireland, as we have been told on high authority, is surrounded by a melancholy ocean which drenches it with unwelcome rain. The owners of its soil are for the most part poor, and their isolated efforts are powerless to rid it of the water which nature only too bountifully supplies. Mr. MacCarthy tells us, on the authority of the Registrar-General for Ireland, that out of 20,227,204 acres of land which might be made available for agricultural purposes, 4,000,000 acres—that is, nearly one-fifth of the whole—are still lying waste. Even if the local proprietors were rich instead of poor, the reclamation of land in such large tracts as alone could be profitably dealt with would need combined efforts and a large outlay of capital. Both these conditions, however, are for the most part wanting, and it was the ostensible purpose of the Bill which was rejected yesterday to supply them. Various attempts have already been made to deal with the subject. Under an Act passed by the late Sir Robert Peel in 1842, 257,000 acres were reclaimed, but the operations sanctioned by that Act were suspended by the famine, and by the dislocation of public industry which ensued upon it, and subsequent Acts have not produced the effects which were anticipated from them. Not more than twenty isolated districts have been reclaimed under the Acts passed after the subject was reconsidered by Parliament in 1856; but Mr. MacCarthy stated yesterday that an area of 2,213,472 acres, amounting to one-twelfth of the soil of Ireland, still remains in a condition that is little better than dismal bog, and drew from that and similar facts the inference that further powers of reclamation were needed. No attempt seems to have been made to question this statement of facts, nor did even the opponents of the Bill deny that the subject was one well worthy of Parliamentary consideration. But the Bill as introduced by Mr. MacCarthy contained provisions of many kinds, tending to a variety of different objects, and thus it concentrated on itself a preponderating aggregate of independent oppositions. Some speakers objected to an undue interference with proprietary rights, others to a State guarantee of the money to be expended, others to the confusion of the question of reclamation with that of arterial drainage,—though it is difficult to see how the two can be kept distinct,—others to the attempt to create a class of peasant proprietors by a legislative side-wind, others to a private encroachment on the province of Government initiative, and so forth. Thus, although a good deal was said in favour of the Bill, and a good deal more on behalf of the objects it ostensibly aimed at, it was rejected on a division, and its promoters will have to be content for at least another year, as Mr. Lowther, the new Secretary for Ireland, recommended them, with having raised a discussion on the subject.

The subject, indeed, is well worthy of the attention promised to it by Mr. Lowther on behalf of the Government. *If it be true, as cannot be doubted, that* 4,000,000 *acres of soil capable of cultivation in Ireland are still in the condition of unreclaimed waste, there clearly must be some want of enterprise, initiative, or encouragement to account for the fact.* Of course there must in all countries be land which will not repay the cost of agricultural cultivation. Some is bog of such hopeless character as would never pay for reclamation; some is mountainous and stony, and its natural herbage, which is all that it can be made to bear, will yield a scanty sustenance to sheep; some is fit only for woodland, and furnishes a precarious profit in periods counted by years; some, as

Mr. Macartney pointed out in the debate, may be so poor as to be worth less than five shillings an acre, and yet may be of use to tenants of cultivated land in the vicinity, because their geese, goats, and pigs can run wild on it. But, if we understand his purpose aright, it is not with irreclaimable waste of this kind that Mr. MacCarthy is anxious to deal. *A good deal of land is only pronounced irreclaimable because there is neither enterprise nor capital ready for the task of redeeming it.* It may be very pleasant for an unthrifty occupier to have the run of a large tract of waste land, where his geese, goats, and pigs may fatten or starve at no cost to himself; but the case is greatly altered if, as Mr. O'Sullivan said, land which is now not worth five shillings can be made worth thirty shillings by drainage and reclamation. Even if the 4,000,000 acres capable of reclamation in Ireland were all reclaimed, there would still remain pasturage for the geese, goats, and pigs whose interests Mr. Macartney defends, and even shelter for the grouse which excite the admiration of Lord Crichton. *But it is hardly fair to expect that those interesting idlers should remain the exclusive occupants of land which, if properly brought under cultivation, might furnish a great stimulus to the industry and a great increase to the wealth of Ireland.* As Mr. MacCarthy pointed out, the present generation has witnessed the reclamation of lands on a vast scale in Holland

and other parts of Europe. The Lake of Haarlem has been pumped dry, and a scheme is now in progress for the reclamation of a great portion of the Zuyder Zee. It is true, as was remarked by Mr. O'Reilly, that the problem in Holland was to reclaim land from the sea, while in Ireland the task is a different one. But it is not necessarily a more difficult task because it is a different one, and it surely must be easier to make water follow its natural course and flow downhill through channels artificially provided for it than, as in Holland, to force it to a higher level and to maintain it there without encroaching on lands reclaimed literally from below its normal surface. We are not concerned to defend the details of the scheme introduced by Mr. MacCarthy; they may have been open to all the objections which were brought against them, and to many more besides ; *but it seems to us indisputable that if, as is not seriously questioned, there exist in Ireland large tracts of land which are now waste and profitless but are capable of profitable cultivation, it should be the business of the Government and of Parliament to devise some means of reclaiming them.*

As regards the actual provisions of the Bill, it will be manifest to any one who reads it that, as Mr. Verner, who moved its rejection, said, it contains a good many more clauses open to question and objection than would be supposed by those who relied solely on the description given of it by Mr. MacCarthy. It may be a good or a bad thing to create a class of peasant proprietors in Ireland, and both views have their advocates; but there can be no doubt as to the impolicy of effecting such an object by a Bill ostensibly dealing with the reclamation of Waste Lands. Arterial drainage is one thing, and a social revolution is another; if an attempt is made to combine the two, we are scarcely surprised to find Parliament looking with hesitation and suspicion at both. It is said that when a certain Head of a College in Oxford wanted to marry, the authority of Parliament was sought and obtained in a clause attached to an Act relating to turnpikes. Some of the legislation proposed for Ireland seems to be modelled on this obsolete and probably apocryphal precedent. A Bill which ostensibly aims at a particular object is found to contain collateral provisions which, even if defensible in themselves, are certainly entitled to independent discussion. We will not say that such was the character of the Bill rejected yesterday, *but it is at any rate safe to assume that the final judgment of Parliament on the reclamation of waste lands in Ireland has not yet been pronounced. Mr. Lowther held out hopes that the subject would receive from the Government the attention which it manifestly deserves.* The population of Ireland, largely reduced by the famine and by the emigration consequent on it, is now again on the increase after long remaining stationary.

As population increases poorer land necessarily comes into cultivation. Waste land cannot be reclaimed on a large scale by private enterprise alone, even in countries where the proprietors are wealthier and more enterprising than is generally the case in Ireland. Arterial drainage is essentially an undertaking which demands a combined effort, a comprehensive plan, and an efficient control. In other words, it is one which needs to be superintended by the State, even if it is not undertaken by it. Much has already been done, as Sir Robert Peel, Mr. Lowther, and other speakers pointed out; much remains to do, as the statistics quoted by Mr. MacCarthy show; but the wide divergence of opinion exhibited by the various Irish members who spoke is a proof that those who are best entitled by local knowledge and experience to a voice in the matter are as yet far from agreed as to the wisest course to be pursued. (See note, p. 128.)—*Times*, 21st February, 1878.

"The Physical Degeneracy of the Artizan Classes.

" *The alleged physical degeneracy of the artizan classes in our great centres of industry is a subject of national importance, which should receive, both from statesmen and from employers, a greater degree of attention than has hitherto been given to it.* We published yesterday the opinions, as stated in evidence before the Royal Commission on the Factory Acts, *of Dr. Fergusson,* who has for *fourteen years been one of the certifying surgeons at Bolton,* and *who describes* himself as having *for forty years taken* a deep interest in *everything relating to the physical well-being of the population.* Dr. Fergusson told the Commissioners that he had kept an accurate record of all the children who were officially brought under his notice, and *that the number of those who were physically unfit to work full time was steadily increasing.* When he commenced his duties he was instructed that he might refuse certificates to these children; but subsequently he found that he had no power to refuse unless the evidence of age was imperfect; and that, whatever might be the physical state, the production of an authenticated certificate of baptism entitled the child to a factory certificate as a matter of right. *When he thus certified a child who was unfit for work he was in the habit of noting down its exact weight and its physical condition generally; and, on watching such children, he found that the lapse of time brought little or no improvement in its train.* At the end of six months many of the children had not increased in weight, and some had even decreased, showing, in his judgment, that their powers had been overtaxed. The effect of working full time upon a feeble child was to stunt its growth, to impair its strength, and probably to shorten its life. *During the five years which ended with* 1873 *quite one half of the children brought to him were unfit to work full time, and the number of this class increased year by year.* He thought it very important that the factory certificate should be withheld even from children who were undoubtedly thirteen years old, unless they were of the ordinary strength and appearance of that age; and unless they were in all respects conformable to the physical standard which the existing test, although manifestly intended to secure, had hitherto failed in securing.

" We shall doubtless be told, and we trust we may be told with some degree of truthfulness, that Dr. Fergusson is an alarmist, or that his account of the conditions which have come under his notice is exaggerated, *or that his standard of physical development is too high, or that the local circumstances are in some respects exceptional. We shall be very glad to believe something of each and all of these statements* ; *but they will not remove the impression that the warning given is important.* Excepting in certain industries, for which a limited number of the sons of Anak will probably always be forthcoming, the *physical powers of the individual artizan were never of less importance than at present, when nearly every kind of hard labour has been transferred from men to machinery. But, notwithstanding this, it must not be forgotten that physical strength forms the natural basis of strength of every other description, and more especially of that strong common sense for which our people were once so conspicuous,* and which they *now so greatly need* as a *defence against the rhetoric of Union leaders* and *other agitators. A community of feeble artizans will not yield a fair average number of men who can think as well as work, who can see the defects of the machinery among which they are employed, who can suggest improvements,* or who can lift *themselves out* of their *own class as successful inventors. Such a community,* on the contrary, would *furnish men who would be driven by muscular fatigue to a craving for shorter hours of labour and for the use of stimulants, and whose weak brains would be easily led into a fool's paradise by the talk of those who would be ever on the watch to prey upon them. The manufacturing and commercial pre-eminence of England depends, in a degree which it would be difficult to exaggerate, upon the maintenance among the artizan classes of a certain sobriety of understanding, as well as of life,* with which *a prevailing physical weakness would be incompatible.*

" It is satisfactory to record that Dr. Fergusson does not attribute the ills which he describes to the labour itself, but *almost entirely to the unwholesome habits of the parents, to their intemperance, and to their excessive use of tobacco.* He states that the latter form of excess is not confined to the parents ; for that at least one-half of the boys in the mills either smoke or chew tobacco, or both; and he adds that, however an adult may be able to bear moderate smoking, there can be no doubt of the prejudical operation of the practice upon the healthy development of a growing child. He also strongly condemns the general substitution in his district of tea or coffee for milk in the food of children; and related what might be called some experiments which he had tried, in having milk given twice a day to feeble children by mothers or managers of mills whom he could trust. The children so treated grew and increased in weight nearly four times as fast as others of the same age who had tea or coffee instead of milk; the increase of weight of the latter, between the ages of 13 and 15, not exceeding 4lbs. a year, while that of the former was as much as 15lbs. a year. To the causes thus enumerated it would probably be necessary to add the influence of very early marriages, and of total want not only of care, but also of knowledge, with regard to the rearing and management of children. Dr. Fergusson mentions, what is well-known to all certifying surgeons, that parents will frequently make false statements in order to send children to the mills at an earlier age than that which the law allows; and that the baptismal certificates of deceased children are often produced as those of younger brothers or sisters. He might have added that in some districts, where infantile mortality is very high, it is not an uncommon practice to prepare for a fraud of this description by registering successive children under the same baptismal name. It is unnecessary to assume that the people who do this care less for their children's welfare than others of their class. They probably think that a child can hardly enter too soon upon that which is to be his future lot.

"*Dr. Fergusson's suggested remedy—that the law* should require evidence not only of the attainment of a *certain age,* but *also of the attainment of such a degree of strength as the age might be taken to imply—is based upon his belief that the parents would then be impelled by self-interest to take more heed than at present to the physical development of their children.* It may be granted that such a provision would be of a salutary tendency, at least if its enforcement were not materially impeded by the differences which might exist between the standards of different Inspectors. Perhaps this difficulty might be met by certain fixed rules with regard to weight and height. But it may still be questioned whether the parents, in many cases, would have sufficient knowledge to modify their conduct in accordance with their interests; and *there is only too much reason to believe that there is a great work to be done by schools and by employers before the law can be usefully appealed to. It might, indeed, remove* from the *vicinity of the dwellings of the artizan class the accumulations of filth against which any single tenant is helpless, and which now sur-*

round those dwellings with a vitiated atmosphere. In other respects, and as regards matters of household management which bear upon the question, the first requirement is to teach the simple laws of health and the necessary consequences of certain lines of conduct. Mrs. Buckton, a member of the Leeds School Board, has already done good work in this direction, by delivering, at Leeds and at Saltaire, lectures to the wives and daughters of working men on the elementary facts of physiology, and on their application to the wants of men and animals. Her lectures, which were models of perspicuity and simplicity, have been eagerly attended by large audiences, and appear to have led many who heard them to renounce common practices, especially with regard to children, which they had previously followed because such were the local customs and they themselves knew no better. *In schools generally there is ample room for a kind of teaching which would at least aim at making children understand the effects of what they do, and the inevitable sequence of these effects from their causes. We must not wonder that artizans should attain only an imperfect physical development, so long as they are exposed to all the insanitary conditions incidental to great aggregations of mankind, and are left without instruction concerning the means by which the evils associated with these conditions may be guarded against."—Times, 7th July,* 1875.

It was gratifying to read in the address issued by Mr. Alfred E. Hardy, the second son of the Minister for War, on the 25th February, to the Electors of Canterbury, the following paragraphs:—

"I am sincerely attached to the principles of the Conservative party, and heartily opposed to all sweeping and radical alterations of the existing Constitution in Church and State. Should you select me as your member I am prepared to give a cordial and independent support to Her Majesty's present Government.

"I am in favour of upholding and consolidating our Colonial and Indian Empire, and keeping our military and naval establishments in the highest state of efficiency.

"With respect to the war in the East, I approve of the policy of conditional neutrality hitherto adopted by the Ministry, and the measures of precaution taken by them to protect the interests of the country. The present crisis demands the utmost vigilance on their part, and ungrudging and unhesitating confidence on the part of the country. A policy of firmness without menace and conciliation without weakness can best secure the peace of Europe and maintain the honour and interests of England."

The consolidation of our Colonial and Indian Empire with the Mother-Country will render us less dependent on foreign countries, and we shall find our reward not only by an increase of trade without any appearance of selfishness, but by being prepared for any hostile tariffs of other nations.

At the dinner given by the Drapers' Company on the 27th February, "replying to the toast of the Auxiliary Forces, Colonel Beresford said he longed to see the day when the army would be at its *full* war complement. We had lost nearly all our old soldiers, and had a great number of young men occupying their places, *who had not the stamina* to *support the fatigues* of a long campaign."

Of the same weakness Lord Raglan complained throughout the earlier part of the Crimean War. We must then find some means of producing a breed of men possessing such stamina.

THE CONDITION OF IRELAND.

Can the article in the *Times* of the 9th of January be more relied on than what is asserted in the following letters? Readers will judge for themselves, but it is all-important that legislation be guided by facts, for truth will ever force itself to the front, in spite of opposition.

"Sir,—In the *Times* of the 9th inst., *an article appears* on *the state of Ireland*, which enlightens me about some facts not generally *recognized in that country.*

" We are told at considerable length *that the condition* of trade, *when viewed in relation to the failure of agricultural produce*, is *remarkably good, and prosperous,* indeed, compared *with that of England; that the social state* of the people *has undergone radical improvement;* and that Ribandism and *agrarian crime are now extinct.*

"I was agreeably surprised to read of such a Utopian condition of affairs, and must only conjecture, either that things in other districts than my own are completely different from what I experience, or that *the writer of that article succeeded in drawing from the fund of a benevolent English imagination an elaborate picture of Irish affairs as he would wish them to be.*

" I am happy to admit that the state of trade is such as to cause considerable satisfaction, but that Ribandism and agrarian crime no more survive I am obliged altogether to deny. The facts of the Mitchelstown case, I should have thought, are sufficient to refute the position assumed in the article, as it is well known that Mr. Bridge, the agent over the property, is obliged, at all times, to go abroad attended by armed policemen, and has been compelled to erect a formidable barrack opposite his hall-door, as a residence for his defenders. He has already within the course of three years been twice fired at and twice wounded.

" Another gentleman in my own neighbourhood

is in constant danger of assassination. He discharged a steward from his service, and employed another, who had not been many months in his employment when he was brutally murdered, and the murderer was never brought to justice. Meanwhile, the master may at any moment share the fate of his servant, and is obliged, to insure even comparative safety, to have the attendance of policemen.

"Were your space to permit I could multiply many similar instances.

"It is a fact that the greater portion of land in the possession of tenants is held at rents considerably below its real value. For this reason— in proportion as the market value of land has increased, landlords have been afraid to raise the rents. They naturally prefer security of life at a reduced income to a larger one acquired with considerable personal risk.

"It is a favourite subject of remark among Englishmen that Irish landlords have no enterprise, that they spend no money in the improvement of their land; but Englishmen do not consider that the real reason of the Irish landlord's apparent niggardliness consists in the fact that, were he to increase the value of his land to double its original value, he could not in the majority of cases increase his rental in proportion without great danger to his life, or the life of his agent.

"*Far then from agrarianism being effete, it has a*

potent influence in lessening the value of property, and checking prosperity in Ireland.

"Your obedient servant,
" 21st January, 1878. " VERITAS."

The *Times* Dublin correspondent writes under date February 27 :—

" The Archbishop of Cashel has addressed the following letter to the Lord Mayor of Dublin, in reply to a circular soliciting subscriptions for the Turkish Relief Fund :—

"'Thurles, Feb. 23.

"' My Lord Mayor,—I beg to acknowledge the receipt of a paper bearing your signature, and purporting to be an appeal in favour of what is called a " Turkish fund for the purpose of affording assistance to certain non-combatants of every creed in Constantinople, Adrianople, Philippopolis, and surrounding districts."

"'I sympathize, I believe, as much as most men with all who are in distress, or who suffer from bodily or other pain, *especially* if it be *in a good cause,* and *is not the result* of any *misconduct* or *perversity on their part;* but in the present instance I cannot help thinking that the Turkish fugitives, on whose behalf this appeal is made, however worthy of being compassionated, are not at all as much entitled to Christian support *as the poor, down-trodden, turnip-fed, and utterly miserable Irish peasants who are being driven in desperation from their homes on the slushy slopes and wilds of the Galtee Mountains.*

"'*Yet I do not find that any one of the many philanthropic personages whose names figure on the subscription list with which I have been favoured has ever expressed a word of sympathy* with those starving mountaineers, "*fugitives*" and "non-combatants" *as they are*, or subscribed a penny to *purchase* for them either *food or raiment*. "Caritas bene ordinata incipit domi."

"'I have the honour to be,
"'My Lord Mayor,
"'Your faithful servant,
"'T. W. CROKE, Archbishop of Cashel.
"'The Rt. Hon. H. Tarpey,
"'Lord Mayor of Dublin.'

"It is a hard measure to visit the sins of their rulers on the poor Turks who have been driven from their homes, and leave them to perish, while at the same time it has not been thought necessary to open a subscription list for the Galtee sufferers."

"RECRUITING IN IRELAND.

"Sir,—The gentleman who signs himself 'A Resident in the County Clare,' in his letter to the

Times of this morning, says I stated to the House of Commons on Thursday last that 'in the event of a war no recruits would be got in Ireland.' I made no such statement. It would, in my judgment, be inaccurate and absurd to say so. I said that in England and in Scotland a patriotic fervour and popular enthusiasm would respond to the call of the Government in defence of the Empire, but *that no such popular enthusiasm or national feeling would respond in Ireland as long as the present unhappy state of things prevailed.* I noticed in the House of Commons what I considered an artifice of debate in *the endeavour to* distort *my words and my meaning;* but I declined to make any correction of even the most absurd misrepresentations. *No honest and courageous public man who knows the two countries dare assert that the same extent of active support or national fervour would in such an emergency just now be forthcoming in Ireland as in England; and he is no true friend of either country who would lure the Government into the belief it would be so. I spoke neither in menace nor ill-will.* Whether such statements are evil threats or evil wishes, or *whether they are honest warnings* of *danger spoken in good faith* and *friendliness*, must always in a *large degree depend* on *the character and general views of the speaker,* for I *grant that one way* of provoking an evil might be to prophesy or suggest it. *I must submit to take my chance of how I may be classed in this instance*—as a man with whom 'the wish is father to the thought,' or *one who honestly warns of a danger he would heartily deplore.*

"Yours very truly,
"A. M. SULLIVAN.

"January 29, 1878."

THE ELEMENTARY EDUCATION ACT.

Look upon *that* picture* and upon *this*—in relation to education—as given in a letter in *John Bull* of 9th March, 1878.

"No Act of Parliament of late years has been so loaded with praise, from all sides, as Mr. Forster's of 1870, and even now, with a great number of people, it holds such a place that we must speak with bated breath if we venture to find fault with it, and many good Conservative papers would refuse a place to a letter, which dared to attempt such a thing as to question the Act of 1870. Why is this? Because very few people know much about *the practical working* of the Public Elementary Schools Act, or of the schools themselves. The Act of 1870 was in fact like the Irish Church Act, a leap into the dark; it took for

* See "Theory of Education," as shown by extract from Mr. Froude's History, vol. 1, p. 44. See *ante*, note, pp. 129 and 130.

granted what any man who is acquainted with our working classes and public elementary schools *knows* is *not* the case; it is believed that the children of this country were, or would be, religiously educated in their homes and at the Sunday Schools. *As a rule,* for the vast majority, they have *no religious instruction at home,* and to trust alone to Sunday Schools is trusting to a broken reed; they have neither time nor power. Teaching is not a heaven-born gift, and an hour on Sunday for *the most important lesson of life is a mockery;* but the *Public Elementary Act of* 1870 *tried to do without religion*—a thing impossible. It is an Act *which strikes a direct blow at all religions alike, and one that is already being felt terribly.* A host of school literature is being put forth, which for the purposes of this Act, are *weeded of all religion.* It is the very *aim of Infidelity to do this:* Don't fight Religion—she is too strong; but cut off Samson's hair *whilst he is asleep.* And as *all pay* depends upon *secular subjects* we are raising an army of teachers who are taught *daily by the cogent argument of money,* to lay aside *the fear of God.*

"Every year a new Code is issued from the Education Department, which, if *well-studied,* shows there is in that department a terrible fear lest they are dealing *with rogues* on every side. *Such a multiplicity of returns are required* that a master in a large school can scarcely be free from Education

Departmental work *half of his school hours.* Surprise visits of inspectors and of managers—all tell a tale. And this with a people's education. Had our Senators truly learned the old proverb—" Si vis fugere a Deo, fuge ad Deum"—they never would have passed an Act which, in practice says, and *is teaching,* " There is no God and so we do not fear Him." I do not hesitate to say I can prove the Act of 1870 to be a failure in all it proposed to do, and I believe it to have failed for the reason that it denied the axiom, which *all* nations except England and her tributaries have admitted, that " the fear of the Lord is the beginning of knowledge."

" Already our gaols are filling with young people who *can read and write well,* and drunkenness, gambling, and other sins increase. Let us, before it is too late, *seek to retrace our steps,* and insist that, in all public elementary schools, the will of the managers and of the parents shall be alone consulted as to the time for religious instruction; that under the fourth schedule, special subjects—instruction in the Holy Scriptures—for Protestant schools in the authorized version, and for Roman Catholics either in the Douay or the Latin Vulgate, at the will of the managers, but subject to parental refusal, be included, and that such subject shall have its place.

" The effect will be, of course, that Her Majesty's Inspectors, if requested, will examine in Scripture, and the Government will pay a modicum for its teaching, and thus remove a fearful blot from our Statute-book.

"In the case of Ireland I hope the Government will propose to pay for all more liberally, and especially if they would give an extra grant for Scriptural Instruction, to be taken or not at will. We should find, ere long, benefits unnumbered arise to Ireland.

"I am sorry to trespass so far on your space, but the subject is one which is indeed *Imperial* in interest.

"H. KNIGHT EATON,
"Vicar of Christ Church, Stafford."

INDIRECT TAXATION.

The following appeared in the *Times* of the 3rd May, 1860:—

A treatise on taxation, written for the eighth edition of the *Encyclopædia Britannica* by Mr. McCulloch, has recently been published in a separate form.* *It comes opportunely to assist to dispel some of the sophisms attempted in defence of the income-tax, and of the cry for a wholesale abandonment of indirect imposts.* After quoting the four maxims of Adam Smith,—1. *That each*

* Adam and Charles Black.

subject of a kingdom should contribute in exact proportion to his revenue, just as the expense of management is divided, pro ratâ, among the joint tenants of a great estate; 2, that the mode of taxation should be such that each may know exactly what he has to contribute, so as not to be liable to fraud or extortion from the collectors; 3, that all imposts should be levied in the most convenient manner for the contributor; and 4, that the expense of collection should be brought to a *minimum—Mr. McCulloch proceeds to show to what extent these requirements have been met in the various plans hitherto adopted.* With regard to Smith's first proposition, it is pointed out that practically it is not possible to attain to anything like perfect equality in taxation. This difficulty, however, is more nominal than real. In *a country whence emigration is free and where Poor Laws exist, all taxes, except those which involve a principle of confiscation, adjust themselves to the question of wages.* The grand object, therefore, should be not *to seek a superficial equality of incidence, for this is a matter that will come as water will find its level; but to select those articles that can be touched with the greatest certainty of not checking commerce, or injuring the public health or morals.* Among the best in these respects are malt, spirits, wine, and tobacco. As regards necessaries, such as tea, sugar, &c., the *amount of duty should be guided so as not to reach a point that would limit their rational use,* or lead to *the employment of substitutes less wholesome.* The doctrine that duties of this description are mainly paid by the poor is a delusion. If a rich man builds a house, the cost of that house comprises the cost of the beer, tea, sugar, tobacco, &c., *consumed by those who were employed in the work. Unless they can obtain what they consider a fair supply of these articles in return for their labour, people will go to the Union, or emigrate to the Colonies.* Their withdrawal from the field increases the occupation for those that remain, and the next bidder for hands must offer more money than ever; that is to say, *must give the equivalent of more tea, sugar, &c., than was previously demanded.* " No doubt, therefore," observes Mr. McCulloch, " *there is a vast deal of fallacy in the statements so frequently put forth in regard to the operation of taxes on the articles principally consumed by the working classes. Their mischievous influence has been grossly exaggerated, sometimes through ignorance, and sometimes, and more frequently perhaps, from less excusable motives.*" Want of providence and dissipated habits are rightly designated as the real sources of the destitution and misery that prevail among the poor. " It is mere drivelling, or worse, to ascribe them to taxes on gin, tobacco, or beer, or even to those on tea and sugar." It must be remarked, however, that although wages invariably adjust themselves to taxation it is always a slow process, and that consequently one of the greatest evils in the government of a country arises when the taxation is unstable. So long as they are not on a scale to affect consumption, to interfere with personal liberty or public honour, or levied at an expense disproportionate to their value, all taxes have nearly equal merits, and in due time will diffuse their pressure with mathematical honesty on every contributor in exact proportion to his means and expenditure. *But the income-tax fulfils not a single preliminary condition, and comes out as the worst that can be conceived. In the manner in which it has been levied for eighteen years it has comprised, not only the principle of confiscation, but also the highest degree of uncertainty.* Let it continue for twenty, thirty, or forty years, with the understanding that it will never be changed, and the natural movements of the labour-market and the general freedom of contracts would go far to counterbalance and destroy even its most gross inequalities; *but laid on as it is from time to time at varying rates, and with a solemn assurance that in a few years it will terminate, it is impossible for persons who may enter into stipulations with regard to their future income, or whose revenues may depend upon fixed professional fees, to insist upon conditions which shall meet their case.* This is an irrefragable argument against its capricious use. But no degree of certainty respecting its duration would mitigate its other vicious characteristics.

In the first place, the principle of exemptions and of subjecting one class to a higher rate of charge than another, involves incurable injustice as well as constant distrust. *The exemption of all persons under £100 a-year is not only in direct opposition to Adam Smith's first maxim, but it operates as a bribe to the whole of that large class to remain silent against the general evils of the impost, and also accustoms them to the idea of insisting that the national burdens shall be placed on any shoulders but their own.* At the same time, the rating of incomes ranging from £100 to £150 at a lower scale than those above that limit establishes a precedent *which, with equal justice, may be carried through a variety of gradations, until in the case of the millionaire nearly his whole income may be confiscated.* If the person with less than £150 is to pay a smaller percentage than the recipient of £200, why may not the recipient of £200 claim an advantage over his neighbour with £500? The latter may apply the rule to one with £1000, and so on indefinitely, until in the case of the receiver of £100,000, the percentage reaches a point which may scarcely leave him the enjoyment of a tenth part of his lawful acquisitions. *The moment individuals or classes are singled out for special contributions, we are thrown back to the old Turkish and Indian systems of spoliation, and as the variations in the scale must depend solely upon the arbitrary fancies of the multitude in whom power* may happen to be vested from time to time, no one can ever calculate as to what may be the proportion of his earnings he will henceforth be permitted to enjoy. Even, however, if all exemptions were removed, the income-tax would still figure as the most "*enormously immoral*" device that can be resorted to for fiscal purposes. " Though theoretically equal," Mr. McCulloch boldly and correctly affirms, " it is in its practical operation the most unequal, oppressive, and vexatious of any that it is possible to imagine." *Owing to the impossibility of establishing inquisitorial proceedings that would enable it to be levied with accuracy,* " *it operates as a tax on honesty and a bounty on and an incentive to perjury and fraud,*" and has probably in recent times done more to weaken the foundation of national probity than any other objectionable influence with which we have had to contend. Of its effect upon the good faith and consistency of statesmen the examples have already been painful, and the glaring instance of the disregard of every consideration but that of might in the treatment of the holders of terminable annuities would in itself have aroused the indignation of the entire country if the exemption clauses had not suborned the masses to look on with indifference. *Happily, as there are no more free trade changes to be worked out, such as have hitherto induced the better part of the public to submit to any sacrifice that might hasten the end in view, the income-tax question will in all future Budgets prove* the prominent one, and must be argued on its intrinsic merits. Although in a House of Commons returned by £6 householders, all of whom will enjoy immunity, the prospect of the doctrines of abstract morality proving triumphant will perhaps be even less encouraging than at present, *it may yet be hoped there is sufficient integrity among us to cause this impost to be a stumbling-block in the way of every Chancellor of the Exchequer who may henceforth endeavour to continue it as it stands, or to evade the recognition of its real features.*

The Six Millions—How to Raise Them.

To the Editor of the " Times."

" Sir,—Now that the country, propelled by the ridicule of united Europe, has very properly at last granted the six millions credit required by Her Majesty's Government towards the probable expenses of maintaining our interests and our honour in the present Eastern crisis, and in view of other no less important though secret foreign complications, which may at no distant period entail even larger demands upon the public purse, the following very incisive questions will not be thought out of place at this moment.—

"How are we to find the money? And out of whose pockets is it ultimately to come?

"The answer to the first question has already been given by Her Majesty's Chancellor of the Exchequer; the answer to the second is much more difficult, and comes home to each one of us individually.

"Is it to come out of the pockets of the freehold householders or of the landowners, most of whom are reducing their rents and unable to let their farms at any price, and who are enjoying the grim prospect of a diminished income with increased necessary expenditure? Or, is it to come out of the pockets of the ratepayers and the tenant farmers of the country, who are nearly ruined by three successive bad seasons, by universally high local rates, by the sensible diminution of good and the present high price of bad labour, and lastly, by huge foreign importations, the result of our one-sided Free Trade? Or, is it to come from the large merchants and tradesmen, or the small shopkeepers whose limited profits are the result of the like cause? Or, from the great manufacturing industries, the iron and coal owners, the cotton, the woollen, the shipping, and all the other various great commercial interests in the kingdom, many of whom are working on short time or shutting up altogether, turning thousands of poor operatives adrift upon the rates, reducing their wages, contracting their operations, everywhere and in every branch of trade, from one cause or other depressed and discouraged, but chiefly by reason of their sheer inability to continue a ruinous competition with the unrestricted importations of foreign countries, without any reciprocity on their part to counterbalance them?

"When I add to these the great moneyed interests, the members of the various professions, and the persons of both sexes in receipt of limited incomes, I think that the above will pretty fairly represent the greater part of the usual taxpayers of the kingdom.

"Sir, if this sum of six millions is to be eventually met by doubling or trebling our present income-tax or by any other approved mode of direct taxation, the burden will chiefly fall upon the overloaded shoulders of the classes above mentioned, and this will be hard enough to bear. But if it is to be raised by any mode of indirect taxation, we shall have to come lower down, and the burden will have to fall with increased pressure on those of the masses and of the still poorer public, and this will be harder still. Which, then, is it to be? The first will be most unpalatable, the second will be positively distressing; but one or the other course will be inevitable, unless some other mode of dealing with the difficulty can be devised which shall extricate us from this necessary, but unwelcome incubus.

"Now, Sir, in the face of this threatened increase

of taxation, why should we not look elsewhere for the means of providing it when they are readily and legitimately at hand?

" For upwards of thirty years past we have been undergoing the experiment of what its apologists are still pleased to call " Free Trade," with varied and doubtful results. It was confidently expected (and any doubts on the subject were instantly ridiculed and scoffed down) that so universally beneficial a measure would be universally adopted and that a new æra of universal reciprocity and prosperity, and a mutually beneficial system of exchange would be immediately and triumphantly inaugurated.

"How vain has been the hope, how delusive these grand expectations our present commercial position but too plainly demonstrates. We find ourselves at the end of this long period with a gradual annually-increasing expenditure which has to be met by a proportionately large annual demand for funds to balance it; with no apparent prospect of any tangible diminution in taxation, but with the exact opposite apparently imminent at this moment.

" We are now undergoing a crisis of almost unexampled commercial depression in every branch of trade and home manufactures, with an Exchequer which will hardly be able to make both ends meet at the end of the financial year, with thousands of operatives literally starving, enterprize everywhere languishing, and with imports from other countries, paying no duty whatever, overstocking our markets with cheap manufactured articles, and almost double in value to the exports of our own.

"Such an alarming state of things cannot much longer be quietly submitted to, and even among the cotton interests, as evinced by their several different deputations, there is already a considerable and anxious discussion.

"Great Britain stands totally alone in its own Free-trade theories, for, as I stated in a former letter last November on this subject, 'not a single country in Europe, beginning with France and Germany, and ending with Spain and Switzerland (to say nothing of the United States of America and our own Australian Colonies), can be cajoled by the most specious temptation into following our example of free importations or of opening their ports to the commerce of Great Britain and of the world unrestricted by safeguards in the shape of duties framed to protect their own native industries.'

"I now ask, Sir, why should we not do likewise? What more ready or more legitimate means of relief could possibly be devised than to make the too-intelligent foreigner who for so long a period (and none more so than 'holy Russia') has profited by our one-sided Free-trade policy without any reciprocity on his part, contribute, in the shape of a limited protective duty as a toll or an octroi on his imports to this country, his quota to our already enormous taxation? Why should we, with such a means of relief at once obvious and apparent, obstinately persist in this isolated policy?

"We do not find foreign countries who profess to be in alliance with us rushing to the front and eagerly proffering their assistance to us in such times of difficulty as the present. We are to all intents and purposes apparently isolated in our foreign as well as in our commercial policy, and, although it pleases some of us to think differently, are being diplomatically duped.

"But that does not prevent them from taking advantage of our commercial liberality. They can button up their own, but they do not scruple to put their hands pretty deeply into our pockets, and under the specious misnomer of Free Trade they rob the manufacturer of his legitimate profits, the working classes of their employment, undersell us in our own markets, take millions yearly out of the country, and leave us nothing behind but the option of re-exporting their surplus manufactured articles.

"It is well known, Sir, that the value of the imports to this kingdom from all countries during the year closing the 31st of December last amounted to the enormous sum of nearly 394 millions, while our own exports were something over 198 millions. Only calculate for a single moment what a Customs-duty, or, let us say, a toll or an octroi of 20 or even 10 per cent. on this sum of

394 millions of imports from foreign countries would bring to the Exchequer of this kingdom, hitherto and at present totally lost to us.

"Let us even deduct from this grand total the sum of 150 millions, which may be said to represent the food supply of the people, and a further sum of 120 millions representing raw materials, and there will yet remain a sum of 124 millions, made up of foreign manufactured articles, tobacco, wine, spirits, and other luxuries, on which a toll might be fairly imposed, and which would produce a sum of 12 millions per annum at 10 per cent., and six millions per annum at even the moderate figure of only 5 per cent., an amount amply sufficient for all we want.

"So simple, so fair, so natural a source of revenue and relief from the horrors of increased taxation must commend itself to every taxpayer without distinction.

"Believe me, Sir, I do not stand alone in my views on this question; they are shared, and I know it, by multitudes of my countrymen and countrywomen, and though it may please the theorists and politicians of the Birmingham and Manchester school to scoff at these suggestions and to ridicule my supposed ignorance on such matters, thank Heaven we are not all of that school nor of that class of politicians who shut their ears to argument and their eyes to facts, and who refusing to be convinced out of their own pet theories, accept them as infallible and endeavour to impose them as facts upon other people.

"There is a pulse in this England of ours which is not always wholly governed by the fluctuations in the cotton market, and it is this healthy, this steady pulse of the British public that I wish to animate, and it is to their calm reflection and to their attentive perusal, in whose interest I write, I have the honour to submit this letter.

"I remain, Sir,
"Your obedient humble servant,
"BATEMAN.
"Shobdon-court, Leominster,
"Herefordshire, March 7th, 1878."

THE CAUSES OF THE PRESENT DEPRESSION OF TRADE.

On Monday, the 4th February, Mr. Edmund Ashworth, President of the Manchester Chamber of Commerce, "entered into a *critical examination* of the causes of the present depression of trade, and the prospects of a revival," and on the 6th February the following appeared in the *Times*:—

"THE MANCHESTER CHAMBER OF COMMERCE.— At the annual meeting of the Chamber of Commerce on *Monday*, Feb. 4, the President, Mr. *Edmund Ashworth*, entered into a critical examination of the causes of the present depression of trade and the prospects of a revival. *He had endeavoured, he said, to ascertain, with at least approximate correctness,* the *proportion* of the *increase of spinning mills and weaving sheds during the last few years, and, as the prosperity of a trade was mainly dependent on the production having some fair relation to the demand, the facts he had collected might, in a great measure, account for the depression under which they were suffering. During the last ten years the building of spinning factories by private firms, and more especially by joint-stock companies, had been in the nature of a mania.* He found that no fewer than 7,228,305 spindles *had been added to the productive power between* 1865 *and* 1875, *representing a capital of nearly* £11,000,000. *So large an addition to the producing power in so short a time is calculated to derange the ordinary course of trade, and cotton spinning had suffered severely from an over-production of yarn beyond the ordinary requirements for many years past. The number of looms also had increased from* 399,992 *to* 463,118, *and even the extension had been unequal to the quantity of yarn spun. Doubtless those who thus converted their capital expected a profitable return, but they had not given due consideration to the probabilities of over-production.* He urged that *more control should be exercised over undue enterprise in cotton manufacture, for these abnormal extensions promoted competition, which at last culminated in these periodical visitations of depression. Another aspect of the question was that of foreign competition.* Germany, Austria, Italy, and Holland had lessened their imports of woven goods, *while Belgium was so nearly our equal that it had imported both woven goods and yarns* into Great Britain for several years, and *America also gained yearly upon us, her exports of cotton goods to this country having increased from £15,830 in* 1870, *to £451,876 in* 1876. The president also dealt with the labour question, and said that when the mill workers obtained the passing of the Act limiting their hours of labour to nine-and-a-half per day, they did it without having a proper regard to the advantage thereby obtained by foreign competitors. The fact was incontestable, that, whatever superiority of manufacture or power of production we might have, it was to a considerable extent thrown away, since the English production of nine-and-a-half hours per day had to compete with the day's work of eleven or twelve hours abroad, with lower wages. At present the English weaver was undoubtedly superior to the foreign; but as the latter would in due time become more expert with experience, this distinction would gradually disappear. *He regretted to say that he could see little or no immediate hope for a revival of trade. A discussion on the question of the Indian import duties followed, and it was resolved to call a special meeting in order to consider what steps should be taken to impress* upon the Government *the necessity either of repealing these duties*, or of placing an excise duty on *goods manufactured in India.*"

What Mr. E. Ashworth said tends to confirm what is said by "Mechanician"—the correspondent of the *Times* at the International Exhibition held at Philadelphia in 1876—in the paragraph on the Title page of this work.

On the 7th February, Mr. Bright wrote a letter, it appears, remonstrating against the course taken by some of his friends of the Chamber of Commerce in the matter of the Indian import duties.

MANCHESTER AND INDIA.—The following letter has been addressed by *Mr. Bright to Mr. Benjamin Armitage, of Manchester:*—" London, Feb. 7th, 1878.—*My dear Armitage,—I am surprised at the line taken by some of our friends of the Chamber of Commerce in the matter of the Indian import duties. It seems dictated by passion and disappointment rather than by reason and a sound judgment. India has an interest in the question as well as England. If the people of India could speak and act as we can in England they would oppose to the last degree of resistance any attempt to impose an Excise duty of five per cent., or of any amount, on the produce of their factories. If they were in theory Free-traders, and wished to be so in practice, they would oppose any such tax, and in my opinion most rightly.* They would say, as we ought to say, an Excise duty on the *produce of the mills is odious on every ground, and cannot be permitted.* They would look for the power to remove the import duties to greater economy in the public expenditure, or the regular growth of the public revenue, or the imposition of some new tax which might raise the needful £800,000 a year. The grievance complained of in the Chamber can only be remedied in one of these three ways, for I feel very confident *the House of Commons will never compel the Indian Government to adopt the odious and intolerable proposition which seems strangely to have found favour with some of the members of your Chamber. I see in the same discussion in the Chamber objection is made to anything being done there which may be termed political. What is more political than a question of revenue and taxation? This dread of all serious questions is the cause of the feebleness and general uselessness of Chambers of Commerce.* I suppose the Excise proposition is merely a weapon to use against the Government and to compel it to act against the import duties. It must fail, for it is impossible to defend it. It would be much more wise to put pressure on the Indian Government to lessen its expenses, to reduce its English and native forces by the amount required, which surely may be safely done if our Indian Government is so intelligent and so just as it constantly declares itself to be. I write this rather hastily after reading the report of the proceedings of the Chamber. I am not a member of the Chamber, but *I shall be very sorry to see it take a course which must lessen its character for wisdom, and therefore lessen its influence.* If you think any one will care about my opinion, you need not conceal it. *I am sorry to be compelled to differ from any of our friends on this question.*— Believe me always sincerely yours, JOHN BRIGHT." A *special meeting of the Manchester Chamber of Commerce was held yesterday for the* purpose of determining the course to be pursued for obtaining the abolition of the Indian *import duties on cotton goods and yarns.* Mr. B. Armitage presided, and there was a large attendance of members. Mr. John Slagg moved, " That, *in the opinion of this Chamber the trade of this district is entitled to a distinct pledge on the part of the Government as to the immediate repeal of the duties on the importation of cotton goods and yarns into India, and that if the condition of Indian finance does not permit* of such a pledge being given, *it is the duty of this Chamber to press for the imposition of an Excise duty* and the removal of the *protective character of the import duties."* Mr. R. R. Jackson seconded the resolution. Mr. G. Lord moved as an amendment that the latter part of the resolution referring to the Excise be omitted, and this was seconded by *Mr. N. S. Symons* and Mr. Jackson, *who condemned Mr. Bright's letter as ill-timed and in bad taste.* He denied that the promoters of the Excise duty were actuated by passion, but said *they were moved by justifiable disappointment.* After a long discussion the debate was adjourned for a week.—*Times,* 13th Feb., 1878.

Yet notwithstanding this very just remonstrance on the part of Mr. Bright, on the 12th February, a special meeting of the Manchester Chamber of Commerce was held for the purpose of determining the course to be pursued for obtaining the abolition of the Indian import duties on cotton goods and yarns, and at that meeting Mr. Bright's letter was, as will have been seen, condemned "as *ill-timed and in bad taste;*" and the result of that meeting of the 13th February, was probably the deputation from the *associated committees of employers and workmen* representing the public meetings held in the cotton manufacturing districts, to secure the abolition of the "Indian import duties," who, on the afternoon of the 14th of February had an interview with Lord George Hamilton, at the India Office, in the absence of the Marquis of Salisbury, who, at the last moment, was summoned to attend a Cabinet Council. As a summary of, and well-deserved comment on what transpired on that occasion, the leader in the *Times* of the 16th February, 1878, is here given:

"'It is simply impossible,' says Lord Macaulay, ' to get Englishmen to interest themselves about Indian finance.' The thing has, nevertheless, been done. *The large and important deputation which attended on Thursday at the India Office to state their views about the taxation of Indian cotton goods is sufficient proof of this. There was scarcely a town in our cotton manufacturing districts which was not represented. Lancashire en masse* had turned out *for the occasion, personally or by deputy, and the speakers to whom Lord George Hamilton gave a hearing on Thursday* may be fairly taken *as expressing the fixed opinions of some hundreds of thousands of Englishmen.* On this occasion there was a charming unanimity between the sentiments of the masters and of the men. Private disputes were sunk for the moment in face of a great question in which the earners and the payers of wages were equally concerned, and Lancashire, for once in a way, was in perfect harmony in all its sections. *We must confess, however, that the interest of all these intelligent persons in Indian finance was not as unselfish as we could wish. It was not so much the effect of taxation on India as its after effect on Lancashire with which they were all busying themselves.* There was no concealment on this point, and scarcely, indeed, the affectation of any. Colonel Jackson, one of the largest cotton manufacturers in Lancashire and the chief spokesman of the deputation, stated his opinions with perfect candour, and explained, moreover, the process of thought which had led to them. His view, and the view of those for whom he was speaking on Thursday, is that the Indian import duties on cotton ought as speedily as possible to be abolished. If they are not to be got rid of at one stroke, they might at least be brought down by degrees to the vanishing point. A reduction at the rate of one per cent. per annum will be accepted as fast enough. The worst of the matter is that this, or something like this, is what the Indian Government has been promising for some time past, while the chances that it will be able to keep its word are becoming smaller every year. This puts off indefinitely the change which Colonel Jackson and his fellows are desirous of seeing accomplished. In the meanwhile India is learning to supply herself with cotton goods from her own mills, and is even invading foreign markets which were not long ago in the undisputed possession of Lancashire. What is to be done, Colonel Jackson asks, in so alarming a state of affairs? He is anxious for justice and fair play both to India and to England. The only question is how these are to be secured for both countries. His key to the difficulty, pending the abolition of the import duties, is the imposition of an excise duty on Indian manufactured cottons. The first effect of this would be to enable English cotton to contend on equal terms with Indian cotton within India, and it would have the further result of reducing the area of competition outside India. Colonel Jackson's wish is not only to be allowed to supply India with cotton goods; he wishes also to be made secure in Japan and China. *It is India, just now, which is threatening him in both these countries, and he claims, accordingly, the same protection abroad which India has been receiving at home.*

There is one point, and one only, on which, as it seemed to the deputation of last Thursday, their position could be open to attack. They are themselves Free-traders, and the excise duty they were asking for on Thursday was not easily to be brought into agreement with Free-trade principles. One of its avowed objects was to restrict the export trade of India, and so to rid *English manufacturers of a rivalry which they are beginning to find troublesome.* It was to the produce of the cotton mills of India, moreover, that the proposed restrictive measure was to be limited. *The hand manufactures were to escape untaxed; but from the English point of view these are of small account, so only that the mills can be kept well within bounds.* The sufferers would be the large Indian cotton manufacturers, who would be placed at a disadvantage both in their own markets and in those which they have more lately ventured to invade abroad. *Unless we assert that free trade is to prevail only where it happens to be suited to English interests, and that in other cases it is to be set aside as no longer of any use,* we cannot go far towards solving the *difficulty with which the Lancashire deputation of Thursday found themselves.* Mr. Hibbert's suggestion is that some part of the import duty goes into the pockets of the Indian cotton manufacturers, whereas an excise duty would go wholly into the pocket of the Indian Government. It is not clear on what principle he bases the distinction. Colonel Jackson sets to work more boldly. He does not even affect to doubt that the excise duty he is asking for is contrary to Free-trade principles. But it is no worse, he urges, in this respect than our own excise duty on spirits or our stamp duty on silver goods manufactured at home. If these restrictions can exist in England, he suggests, they can be imposed just as well in India without offence to Free-traders. The effect they are intended to produce is, however, not quite the same in the two cases. An excise duty which is intended to check trade is not to be defended by reference to another excise duty which is imposed only for revenue purposes, and which would not be tolerated for a moment if it had the kind of effect expected from an excise on Indian manufactured cottons. *If the people of India were self-governing,* CAN WE SUPPOSE THEY WOULD SUBMIT TO THE TREATMENT THE LANCASHIRE DEPUTATION SUGGESTS FOR THEM? *The import duty on cotton goods would certainly not be the first burden from which the Indian taxpayer would seek relief. He would place the salt duty far higher on his list of grievances.* The fact is that as long as English cotton manufacturers were content to appeal to trade principles which we all recognize as true, they had a good-standing ground for demanding the abolition of the cotton duty. The new attitude they have taken puts them in a wholly different position in this respect. *Their wish to preserve a foreign market for their goods is natural enough, and, within decent limits, praiseworthy enough.* We can scarcely say as much for them when they ask *not only that Indian finance shall be regulated for their convenience,* but that *the export trade of India shall be kept within the bounds they wish to assign to it, and shall be crushed out of existence when it introduces itself as their rival.* It was nothing less than this that the deputation of Thursday were asking for, and with scarcely a disguise as to their real meaning. Whatever they may find to say about the old grievance of the import duty, it would have been hard for them to make out that India was likely to be suffering by the extension of her foreign trade with Japan or China or any other country, and there is a charming frankness in the request that this trade shall be knocked on the head because it is beginning to interfere with the trade of Lancashire. We wish well both to the operatives and manufacturers of that important county, for whose difficulties just now much sympathy must be felt, but *we fancy that the rest of the world exists for some other purpose than for Lancashire cotton-spinners to make their fortunes in, and that the fine names of Justice and Fair Play point to conclusions somewhat different from those which they have been endeavouring to draw from them.*

" Lord George Hamilton, in the reply he made to the deputation, acquitted himself exceedingly well. His task was in some respects a difficult one. He has been so long assuring the House of Commons that the finances of India are in a very flourishing state that he could not fairly take objection to the rose-coloured view of them presented by the deputation. His actual line was chosen with great discretion. He still held out the hope that the obnoxious import duty on cotton might, before long, be dealt with. With this change in prospect, it was clearly not necessary to impose new taxes on cotton. Moreover, to impose an excise duty would, Lord George Hamilton declares, have the result of postponing indefinitely the abolition of the import duty. *It is a strange thing, we cannot help remarking, to observe the new quarters from which proceed, in the case before us, the attack on Free Trade and the defence.* Lancashire and a good many staunch Lancashire liberals make up the assailing party. The deputation of Thursday was collected together from all regions, from all strata of society, and from all political camps. Opposed to it, and strong chiefly in the rectitude of his cause, was Lord George Hamilton, a Conservative placeman, and by some freak of destiny, *a defender for the nonce of Free-trade principles* against the assault of united Lancashire. *In such an assault it would be unjust to find nothing beyond proof of the ease with which convictions, however sound, however deeply rooted, may be set aside when it becomes convenient not to hold them.*

Yet political cynics will not fail to say that this must be the view taken about it. *A direct proposal to tax India for the benefit of Lancashire would have been less plausible than what actually was proposed, but it might, perhaps, have been agreed to with less mischief. The contention that India and England meet as rivals in the Eastern markets, and that the dependency ought, therefore, to be made to give way to the governing country, does, in fact, sound a little cynical when it is thus baldly stated. It was this in substance, and a good deal more of the same kind, that the Lancashire deputation was urging last Thursday, and with no seeming consciousness that there was anything unreasonable in the demand.* With persons thus minded, Lord George Hamilton did the only thing that could be done pleasantly. He did not get rid of them by telling them, as Mr. Bright has done in a letter we published last Wednesday, that *their request was such as no decent Government could listen to for an instant, and that they ought to be ashamed of themselves for making it.* He brought the interview to a more agreeable close by making promises of something else than what his visitors were asking for, without fixing any precise date for its fulfilment. His trust, no doubt, is that in the meanwhile trade may revive elsewhere, or that Lancashire, with or without a trade revival, may come back to its sober senses."

There was one passage in Lord G. Hamilton's reply to the deputation, not touched upon in the *Times*' just and able article, to which it is important to call attention. He said "As to the depressed condition of the cotton-trade, to which Mr. Whalley had referred, he might observe that he had before him some figures that during the first eight months of *this year* the imports in India *were* 13 *per cent. over the corresponding period of the preceding year, the value being* 9 *per cent. greater.* Mr. Jackson* had, no doubt, to a certain extent, accounted for that increase, but

---

* In concluding his address, Mr. Jackson observed:—

"It might, however, be said that the Manufacturers of Lancashire were coming before the Government with an unnecessary complaint, when it was borne in mind that the exports to India had increased of late; but it so happened that our Trade to all parts of the world had been for some time past in a most unsatisfactory state. But there were very few markets which took goods of the same staple character as India, and when there was a large accumulation of those goods in stock it became necessary to force them forward at any price. He might state as a fact that he could not stop his own works at a less cost than £10,000. per annum; so that if he could by shipping goods lose under that amount, and keep his work-people together, it would be more to his advantage to do so then than to stop the works altogether. He could assure the Government the Trade in Lancashire was extremely bad."

Whether inundating India with such goods at any price was quite fair towards the Indian Manufacturer may be a question. At least such practices afford an additional justification for the maintenance of the 5 per Cent. Import duty for the present.

it was, nevertheless, he thought, clear that the depression spoken of was not so much due to a falling off in the imports to India as to a DECREASE *of* CONSUMPTION ELSEWHERE."

As will have been seen in the earlier part of this volume, Mr. Hoyle, a great cotton-spinner, himself told us that this "*decrease was in the Home Market,*" which he ascertained by investigating, in the year 1869, how it happened that at the time our exports were higher than they had ever been, there was such distress in the manufacturing districts. (See pp. 69, 70, 71.)

In the *Times* of the 27th February the following appeared:—

"ASSOCIATED CHAMBERS OF COMMERCE.—Yesterday the delegates from all the Chambers of Commerce in the United Kingdom assembled at the Westminster Palace Hotel to discuss the steps which should be taken by the Associated Chambers in various matters affecting commerce, trade, and manufacture. Mr. Sampson Lloyd, M.P., presided, and among those present were Mr. Samuel Morley, M.P., Mr. Monk, M.P., Mr. Whitwell, M.P., Mr. J. S. Wright, of Birmingham, and representatives from all the great towns in the United Kingdom. The Chairman, in his opening speech, reverted to the matters which occupied the particular attention of the Chambers last year—the Bankruptcy Act Amendment Bill and the Bills of Sale Bill—and pointed out that if the Chambers desired steps to be taken on these and other measures in Parliament, the members for the various localities must be requested to direct attention to them, and the Chambers must present petitions on the subjects. The annual report stated that the usefulness and activity of the Association had been fully maintained. The report discussed the various questions brought before Parliament in the last Session, and in regard to the Railway Commission the Council suggested that it would be desirable to recommend the continuance of the Commission. It also called attention to the new treaty between this country and Italy, the proposed alterations in the Austrian tariff, and *the hopeful signs* of *change in the American system of protection*. It was stated that the question of the Swiss tariff would be decided in the next Session of the Swiss Parliament. The report was unanimously adopted. The first subject discussed was the question of the amendment of the law respecting patents for inventions. Mr. J. S. Wright, of Birmingham, proposed a resolution to the effect that in the opinion of the Chambers the Patent Law should provide for a considerable reduction in fees; that any preliminary examination should not go further than the point of novelty; that no patent should be granted to foreigners unless with the condition that licences be granted to manufacturers in England; that provisions should be made for cases of infringement being brought before local magistrates, as provided by the Merchandise Marks Act, 1862; and that a memorial on the subject should be forwarded to the Government. Mr. Bartlett seconded the motion, which was adopted. *Mr. Longdon, of Derby, proposed " That while fully approving the principles of Free Trade which have for some time past mainly guided the commercial policy of this country, measures be at once adopted by this association to enforce upon Her Majesty's Government the inadvisability of signing Treaties of Commerce with those foreign nations which have imposed,* or intend to impose, higher import duties upon English manufactures than those existing under the previous or present treaties or tariffs, or *which exclude Great Britain from the most-favoured nation treaty."* Mr. Edge, of Burslem, seconded the motion, which was carried. *Mr. Britain, of Sheffield, moved a resolution to the effect that the attention of the Colonial Office should be called to the " heavy duties which British colonial manufactures are liable upon their importation into France, and to suggest that in case the treaty negotiations with France be renewed, an effort be made to secure for our colonies the same treatment as that accorded to the Mother-Country."* Mr. Wilson seconded the motion, which was carried. The representative of the Newcastle and Gateshead Chamber moved, " *That this association urge on Her Majesty's Foreign Secretary, by deputation or otherwise, the necessity of taking immediate action in such way as he may deem best, with the object of getting the recently promulgated Spanish tariff modified—at any rate, to such an extent as shall place English goods on the same footing as the goods and shipping of any other nation as regards import duties.* Mr. Ripley, M.P., seconded the motion, and said that the association ought to express *its strong disapprobation of the system in Spain of having more favourable terms for the admission of goods from countries other than Great Britain.* The motion was carried and a deputation appointed to seek an interview with Lord Derby upon the subject. The subject of the Governmental management of commerce in this country was discussed at very great length, and there was a decided expression of opinion that *commerce should be under a separate Department of the State, presided over by a Minister of Commerce.* The Chambers then adjourned until to-day.

The writer of these pages was very pleased to find that the resolution embraced the suggestion that *in case* the treaty negotiations with France be renewed, an effort be made to *secure for our Colonies the same treatment as that accorded to the Mother-Country.* "Such sentiments will tend to promote that all-important measure, the consolidation of our Colonies with the Mother-Country."*

* FOREIGN AND COLONIAL TRADE.—At the Royal Colonial Institute on Tuesday night, the Duke of Manchester in the chair, the hon. secretary, Mr. Frederick Young, in the

On the 27th February the Yorkshire Chamber of Commerce and the Associated Chambers of Commerce held an interview with Lord Derby

author's unavoidable absence through sudden indisposition, read a paper by Dr. Forbes Watson, Director of the Indian Museum, on "The Character of the Colonial and Indian Trade of England contrasted with her Foreign Trade. Our colonial trade was, he said, distinguished from our foreign trade by certain characteristics which considerably enhanced the importance it already possessed. Dr. Watson grouped the colonies as—1, Trading and military stations; 2, plantation colonies; 3, agricultural, pastoral, and mining. Taking first these last, such as Australia, Canada, and the Cape, he found that while English trade with the United States, our best foreign customer, would be £2. 5s per head, that with Canada was three-fold greater, with Australia seven-fold greater, and that with a colonist at the Cape fifteen-fold greater. In the plantation colonies, such as the West Indies, Ceylon, and Mauritius, the trade per white inhabitant amounted to £310, of which £165 was English. In the case of the trading stations, such as Honkong, Singapore, and Malta, the few European residents were but the intermediaries of a vast trade with the adjacent foreign countries, so that the amount of total trade for each white inhabitant was £10,000, of which £2000 was English. The returns for 1876 placed India ahead of every other country in the absorption of British produce and merchandise, whereas in 1869 it ranked third only, standing behind the United States and Germany. He stated that between 1869 and 1876 the exports of British home-produce to the British possessions had increased £17,000,000 while the exports to foreign countries sunk £6,000,000. Foremost among the leading export trades of England, constituting about one-third of the whole, was the cotton trade, and in 1876 the British possessions absorbed 40 per cent. more cotton manufactures than in 1869. In 1876 the colonial demand for our cotton wares rose to two-fifths of our whole export, while against its increase during the eight

at the Foreign Office on the subject of treaty arrangements with foreign countries. In his reply, Lord Derby evinced the same wisdom, acumen, and prudence as has marked his answers to deputations which have sought him and questioned him in relation to that most difficult of all questions for the Foreign Minister to trust himself to speak on—the Eastern Question. Much credit is due to him for his answering at all times with candour and good temper, though reticence, to a certain extent, was imposed on him in relation to the latter, by a due regard to the national interests involved.

In the course of his reply to the deputation, on the 27th February, he said:—

"If I were to look at the resolutions (2), which have been put before me, in a critical spirit—which is not at all my purpose—I might point out to you some little discrepancies between the first and the succeeding one. You began by impressing upon me the unadvisability of signing treaties of commerce with foreign nations which do not give the 'most-favoured nation' treatment, and then you go on to contend, with considerable force, that the 'most-favoured nation' treatment is *not nearly sufficient* . . . .

years of £6,300,000 we had to set a falling off in the foreign demand amounting to £4,500,000. Similar observations applied to most of the other trades, the foreign demand being either stationary or declining, while the exports to the British possessions were rapidly rising. 28*th February*, 1878.

"It is one of those cases where it is very *much more easy to point out the evil which you wish to remedy than to apply a remedy which is efficacious,* because, to look at it in a broad point of view, all commercial treaties which are entered into with foreign nations are matters, more or less, of bargain and reciprocity, and as I have had, *more than once,* to remind similar deputations, *we are not in a position in which we can enter into transactions of the kind, because we have not gone upon a system of reciprocity, and this brings with it the one particular inconvenience to which I refer, for we have not the means of insisting upon reciprocity; we have given away freely what we had to give, in the first instance, and now we have nothing left to bargain with.* The strength of our position was the *commercial point of view,* and when we come to matters of *bargain and negotiation and the large returns upon our manufactures, that* circumstance *constitutes* the weakness of our position." —See report of *Times,* 28th February.

This surely ought to convince Free-traders of the hopelessness of gaining reciprocity.* Notwithstanding, however, Lord Derby was again besieged by members from the Manchester Chamber of Commerce, " to ask that in all further treaties with foreign powers a fuller application of the principles of Free Trade should be embodied in them."

* Why seek it, as the *Times* has said it is not necessary?—Q. E. D.

What could Lord Derby say but what he had said only a few days previously to a deputation seeking the same object?

After what Mr. E. Ashworth had said, on Monday, the 4th February last, was the cause of the depression of the Manchester cotton manufacturing trade, one cannot but feel surprised that he should have been one of the deputation on the 7th March to Lord Derby.

LORD DERBY ON COMMERCIAL TREATIES.

Yesterday, Messrs. B. Armitage, *E. Ashworth*, J. M. Bennett, C. P. Henderson, jun., and Thomas Browning, from the Manchester Chamber of Commerce, had an interview with Lord Derby, at the Foreign Office, to ask that in all future treaties with foreign powers a fuller application of the principles of Free Trade should be embodied in them. They pointed out that Continental nations were making very unfriendly treaties with us, and that our Consuls were somewhat under the influence of the manufacturing classes abroad. They asked that in making future treaties commercial men should be consulted upon the subject, so as to afford the Foreign Office information on those points which would more immediately affect their interests; and they complained that Roumania had recently terminated a provisional arrangement whereby our goods were suddenly stopped *in transitu.*

Mr. Armitage and Mr. Ashworth having spoken to this effect,

Lord Derby, in reply, said : Well, gentlemen, I am very glad you have come here. It is always agreeable to me to discuss these matters with the local representatives of our trades and manufactures, and I hope that you will no longer have to complain that questions of the kind with which you deal are neglected or ignored at this office. As to what has been said about our representatives not being as active as they should be in the way of securing advantages for their own country, *I am not aware that there is any want of vigilance or want of activity upon their part, but in the way in which matters are actually arranged between Continental Powers, every tariff is, more or less, a matter of bargain and arrangement.* We have never approved the system in this country. We have, as a rule, disclaimed it, and gone to what I may say is a much safer and wiser provision of making reductions in our own tariffs irrespective of those of foreign countries. *But you cannot eat the cake and have it too, and, having made these reductions for our own country, we are, as I said to a deputation the other day, not in the same position when it is a question of bargaining for our advantage in making up a tariff; we are not, I say, in the same position as those states are which have been and are in the position to give, and still do give, a great deal.* There is not much gratitude among communities for past favours, and in the very case which has been referred to—*the case of France and Italy*—I apprehend that if French goods have got any advantage over ours—which I am afraid in some cases seems to be so—the explanation is simply this, that the Italians are extremely anxious to secure the good will of the French Government, in order to obtain some corresponding reductions from France. *They are perfectly well aware that we are not in any case likely to adopt differential treatment, and therefore they have not the same inducement to treat liberally and generously with us.* At the same time, I think you will find whenever representations have been made by the Chambers of Commerce to this office, that they have been immediately forwarded to our representatives in those countries which were concerned; and, where it could be possible, that action has been taken upon it.

But yet another deputation from the Manchester Chamber of Commerce on the subject of the Cotton Frauds Act and the Abolition of the duties on Cotton goods and yarns into India, attended at the India Office, and Mr. Ed. Ashworth was one of the deputation.

In the course of his reply, Lord Salisbury (may we not think in a spirit somewhat savouring of rebuke, and if so, very properly) reminded the deputation that—

Every penny added to the taxation in India makes a very serious addition to the burdens upon the people. For example, when you increase the *Salt-tax* in India, you run the *chance of* making *salt so dear that the peasant cannot have that which is absolutely essential for his health;* or if you go to the source to which Indian legislators are *naturally tempted*—(he might have added—and English legislators also as regards the law of England)—though they generally have *the wisdom* to resist the *temptation* where they can, if you impose an increase of burdens upon land, you run the risk of making tens of thousands of poor ryots lose that *wretched margin of profit* which to *them now constitutes the difference between existence and starvation.* Therefore, it is no easy matter to talk of raising this £800,000 by additional taxation in India.

Just look at the difficulties arisen in the finances of India. We have had two famines, which for intensity and severity, have been almost unexampled in Indian history; and we have had another calamity, apparently not so severe, which has disturbed and crippled the finances of India; I mean the disturbances and the fluctuations in the *silver market*, which have seriously affected the finances of India.

The deputation then alluded to the operations of the *Cotton Frauds Act, and asked that it should be repealed, on the ground that it was no prevention of frauds, that it harassed trade, that it placed in the hands of the officials in India a weapon which they frequently used to the great inconvenience of a legitimate trade,* and which not unfrequently provoked animosity between the traders and the Government officials.

Lord Salisbury.—The information that you have been kind enough to give me is exceedingly interesting, and I have listened to it with great attention. There is no doubt that matters have changed of late years. I remember being at Manchester some twelve years ago, and I saw a bit of iron as big as my two fists, which had come over inside a bale of Indian cotton. Matters, as you say, have considerably improved since then, but there is a considerable difference of opinion upon these matters among persons whose opinions on both sides are entitled to respect. For instance, I think I am not breaking confidence in saying that the able and experienced gentleman, Mr. Andrew Cassels, upon our Indian Council here, and who represents Lancashire interests, takes a different view from what you do.

The Deputation.—He represented Lancashire a long time ago.

Lord Salisbury.—Undoubtedly there is a certain amount of opinion both in Lancashire and India which is opposed to the view you take, but I think the preponderance is the other way, and the

Government of India, I think, have a distinct leaning in opposition to the policy of the Act. The matter is still under discussion between us, and I should be sorry to pronounce a definite opinion until I have their latest expressions upon the subject. But you may be sure that the greatest weight will be given to the representations you have made, and that we shall earnestly strive to arrive at some result that may be best for the interests both of those in India and here.

The following letter, written by a Scotch gentleman, an experienced agriculturist in England, or at least Scotland, and a quondam Indian planter, is valuable, as showing there are still measures wanting for the fuller development of the resources of India. Though, since the Government was transferred from the East India Company to the British Crown, her resources have been greatly developed, as shown by Dr. Watson in the following paper :—

AGRICULTURAL PROSPECTS OF INDIA.

To the Editor of the " Times."

Sir,—Will you allow me to direct attention to the very serious question of the miserable condition and melancholy future prospects of agriculture in India, and, at the same time, indicate such remedial measures as have been suggested by my practical experience as an Indian planter.

As to the facts of the existing condition of Indian agriculture, I may observe that they are too well known to require my entering into any lengthened particulars, and may be both briefly and accurately described by saying that, with the exception of land irrigated by rich river water, and of certain wooded tracts, where the feed for cattle is abundant, and the agricultural area very limited, the people have been living for a very long period, not on the interest, but very largely on the capital of the soil. Nor does it require many words to show how this must be the case; for if, for instance, you go into the interior of the Province of Mysore—a Province generally admitted to be above the average of Southern India—and examine the scanty manure heaps, you will find that they consist almost entirely of the dung of lean cattle, and of the ashes of such part of the dung as has been used for fuel ; and the value of this manure may be estimated by stating that even the dung of grass-fed cattle only contains, out of every 1000 lb., about 11 lb. of valuable matter. Whence, then, asks the practical agriculturist, is to be supplied the phosphoric acid, lime, potash, and nitrogenous matter, which is carried off by the land, partly to be eaten by the farmer, and partly to be exported to enable him to pay his rent, and whence that vegetable matter which is entirely consumed by cattle, but which is so necessary, not only for its constituents, but for the effect it has in maintaining the texture as well as the radiating and absorptive powers of the soil ? The answer is, that there is no means of adequately supplying them at all. The land, as we have seen, is deprived of its matter, because that is needed to feed cattle, and from the absence of trees there is no means of procuring leaves ; nor is there any practicable means of supplying vegetable manure. It is deprived of its phosphoric acid, lime, and nitrogenous constituents, which are but very partially replaced by the infinitesimal quantities of these substances to be found in the dung of lean cattle, and it is deprived of its potash and other mineral constituents, which can hardly be said to be replaced at all. And what is true of the interior of Mysore is true generally, as far as our information goes; and were I not afraid of wasting your space, I could easily bring ample evidence to show that the soil of all India is, with few exceptions, bordering on exhaustion.

Now, let us look at the future agricultural prospects. We have seen that the manure at command is both poor in quality and small in quantity ; but, as the population increases, even these paltry resources must steadily diminish, for, as more and more of the grazing lands are broken up, it is evident that fewer and fewer cattle can be kept in proportion to the cultivated area. Even already complaints have been made as regards that extension of cultivation, which, to persons unacquainted with the agricultural circumstances of the country, seems to be a sign of steady progress. And if that is the case now with a population of only about 240 millions, what will the state of things be in twenty years, when the people will have increased to 293 millions, or, to look a step further, in forty years, when we shall have a population of 357 millions? It would seem ridiculous to look on to a further period, but the question as to whether the Government should take over the Indian railways now or eighty years hence makes it worth while to point out that by that time these exhausted soils will have to support about 530 millions of persons.

In conclusion, let me state what is practicable, in order, not to raise Indian soils to a fair state of fertility—for unless some undreamt-of manurial resources be discovered this would be impossible—but at least to prevent matters going from bad to much worse than they are at present.

In the first place, then, the grazing lands attached to or in the vicinity of each village must not be encroached on, unless it can clearly be shown that they are far in excess of the requirements of the community. In the second place, wherever it is practicable, each village should be compelled to plant, fence, and maintain a considerable block of forest trees, partly to improve the climate and the grazing by sheltering it from drying winds, partly for wood for building and firewood, but mainly for the supply of that great want in the plains of India, a sufficiency of leaves, which, by being used as bedding for cattle, would absorb the most valuable constituents of the manure, and especially of that liquid portion of it which is now entirely lost.

One word more. It is grievous to see how much we have failed to accomplish in India owing to the fact of our officials knowing nothing about agriculture. Take Mysore, for instance. We have governed it for about 43 years, and, if some of our most intelligent Scotch factors—acting, of course, in conjunction with the advice and co-operation of the most able natives in the country—had been employed and allowed to have their way, the whole face of the country might now have been altered, and its climate largely modified for the better. At a very trifling expense it might have been studded with woods and plantations, its manurial resources and grazing capabilities largely increased, and its agricultural area kept well and evenly within the bounds of its manurial resources. Does any proprietor here allow moor and grazing land to be enclosed and broken up without seeing that suitable plantations are formed both for wood and shelter, that the cultivator has the means of doing it justice, and that such restrictions are imposed as will fairly protect him from having his land run out and utterly destroyed? Why then, should the greatest landed proprietor in the world—Her Majesty the Queen—have her Indian estates managed on principles exactly at variance with those which are generally accepted here?

Obediently yours,
ROBERT H. ELLIOT.

Clifton Park, Kelso,
Saturday, 2nd January, 1875.

The second admirable letter of Lord Bateman, "The Six Millions—How to Raise Them," in the *Times* of the 11th March, may well lead to grave reflection as to whether we should continue to "give away all," as Lord Derby said, and get nothing in return. Also, how the *Home Market* can be improved.

Twenty Years' Progress in India.

The official account of the products of India which were shown at the Philadelphia Centennial Exhibition of 1876 is accompanied by a report prepared by Dr. J. Forbes Watson, of the India office, on the progress of India in the last 20 years—namely, from 1858, when the Government was transferred from the East India Company to the British Crown, to the present year 1877. In those 20 years, he says,

India has undergone a profound transformation. Two causes have mainly contributed to bring about this result—the gradual progress of education, and the extraordinary development of means of communication. The expenditure on education, as far as the Government is concerned, has increased fourfold, and now exceeds a million sterling in the year, and the number of pupils has increased from about 200,000 in 1857, to about 1,700,000, and is rapidly increasing. Small as this number may seem, it being below 1 per cent. of the population, it shows extraordinary progress, and proves that education is beginning to affect the masses. At any rate, it compares favourably with the number in other semi-civilized countries; the school attendance in Russia is about the same. The progress of education in India is also shown by the increasing number of graduates of the Universities of the three Presidencies, and the large number of pupils in the special engineering, art, and medical schools; and equally striking is the rapid growth of the native Press and literature. But the results of the progress of education are at present valuable chiefly as the promise of a better future, when the present generation shall have grown up. The changes wrought by improved means of communication have been, on the other hand, almost instantaneous, and have already transformed the whole face of the country. The length of railways open in 1857 was 274 miles; in 1876 it had become 6497 miles. The passengers carried in 1857 were 1,825,000; there were 26,779,000 in 1875. The miles of telegraphs increased from 4162 miles to 16,649 miles; the letters and packets conveyed by post from less than 29 millions to more than 116 millions in the year. The opening of the Suez Canal in 1869 also marks a turning-point in the trade of India and the East generally. The revenue of India has advanced from £31,691,000 in 1857 to £55,422,000, Imperial and provincial, in 1877; the expenditure from £31,609,000 to (estimated) £61,382,000 in 1877. The excess of expenditure over income in 1877 is due partly to the famine and partly to the outlay on remunerative public works. Adding together the cost of public works, of education, and of surveys and other scientific operations, we find about £10,000,000 now yearly spent by the Government in India for the permanent improvement of the country and its people. The trade and shipping returns show a vast increase in wealth and prosperity. The tonnage entered and cleared in the foreign and coasting trade was 4,549,000 tons in 1857, and rose to 9,887,000 tons in 1875. The value of the imports was £28,608,000 in 1857, and £48,697,000 in 1877; of the exports £26,591,000 and £62,975,000 respectively. These figures include treasure as well as merchandise. The imports of treasure amounted in the 20 years, 1858-77, to £267,582,677, but the exports of treasure to only £28,804,567, showing an increase in the precious metals to the amount of nearly £239,000,000, or about £1 for every head of population in the whole of British and Native India. The imports of merchandise have risen from £14,000,000 to £37,000,000 in the 20 years, an increase of 163 per cent.; the exports of Indian produce and manufactures from somewhat over £25,000,000 to £59,000,000 an increase of 133 per cent.; the total of imports and exports of merchandise showing an increase of 140 per cent.

While the trade of India has thus increased in volume, it has completely changed in character. Many of the old staple articles of Indian trade continue stationary, or are even declining. This is the case with silk, and silk manufactures, formerly such an important item in Indian exports; in fact, in the current year there have actually been more silk and silk manufactures imported into India than exported from it. A like decrease may be observed in the export of Cashmere shawls and other woollen manufactures, and also in saltpetre, another characteristic Indian produce. The export of sugar also has largely decreased, India being beaten by Mauritius and other plantation colonies in international competition; but her internal consumption of sugar is enormous, and its cultivation still hold the first rank in Indian agriculture as the most valuable crop, the various grain crops alone excepted. The best ground is devoted to it, and the total value of sugar and molasses annually produced in India is probably not less than about £20,000,000, or considerably more than the value of the cotton crop. On the other hand, a gigantic trade has sprung up in articles which were formerly of very small importance. They belong mainly to three classes. There is, first, the bulky agricultural produce which, in consequence of the improved means of communication, can now be thrown upon the markets of Europe. The trade in grains and seeds of all kinds sprang up about the time of the Crimean War, in consequence of the closing of the Russian ports, from which the main supply had been derived. The total trade in grains and seeds increased in value from £3,885,000 in 1857 to £13,560,000 in 1877, or about 274 per cent., and now constitutes 23 per cent. of the entire exports instead of the 16 per cent. of 1857. The most extraordinary development is shown in the trade in wheat, now approaching two millions sterling. The export of hides and skins also shows considerable progress, and the export of opium has risen from £7,057,000 in 1857 to £12,405,000 in 1877, but this last high figure is due not so much to the prime cost of the articles as to the duties placed upon it. A second group of articles comprises raw textiles, the vegetable and animal fibres which now form the most important item in Indian exports—namely, cotton, jute, and wool. The exports of these have grown in value from £2,027,000 in 1857 to £15,460,000 in 1877. Of this last sum raw cotton accounts for nearly 12 millions. In 1865 the Indian exports of cotton shot up to above 37 millions sterling, and, notwithstanding the fall in value after the close of the American Civil War, the quantity has been very fairly maintained, and cotton holds its place as one of the most important articles of Indian trade. The trade in jute has been entirely created within the last 30 years and has a great future before it. The development of the wool trade is also comparatively recent. The third group of the new growth of Indian export trade—namely, exotic products recently acclimatized in India by means of European capital and enterprise—is perhaps the most interesting. The exports of tea show an increase from £121,000 in 1857 to £2,607,000 in 1877, and of coffee from £133,000 to £1,346,000. The production of tea in India in the past year is equal to the total quantity consumed in the United Kingdom so late as in the year 1840. Another exotic, the cinchona, promises to become important. Introduced by Mr. Clements Markham so late as 1861, there are now nearly three millions of trees in the plantations in India, and the Government sales of bark amounted to £29,000 in the past year. Several other Indian products, such as tobacco and india rubber, also begin to attract attention, as showing how greatly the consuming power of India has increased. The principal articles are cottons (the cotton manufactures reaching nearly 16 millions sterling in the last year), woollens, metals, and metal work, machinery and mill work, railway materials, beer, wine, and spirits, the increase ranging from 160 to 533 per cent. In respect to several of these articles considerable progress has been made in establishing manufactures for their indigenous supply. A large and rapidly increasing number of cotton-mills has been established in India, and successful attempts have been recently made to manufacture iron on the European method. The output of coal in the Indian coal mines has considerably increased of late, and already supplies some of the Indian railways with the whole of the fuel required. The total area over which coal rocks may be presumed to extend is above 35,000 square miles. Dr. Forbes Watson observes that the statements thus made show that India, known usually as the country of caste and immutable tradition, shows herself possessed, under her present rule, of a remarkable power of expansion as regards trade and commercial development. It must also be remembered that the above figures refer to the seaborne trade, and that of late years the land trade with Central Asia and Thibet has been acquiring some importance. If once the communication with these countries and with China is improved, we may expect a considerable increase of trade in these directions. We may just add that British India comprises an area of nearly 1,500,000 square miles, and contains about 240 millions of inhabitants. The greater part of the country—three-fifths of the area and nearly four-fifths of the population—is placed directly under British administration; the remaining portion continues under the rule of different native Princes, who, however, all acknowledge the supremacy of the British Crown.

November, 1877.

Whilst the foregoing pages have been in the press, "Senex" has found with great gratification that our *Home-supply of food* is likely next year to receive that further consideration, and, let us hope, stimulus, which it has been the earnest desire and chief aim of "Senex" to promote, and which alone induced him to commence and have enabled him to carry through his labours.

On the 14th of March the *Times* announced that a large and influential meeting had been held on the afternoon of the previous day at the Mansion House, at which it was proposed that an Agricultural Exhibition should be held in London in 1879. And on the 23rd of March there appeared in the *Times* an admirable letter from the Right Hon. the Lord Mayor inviting subscriptions towards the expenses necessary to be incurred for holding such an Exhibition. In that letter occurs a passage justly calculated to excite the sympathy and arouse the energy of the nation—of all who recognize in Agriculture the *basis* of our national wealth, greatness, and honour.

"The food-supply of the people is *continually* acquiring an *increasing importance in the large centres of population*, and this holding of an Exhibition having for its objects the *improvement* of *all* the *means which can be adopted* for *stimulating the Home supply* cannot fail to be of great interest and use to the *consumer* as well as to the *producer*."

A deep and strengthening conviction year by

year during the last quarter of a century, that stimulating the means of providing a much larger Home supply for the people is the first and highest interest of the nation—far, far higher than any attempt to stimulate mutable foreign commerce, though that too need not be neglected, trade would certainly receive a great stimulus by the increased demand in the Home Market arising from stimulating the means of providing a much larger supply from Home-cultivation of our soil—has alone prompted this publication.

The following recent return tends further to show the imperious necessity of lessening our dependence on foreign nations for our supply of food by using every exertion in our power to increase our Home produce.

IMPORTS OF CORN.—The Custom-house accounts show that *in the six months since last harvest*—the half year from September to February inclusive—the imports of corn into the United Kingdom—namely, wheat, barley, oats, peas, beans, and Indian corn, amounted to no less than 64,442,650 cwt., equal to 16,266,156 qrs. About half consisted of wheat, which, including wheat flour, was imported to the extent of 33,658,857 cwt., *equal to* 8,011,635 *qrs.* These figures will not be much reduced by the accounts of the re-exports, which in 1876 averaged about 100,000 cwt. per month for corn of all kinds together.—*Times*, 20th March, 1878.

Whilst the late Sir Robert Peel, alarmed at our being dependent on foreign nations for five million quarters of corn, justified the sliding scale, we now find, that 8,011,635 quarters of corn have been imported during the six months since last harvest, being at the rate of 16,023,270 quarters for the year.

In the Estimates for the Civil Service and Revenue Departments for the year ending the 31st of March, 1878, issued on the 12th of March, we have another painful proof of the great and regular increase of lunatics amongst the poor.

In Class 6 the vote for pauper lunatics *in England amounts to* £380,000, *an increase of* £40,000; *for Scotland the estimate is* £68,000, *an increase of* £3000, *and for Ireland* £83,000, *an increase of* £2700. In Class 7 there is an increase of £1910 in the vote for temporary commissions. The total amount of the grants in aid of local taxation in Great Britain and Ireland is £4,961,594, against £4,323,313 in 1877-78, an increase of £638,281.—*Times*, 13th March, 1878.

On the 12th of March the following appeared in the *Times* :—

CONSUMPTION OF SPIRITS.—In the year 1877 duty was paid on 29,888,176 gallons of home-made spirits for consumption in the United Kingdom as beverage, this quantity being less by 62,112 gallons than in the preceding year. *The* 16,853,082 *gallons for consumption in England, show an increase of* 414,947 *gallons, and the* 6,987,189 *gallons for Scotland an increase of* 16,051 *gallons; but these increases are more than counterbalanced by a decrease of* 493,110 *gallons in Ireland, where the quantity fell to* 6,047,905 *gallons.* The 10,618,564 proof gallons of imported foreign spirits (not sweetened or mixed) entered for consumption in the United Kingdom in 1877, *were less by* 883,176 *gallons than the quantity in the preceding year.*—*Times,* 12th March, 1878.

Let us remember here, that "what to us *seems* vice may, in very many cases, be but woe." And lastly, the following letter in the *Times* of the 21st March shows us why we have required such an increase in our importations of foreign corn.

Modern Farming.

To the Editor of the Times.

Sir,—The opinion of Baron Liebig, quoted by Mr. Mechi, as to the decreasing fertility of English soil is strongly confirmed by the crop returns published by the *Mark Lane Express during the last ten years.* These returns are supplied each year by more than 400 contributors, who report separately as to the wheat, barley, and oat crops, whether they are average, over average, or under average. For example, as to the wheat crop of 1877, only six out of 409 returns represented it as over average, and no less than 369 described it as below average.

Four hundred or more reports, then, are sent in each year after harvest as to the wheat crop, and the total number sent in for the last ten years is 4577. Of these, 973 were over average, 1112 average, and 2492 under average. The barley crop returns for the ten years were 592 over average, 1855 average, 2003 under average, the oat crop returns being 540 over average, 1746 average, 2032 under average. These figures show at once that, in the judgment of these 400 observers, *the crops for the last ten years have been under average, and that very considerably;* for if not, the number of reports over average would equal the number under average. Surely this is strong evidence that our crops are not what they used to be ; and, unless the result can be laid to the charge of change of climate, it must be concluded that the fertility of the soil is decreasing.

I am, Sir, your obedient servant,
March 19-21, 1878.   H. J.

It may fairly be assumed that a want of due cultivation of the soil (no doubt in a great degree from a want of capital amongst farmers generally, and a consequent rapid decrease of able-bodied agricultural labourers, till at last there are not a sufficient number to cultivate the soil as it should be cultivated), has been *one* cause of " the decreasing fertility of English soil during the last ten years." But let us not forget that the seasons of late years have not been propitious, and that we have had frequent recurring diseases amongst our cattle.

Let us, then, bear these alarming and painful facts in remembrance, and humbly pray, in the language of the Psalm lxvii, used in the Evening Service of our Church.

" Let the people praise Thee, O God ; yea, let *all* the people praise Thee.

" *Then* shall the earth bring forth her *increase*, and God, even our own God, shall give us *His* blessing."

Is this duly reflected on when sung or said every Sunday, at least in our Churches.

The writer of the foregoing pages cannot but think that it augurs well for the future interests of this country that one member at least of the present Conservative Administration has become *convinced of the injurious effects* of the one-sided Free Trade—or rather the Free Imports—policy of 1846.

On the evening of Thursday, the 2nd of May, the Right Hon. R. A. Cross, M.P., the present able and indefatigable Home Secretary, the real friend of the working-classes, addressed a large meeting of Conservative working-men in the Corn Exchange, at Preston, " at which about 5000 people were present," says the *Times*, of the 3rd of May. And after him,

Sir John Holker, M.P., Her Majesty's Attorney-General, having expressed the pleasure it gave him to find himself once more among his constituents, said :—" He could not *contemplate the stagnation* of trade—especially the cotton trade—which had existed throughout the manufacturing districts for some time, without feelings of the *deepest concern. The depression of trade had entailed suffering upon the whole community*—more especially of those whose livelihood depended upon the prosperity of the industries affected. The distress, however, had been nobly borne both by the employers and the employed. The masters and men no doubt entertained different views as to the most effectual mode of grappling with the calamity;

but in the main the contending parties had put forward reasonable arguments, and without semblance of heat or passion. He hoped that before long better times would return, and that the glut of the old markets would be removed and new markets opened. He knew not whether the evil had any political source, but he could not help saying, even at the risk of being pronounced for his declaration a stupid old Tory, that much mischief had been occasioned by the firm determination which had, in recent years, been evinced to bind this country to a policy of Free Trade" (rather of Free Imports) " without taking care that the principles of Free Trade should be embraced also by other countries with which we had Trade transactions." (Cheers.) See *Times*, 3rd May, 1878.

Let us hope that the sentiments here enunciated by the Attorney-General as regards the results of Free Imports policy are entertained by other members of the Administration, as they assuredly are by fast increasing numbers, both in the Mother-Country and our Colonies. Experience is the test of a sound policy as it is of truth. To enforce which has been the sole object of the writer of these pages. He has been pleased to find from the following recent paragraphs which have lately appeared in the *Times*, that the measures he has so strongly urged as the surest means of alleviating distress, and at the same time of ultimately increasing the wealth of the country, and our breed of labourers, are of necessity being partially adopted. May they be generally—though gradually—adopted throughout the United Kingdom—or Empire!

RECLAMATION OF WASTE LANDS IN CORNWALL.—In consequence of the distress prevailing and the dearth of labour through the stoppage of several mines in the district, the Guardians of Helston, Cornwall, have addressed the *local landowners on the subject of improving their waste lands.* Several of these gentlemen have stated that, owing to their lands being out on leases which are unexpired, they are unable to act as they would wish; but the Duke of Leeds has written in a different strain, and *set an example which it would be well for others similarly situated to follow.* He has issued instructions for an immediate outlay of £400 in labour on waste lands in the parish of *Breage,* known as *Godolphin Warren. Lord John Thynne* has also applied to the Lands Improvement Company for a *loan of £10,000 for improving lands in the parishes of Morwenstow, Stratton, and Poughill, in Cornwall, and two parishes in Devonshire.—Times,* 7th May, 1878.

May the example set by Lord John Thynne be followed as early as possible by others, encouraged by the feeling that, as years roll on, they will have done their best

To scatter plenty o'er a smiling land.

LONDON:
G. NORMAN AND SON, PRINTERS, MAIDEN LANE,
COVENT GARDEN.

www.ingramcontent.com/pod-product-compliance
Lightning Source LLC
Chambersburg PA
CBHW032018220426
43664CB00006B/291